Shakin' All Over

# **Corporealities:** Discourses of Disability

# Shakin' All Over

## POPULAR MUSIC AND DISABILITY

### George McKay

THE UNIVERSITY OF MICHIGAN PRESS
ANN ARBOR

Published in the United States of America by
The University of Michigan Press
Manufactured in the United States of America
⊚ Printed on acid-free paper

2016    2015    2014    2013       4   3   2   1

A CIP catalog record for this book is available from the British Library.

Library of Congress Cataloging-in-Publication Data

McKay, George, 1960–
     Shakin' all over : popular music and disability / George McKay.
          pages      cm
     Includes bibliographical references and index.
     ISBN 978-0-472-07209-5 (cloth : alk. paper) — ISBN 978-0-472-05209-7 (pbk. : alk.
paper) — ISBN 978-0-472-12004-8 (e-book)
     1.   Disabilities and popular music.   2. Musicians with disabilities.   I. Title.
ML3470.M44       2013
781.64087—dc23

2013028357

... *anything* that rhymes with "me."

—Kevin Coyne, In Living Black and White (1976)

... although it amounts to rebellion and a near-utopia:
let's love the difference.

—Henri-Jacques Stiker, *A History of Disability* (1997, 10–11)

*For Dora*

## ACKNOWLEDGMENTS

THIS BOOK WOULD not have been possible without an Arts & Humanities Research Council research leave grant in 2010 (project title and number: "Spasticus: Popular Music and Disability"; AH/H005021/1), and a University of Salford sabbatical the same year. I am hugely grateful for both.

I owe thanks to musicians Steve Harley, David Rohoman, Penny Rimbaud, David Liebman, for discussions about music and disability; to Tony Gould for the transcription of his 1991 Ian Dury interview; to Peter Cox for sending me a transcription of his interview with Peggy Seeger about *The Body Blow*; to Christopher J. Rutty for sending me a copy of his Neil Young "Helpless" essay; and to Jessy Franklin and her brother Sean Stanley for the photograph of his tattoo.

To my University of Salford colleagues Dave Sanjek (RIP), Gareth Palmer, Tim Wise, Ben Halligan, Tony Whyton, Nicola Spelman, Beth Hewitt, Deborah Woodman, Michael Goddard, Adam Garrow, Peter Buse.

Also to Petra Kuppers, Neil Foxlee, Les Back, Andy Bennett, Charles Fairchild, Tony Mitchell, Hilary Pilkington, Mat Fraser, Ross from the Cripples, Bruce Johnson, Barbara Bradby, Simon Warner, Andy Simons, Gillian Pitter, Alison Wilde, Irene Rose, Rebecca Mallett, Claire Molloy, David Bolt, Paul Carr, my Scottish neuromuscular consultant Prof. Douglas Mitchell (RIP), Hilary Boone, Pauline Eyre, Mark Goodall, Paul Long, Ben Higham, Maran McKay Senior, Ken Johnson, Nick Gebhardt, Mike Weaver, Paul Dumke, Jorge Cortes, Chris Lines, Micah Levi Spangler, Petina-Dixon Jenkins, Giselle R. Bratcher.

To the contributors to and reviewers of a special issue of *Popular Music* on disability I edited in 2009—in particular, Nikki Dibben, Laurie Stras, Cheryl Herr, for critical or musical suggestions. The anonymous reviewers of AHRC grant applications in the UK and proposal and manuscript for University of Michigan Press in the United States all helped me sharpen up my ideas. The International Association for the Study of Popular Music list members kindly and informatively responded to several queries.

At the University of Michigan Press, thanks first to Chris Hebert for commissioning and supporting the book throughout, and David T. Mitchell for initial interest from the series editors. Also to Christopher Dreyer, Susan Cronin, Marcia LaBrenz, and Jessica LeTourneur.

For those who lived with me when I was writing the book—Emma McKay, Ailsa McKay, Dora McKay—first, apologies, I didn't realize it was going to take that long, and second, thanks, with love, as always.

Versions of parts of this book have been presented at Lancaster University Institute for Cultural Research research seminar (2006); Vytautas Magnus University, Kaunas, Lithuania, Society and Lifestyles project meeting (2006); Salford University postgraduate conference on Authenticity keynote lecture (2006); Liverpool John Moores University Cultural Disability Studies Research Network keynote lecture (2007); Warwick University Transnormative Cultures symposium (2008); Community Music East, Arts 4 All conference, Norwich keynote lecture (2008); Glasgow School of Art annual research conference lecture (2009); at Kendal Calling pop festival while I was professor in residence there (2011). I am grateful for all the invitations and the organization. Also I am grateful for a University of Sydney International Visiting Fellowship in 2008, which enabled me to talk about the work there and at Royal Melbourne Institute of Technology, Griffith University, Brisbane, and University of Technology Sydney.

An earlier version of chapter 1 appeared in the special issue on disability I edited of *Popular Music,* as the article "'Crippled with Nerves': Popular Music and Polio, with Particular Reference to Ian Dury," vol. 28, no. 3 (October 2009): 341–66. Parts of chapter 4 appear in my piece, "To be Played at Maximum Volume: Rock Music as a Disabling (Deafening) Culture," in *Resonances: Noise and Contemporary Music,* ed. Michael Goddard, Nicola Spelman, and Benjamin Halligan (London: Bloomsbury, 2013).

Arts & Humanities
Research Council

# CONTENTS

# Introduction

## Cultural Disability Studies and the Cripping and Popping of Theory

Well, my hands are shaky and my knees are weak
I can't seem to stand on my own two feet
Who do you thank when you have such luck?
— Elvis Presley, "All Shook Up" (1956)

THE OUT-OF-CONTROLLABILITY of the pop body has been a persistent feature since the music's early days. From "All Shook Up" in the United States and Johnny Kidd and the Pirates' "Shaking All Over" (1960) in Britain, songs about uncontrollable neurological tremors, as physical symptoms conflating the ecstasy of sexual attraction and of dance, are heard from rock and roll on—and are themselves prefigured in the pleasure and fear of the transcendent body in the jazz and dance musics of the first half of the twentieth century as well.[1] There are identifiable and powerful links between popular music and the damaged, imperfect, deviant, extraordinary body or voice, which can be, and surprisingly often *is,* a disabled body or voice; these links have been overlooked in much critical writing about popular music. Popular music has always been about corporeal transformation or excess and the display of those—there has always been "a whole lot of shaking going on"— and reading that shakiness in the context of the disabled body is the starting point for opening up fresh insights into both popular music studies and cultural disability studies. The purpose of this book, then, is to explore the common cultural and social territory of popular music and disability, which has been a hitherto neglected topic. It is situated at a nexus of disciplinary or subdisciplinary concerns: disability studies, popular music studies, cultural studies, performance studies, gender studies, and theory. It is intended as a timely musical contribution to the critical dialogue of recent years around disability culture, as one corrective to the relative silence of popular music studies here. *Shakin' All Over* is the first book looking right across the popular soundtrack of "our time, crip time" (McRuer 2006, 200).

From disability studies, Colin Barnes has reminded us that an "element in the development of disability culture and the arts that should not be overlooked is the relationship between disabled people and the 'entertainment' industry. Historically, people with perceived impairments or 'abnormalities' have provided an important source of entertainment for the non-disabled majority" (2003, 12). Such entertainment ranges from nineteenth-century freak shows to twenty-first-century performance art, and there are now extended academic studies of each of these (see, respectively, Thomson 1996; Thomson 1997; Fahy and King 2002; Kuppers 2003; Sandahl and Auslander 2005; for instance). We can go back further to make tentative connections: in the early modern period, courts made space for dwarves and fools to explore misrule and satirize their masters and mistresses—an allocation of a dedicated disability performance facility and role. Rosemarie Garland Thomson has drawn our attention to the common etymology that connects the freak, the corporeal deviant, with the act of showing, display, performance: "the Latin word *monstra*, 'monster,' also means 'sign' and forms the root of our word *demonstrate*, meaning 'to show'" (1997, 56). As we will see, such a cultural or musical demonstration can be a sign of dissension, critique, too, as the monstrous, deviant, or different stigmatized identity is claimed, staged, sounded, flaunted—we can say that it is popped and it is rocked: "performing difference, when that difference is a stigma, marks one as a target, but it also exposes and resists the prejudices of society" (Siebers 2008, 118). In work that crips Laura Mulvey's highly influential feminist film-theory work on the female gaze, Thomson proposes not the gaze, but the stare. And, "as anyone with a visible disability knows, persistent stares are one of the informing experiences of being considered disabled. . . . The disabled body is at once the to-be-looked-at and the not-to-be-looked-at" (Thomson 2005, 31). That being the case, what better cultural location for managing and challenging that discomforting dialectic can there be for the visibly disabled "staree" (Thomson 2005, 32) than the stage or the screen, particularly when his (mostly) moving (dancing) body might be accompanied by a deviant gang (band) making super loud noise (amplified music)?[2] And how does a staree get to be a star?

So disability studies has indeed begun to formulate a body of work that is altogether more substantial than a "subfield in literary criticism and cultural studies," as Thomson called for some years ago in her groundbreaking book *Extraordinary Bodies* (1997, 16).[3] Indeed, cultural disability studies is arguably now a recognized, more than emergent, field, with its own dedicated journals, book series published by academic presses, and research centers and networks. But why should we look at popular music and disability, together? Because, we might argue, *they were invented at the same time.* That is, there are identifiable links between modernity, mass media and popular culture (including popular music), and disability. In fact, "as Lennard Davis argues, *normal*—a concept and indeed an English word less than 160 years old—is an outgrowth of the development of statistics" (Lubet 2011, 27; emphasis in original). To historicize a little further, we can see that the shifts in perception of and engagement with people with disabilities took place in the late nineteenth and early decades of the twentieth centuries. These shifts were due to the increasing visibility of disability—caused by, in Henri-Jacques Stiker's view, the increase in workplace accidents in the mechanized and pressured workplace of the later Industrial Revolution, and the large numbers of World War I disabled veterans (we can make a similar presumption about the postbellum situation in the United States a few decades earlier). So, effectively one could say that the new century (the twentieth) saw a "new way, both cultural and social, of addressing disability" (Stiker 1997, 121). From the perspective of popular music, this is also the period of the development and dissemination of mass media and communications technologies. Marc Shell illustrates the connection in the specific context of polio from the late nineteenth century on: "during the seventy years in which polio epidemics were widespread, the various electronic media—cinema, radio, and television—were also coming into their own" (2005a, 1). More generally in the context of the rise of mass media, one can understand the representation of the body as an ideal through which different (which are in their mundanity ordinary rather than extraordinary) bodies are excluded or marginalized. Eugenics, for example, "spread into mass culture in the form of product promotion" in advertising (Snyder and Mitchell 2006, 30). Like some of the sonic arts we are considering in popular music, mass visual technologies could offer ways of compensating for disability, as well as ways of disabling people, as Shell astutely notes.

Many polios [including Lord Snowdon, Bert Kopperl, Dorothea Lange] took up photography: angled or telephotographic lenses bring closer what a paralyzed person cannot reach. . . . Cripples, usually the victims of the voyeurs and the "rubberneckers," could turn the tables on the observers thanks to the cameras. . . . Early movies . . . made even "normal" people look odd when they walked—Charles Chaplin's quasi-stumbling gait is still celebrated. Thanks to the slow rate of shutter intervals in early movies, nonparalyzed walkers seem to suffer from the same walking disorder [as] . . . paralyzed walkers. (2005a, 130, 137)

In the United States, "'disability' as a socially composed grouping is less than two hundred years old" (Snyder and Mitchell 2006, 22); indeed, it is both part of modernity, and in some cases—in disabilities which are associated with polio, autism, AIDs, for instance—of modernism and even postmodernism.

Scholars have recently considered the practice of music within the frame of disability. So, for Rod Paton, because playing an instrument, say, is a complex and specialized form of the development of body control—it is a discipline—down to the nerves and muscles of the fingertips or mouth—"where music is concerned, we all have a degree of disability" (2000, 27). Alex Lubet sees not so much a connection between music and disability as a discontinuity which has a profound potential for generating discourse: "because music is understood within many cultural systems to be a manifestation of 'talent'—extraordinary ability—its juxtaposition with disability—understood as talent's opposite—offers an exceptional window on social praxis" (2008, 4). The arguments get more ambitious. Elsewhere, Lubet argues that in certain anticultural societies the practice and love of music is itself a form of disability (Lubet 2011). Neil Lerner and Joseph N. Straus have proposed that "the special fluidity of music, unfettered by language or concrete referentiality . . . [contains the] power to disrupt the seemingly hard and fast distinction between ability and disability" (Lerner and Straus 2006a, 10). My own interest is in popular music, which includes formal aspects of music itself, but also the many fascinating extramusical facets that make popular music studies such an impure, imperfect, and marvelously messy discipline: audience, industry, body, mediation, style, language, theory, and so on. Primarily, as the title of my book—itself taken from a song title and hit single from 1960—signals, the popular music I am discussing is that from the 1950s, from American and British rock and roll,

Fig. 1. Earlier music and disability: Blind Tom, sheet music for "Oliver gallop" / "Virginia polka" (1860). © Thomas Bethune/Thomas Wiggins/Blind Tom Collection, Columbus State University Archives, Columbus, Georgia. Used with permission.

Fig. 2. Earlier music
and disability: Squire
Hughes, early 20th
century (?) disabled
singer's publicity card.
Author's collection.

SQUIRE HUGHES,
Wonderful Cripple Basso
and Character Vocalist.

onwards. Occasionally I move further back—to, say, the 1930s—or outside
the strictly pop and rock—a jazz interlude—or away from the mass mediated transatlantic nexus—Jamaican reggae, or Congolese dance music—
where these bring light or nuance to the discussion.

Broadly articulated, the theoretical framework of this book is threefold,
drawing on and interweaving popular music studies, cultural and media
studies, and disability studies. In terms of popular music studies, I focus on
popular song, the pop industry, live performance, mediation and marketing, the voice, and fans—that list should make clear that mine is not a mu-
sicological approach, though I do discuss the music itself, if not through the

dots and staves of notation, and with only intermittent use of music's "forbidding technical vocabulary" (Strauss 2011, 11). From cultural and media studies I take questions around subcultures and post–subculture theory, identity, the body, pleasures, race, gender, sexuality. These two theoretical groupings can be seen as related, and indeed it is the case that many cultural studies scholars have written extensively and convincingly about popular music, for example. In terms of disability studies, I am interested in ways in which theories of enfreakment, questions of performing difference, the post-social and cultural models of disability, the stare, and, to a lesser extent, the problematic of passing, can help in our understanding of popular music. And of course I am interested in how popular music can *resound* disability studies. The plethora of "studies" here should stand as pretty clear evidence of a crossing (perhaps it is time to say "cripping") of disciplines—an activity I have tended over the years to view as producing a rather positive critical positionality, as offered by the kind of academic I like reading, and that I aspire to be—but I want to point out one issue in this triangulation. Since mapping matters in theoretical questioning, I should (briefly) explain my own journey through the terrain, my statement of prior positionality. I come from cultural and media studies, and write a good deal about popular music—as my personal website puts it, I do "cultural studies with a soundtrack" (McKay n.d.b, website). So for this book, it was the disciplinary frameworks and limitations of popular music and cultural studies, even at their blurring boundaries, that set me off. *I then came to disability studies,* in which I dipped my toe before putting my head under. I was not first and foremost a disability-studies scholar (though I gladly acknowledge that my immersion in it has demonstrably changed my cultural and interpretive thinking; I have a new lens). With *Shakin' All Over* I come in a spirit of openness. I want disability-studies readers, as well as music and cultural studies ones.

The founding binary of the social vs. medical model has remained important and influential in disability studies, no doubt in large part because the social model has an advocacy imperative inscribed within it. But the social model has also been challenged and nuanced, and the aspect of that challenge that has most relevance for us is in work placing the complexity of cultural representation and expression within it (see Riddell and Watson 2003a, 4). The cultural nuancing of the social model matters. I concur with, for instance, Sharon L. Snyder and David T. Mitchell that "impairment is both human variation encountering environmental obstacles *and* socially mediated difference that lends group identity and phenomenological perspective. . . . Many cultural model scholars understand 'disability' to function both as a referent for a process of social exposé and as a productive locus for identification" (2006, 10; emphasis in original). I take the cultural model into an important, high profile, and relatively neglected part of the contemporary cultural realm—popular music. I also present what I think of as a more affirming version of the cultural model—"'disability' in this book," write Snyder and Mitchell in *Cultural Locations of Disability,* "is largely . . . synonymous with sites of cultural oppression." In *Shakin' All Over* disability is also, as they go on to put it, designated "a source of cultural agency" (Snyder and Mitchell 2006, 6, 10). There is the powerful potential for, if not quite—or rather not always—cultural resistance or liberation, then at least for what Danny Goodley has termed "a politics and culture of resilience" (2003, 105). We will see how this potential has been shaped, and is fulfilled, or indeed missed, in the advocacy and campaigning activities of musicians around disability issues.

I aim to widen the cultural scope of disability studies by looking at the arena of popular music. Notwithstanding the small but important number of studies that write either about music and disability or about popular music and disability cited elsewhere in this introduction, I am struck by the extent to which pop and rock in particular have been neglected in cultural studies of disability performance, especially because I am *also* struck by the quite common occurrence of, for want of a better term, disabled pop.[4] This really is the heart of the book—popular music as an interdisciplinary cultural form and practice, with a related critical approach drawing on cultural politics and cultural and media studies. That's my bag. I was a pop fan before (I knew) I was disabled; my academic and popular writing on cultural politics has most often at least had a soundtrack, and frequently been directly about the relation between popular music, society, ideology, social movements. Only in recent years have I begun to embrace (my) disability—a muscular dystrophy—and seek to understand its plural meanings and effects. But then I thought back, back on my identity as an uncompromising young punk rocker of thirty-five years ago, with (to quote my school teachers) an "attitude problem"—with my gait? What did they expect?—anarchist sympathies, and a suddenly surprisingly fashionable weird way of walking, and I drew inspiration from a troublesome singer I'd first seen at sixteen in 1977, playing drums for a singer called Wreckless Eric, and who, puzzlingly, seemed to speak to me once more as I was in my forties and going to hospitals again: Ian Dury. Not that I had external obstacles to the idea of the book, nor critical voices seeking to dissuade or undermine—quite the contrary; really I was just up against myself. The anxiety and insecurity, which both surprised me, were not really about writing, or trying to understand new theory and discourse, of course—they were bound up with the act of self-recognition and the process of acceptance. Popular music has helped me to understand myself in transition. (Contrary to much belief, pop can be wise and generous.) And now I understood why I had listened to Dury as a youth—or stared past Sid Vicious, asking me for a fight, at Johnny Rotten onstage singing "Bodies"—and before them to that great lost northern English singer-songwriter Kevin Coyne, with his anti-guitar playing and repertoire of songs about hospitals and suffering and "anything that rhymes with 'me'"—a tiny phrase that, like one of Oliver Sacks's musical "brain worms," has stayed in my head for thirty-five years, waiting patiently for me to write the book it would be an epigraph to. (Pop can be wise and generous.) Tom Shakespeare wonders whether "disability scholars often emphasize the dimension of disability which they most directly experience" (2006, 4)—though not a polio survivor, I was put in the polio ward at Mearnskirk Hospital outside Glasgow, Scotland, as a child in the mid-1960s, alongside other wee boys who were in iron lungs. It is polio that starts this book, and it was polio that started me writing it; it seems clear to me (now) that this interest in polio is because it spoke to me both in my own neuro-muscular specialist embodied knowledge, and of my own childhood.

In the course of the book we will see that some artists sing of disability in compelling and sustained ways—drawing on autobiographical lyrics and experiences, singers and musicians as varied in musical style, sartorial image and lyrical language from Neil "Shakey" Young to Ian Dury share the profound and formative experience of each being a polio survivor from childhood. Here the deployment of autobiographical authenticity within singer-songwriter practice portrays a different kind of childscape, which may be diseased, scar(r)ed, crippled. Young's "sensitive" falsetto and Dury's "coarsened" poetics (as we will see, their descriptions of their own voices) are discussed as alternate vocal representations of their embodied experiences. These are autopathographical texts and readings (see Auslander 2005; Cizmic 2006), in which disability is framed in autobiographical and experiential terms (Siebers 2008, 47; Snyder and Mitchell 2006, 4)—the very forms of authentic text production favored in much rock lyric.[5] Yet it should be noted that even popular music forms centered on the autobio-

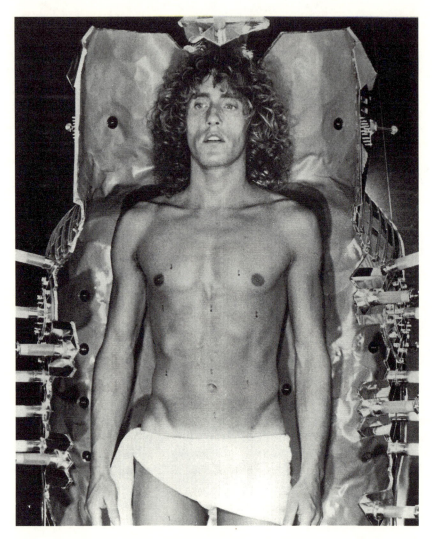

Fig. 3. "That deaf, dumb and blind kid" (with the perfect body): Roger Daltrey in the Who's crip musical film *Tommy* (1975). Author's collection.

graphical lyrical narrative do not always make space for autopathography. In *The Songs of Blind Folk*, Terry Rowden argues that few blind African-American musicians have explicitly referenced their experience of disability, preferring to "minimise and deflect attention away," or to "lyrically pass" (singing words that suggest the capacity to see, as in Blind Blake's "Early Morning Blues": "When you see me sleepin' baby don't you think I'm drunk

/ I got one eye on my pistol and the other on your trunk") (Rowden 2009, 39–40). This seems a remarkable absence in a musical culture like the blues, which is, after all, largely predicated on an autobiographical lyric frequently drawing on experiences of struggle and suffering.

We will see that some music-centered subcultures have opened up new cultural spaces and corporeal expectations—so punk and post-punk enfreakment were embodied in the seminal example of the staring, sneering, spiky-haired, hunched, pierced, swearing, and spit-covered figure of Johnny Rotten, punk dwarves graced the shop floor of Vivien Westwood and Malcolm McLaren's King's Road London boutiques and the film backdrop of Derek Jarman's *Jubilee* (1978) alike, while bands with names like the Epileptics (see fig. 19), the Subhumans, and the Happy Spastics (all UK), another Subhumans (Canada), Disability, and the Cripples (both U.S.) have made minor provincial waves. Here theorizations of the body and the expressions of the blank generation are employed in order to further nuance the understanding within post–subcultural studies of the differently abled (see also Church 2006; Calvert 2010). We will see that some musical acts explore and return to tropes of disability over lengthy pop careers. To offer one illustrative example, English rock group The Who stuttered the attitudinal voice of English youth in 1964's "My Generation" ("People try to put us d-d-down"), sang and acted "That deaf dumb and blind kid [who] sure plays a mean pinball" in the film *Tommy* in 1975, while guitarist Pete Townshend was widely reported when he spoke out recently about the experience and the dangers of rock-music-induced hearing loss: "I have unwittingly helped to invent and refine a type of music that makes its principal proponents deaf" (quoted in Anon 2006). From youthful stutter to a hearing impairment more readily associated with older people, from the band that first sang, when they were young, "I hope I die before I grow old" (it didn't happen: not to the songwriter or the singer, anyway): cripping The Who offers us a different set of insights into the band's body of work across the decades, which is also to do with refiguring the generational pull of youthful pop and rock. As singer Roger Daltrey said in 2006: "Can you see us onstage in wheelchairs? . . . It will still be us, still be the same music. . . . Pete may have trouble with the guitars, I suppose. He does like to jump around" (quoted in Garfield 2006, 33). From another perspective, we will see that some pop musicians have displayed a fascination with the otherness of disability: Morrissey on BBC television's weekly chart programme *Top of the Pops* in 1984, singing "Heaven knows I'm miserable now" while controversially sporting a Johnnie Ray–era hearing aid and National Health Service glasses, Kurt Cobain being pushed onstage in a wheelchair and hospital gown at the 1992 Reading Festival, the is-she-or-isn't-she-blind music press debates about eye-patch-wearing British singer Gabrielle in 1993.[6]

*Shakin' All Over* is intended to form part of a recent development within the emergent discipline of cultural disability studies—at the forefront of which were performance/theatre studies, and theory—as (popular) music research has begun to critically discuss the impaired or damaged pop body and voice, finding their presence to be surprisingly common in a cultural practice more readily associated with the youthful and sexual pleasures of the ideal body. Recent works focused exclusively on music and disability provide evidence of the development of an intellectual project by academics from each discipline, if predominantly a project led by music rather than disability scholars. Here I have in mind two collections of academic essays: Neil Lerner and Joseph N. Straus's wide-ranging book, *Sounding Off: Theorizing Disability in Music* (2006), which encompasses some popular music examples alongside a greater number of classical ones, and the 2009 special issue on disability and pop of the journal *Popular Music,* which I edited (McKay 2009b). More substantial still is a quartet of book-length, single-author studies, which have focused on either music in relation to a specific type of disability, or, like *Shakin' All Over,* look at a range of musical, theoretical, and disability questions and clusters.[7] In the case of the former I am thinking of Oliver Sacks's 2007 neurologically oriented set of case studies, *Musicophilia: Tales of Music and the Brain,* which, though firmly embedded in the medical model, sparkles with intelligence and insight. Also I am thinking of Terry Rowden's *The Songs of Blind Folk: African American Musicians and the Cultures of Blindness* (2009), the book that moved me toward *not* including in *Shakin' All Over* a chapter on visual impairment and scopophilic pop, as I had originally intended. For the latter I refer to Alex Lubet's *Music, Disability, and Society* (2011), which contains also an essay on blindness and music, and has several chapters on some forms of popular music, even if the case studies might seem less than accessible for many readers. Finally, Strauss's *Extraordinary Measures: Disability in Music* (2011) has important insights about the formal understanding of the music itself (rather than, say, lyric or vocal delivery, or corporeal comportment onstage) as a representation of the experience of disability. Despite its inclusive subtitle, Strauss's book contains no popular music whatsoever, focusing instead on

Fig. 4. 1970s British chart-toppers Peters & Lee, featuring blind singer Lennie Peters. Author's collection.

what Lubet has called "the rigid, ungenerous cultural system" of Western classical music, with its central institution of the orchestra, or "sonic Sparta," as he powerfully describes it (Lubet 2011, 33, 77). In the context of popular music, I have of course used each of these—all of which have been published during the very half decade when I was first thinking about and then writing this book—as intellectual and cultural aids and prompts. Together they present compelling central evidence that pop, rock, and classical music academic critiques are, shall we say, embracing their inner and outer crips. I would like to think that *Shakin' All Over* contributes to that emerging field, while moving it in a significant new direction, into the cultural detail and trashy ephemera of pop and rock.

Let me develop a point here, about the relative absence of visual impairment in this book. As just stated, originally it was my plan to include a chapter on blindness and music—I was thinking of all those early African-American blues musicians whose very names signaled and marketed themselves as disabled: Blind Lemon Jefferson, Blind Willie McTell, Blind

Boy Fuller, possibly Sleepy John Estes (see Rowden 2009, chapter 2). Or later jazz and soul stars like Rahsaan Roland Kirk, George Shearing, Ray Charles, and, of course, Stevie Wonder. But as the book in its writing became less pre-rock-and-roll oriented and less jazz-focused, many of these figures became less central to my narrative. And, on a purely pragmatic level, as I have just outlined, their musics and disabilities were beginning to be written about by other academics. Part of me regrets this absence here, particularly with Roland Kirk—my father was a jazz musician whose flute solos often featured vocal overblowing, and who occasionally played two saxophones at once—both techniques picked up from Kirk. So Kirk was a kind of family hero for us McKays. Also, I was aware of the discourtesy toward him by at least one leading British jazz critic in the 1960s, who was obediently keen to join in the dismissal of Kirk as a circus clown or freak, and I wanted to address that controversy.[8] And I regret it with George Shearing too, now pretty much absent from these pages, even though his extraordinary jazz journey took off with him playing accordion and piano in Claude Bampton's All-Blind Orchestra from London during the 1930s (see Shearing 2004, chapter 4). (Us Brits don't have too many major successes recognized and embraced by the American jazz world on its own patch—see McKay 2005—and we can still get excited when a local boy makes good across the pond.) It may appear a truism that, as Rowden points out critically, "no role has been more strongly linked to disability than musicianship has to blindness" (2009, 11), or that blindness is a means to a precious "enhanced interiority" for musicians (Strauss 2011, 6). Yet Shearing himself rejected "the theory that blind people actually hear more or have the ability to memorize more than sighted players" (2004, 30). Further, in our observation that there have been many blind musicians, we should bear in mind Lubet's stark and well-put conclusion that "blindness may not be an impairment at all when the musician . . . is actually making music" (2011, 43). As for Stevie Wonder—he is here, the stage is being set for his entrance.

Shakespeare makes the point of critiquing the social model by quoting a popular song lyric: "people with impairments will always be disadvantaged by their bodies: they will not be able to climb every mountain" (2006, 46). My book probably is not inclusive either. Its musical choices, it should be clear, are being made mostly on the basis of the extent to which songs, artists, performances, autobiographical utterances, public interventions, *do* engage with disability in some way. For instance, in the course of writing it,

I was surprised to find that there are not that many women here. I should not have been. I should earlier have noted Lucy O'Brien's stark observation in *She Bop II* that "women with disabilities . . . are almost invisible" in pop and rock (O'Brien 2002, 245): as we will see, the body limits of the industry seem rather starkly gender fixed. Lubet identifies the source of anxiety as not the industry but the audience: "This gender bias may owe to the expectation in music that women performers be decorative as well as proficient. Music audiences prefer not to view women's impairments, but have less difficulty gazing at those of men" (2011, 160). More generally, Rowden argues that disability—or rather, the discussion of its experience—is traditionally written out of popular entertainment, and specifically music, as the sort of thing people "would rather not dwell upon when they are trying to have a good time" (2009, 100); disability as ectopic. (This is partly to do with the nondiscursive reality of discomfort and in fact pain that people with disabilities may experience or embody, and "disability identity . . . is the identity most associated with pain" (Siebers 2008, 20). After all, how many pop fans want pain—physical pain, that "most subjective of phenomena" (Siebers 2008, 60)—in the pleasure-dome?) But I am more interested in the topic than the ectopic. So, while, extraordinarily, Joni Mitchell and Neil Young each contracted polio in the same epidemic in Canada in 1951, there is much more about Young than Mitchell in this book because he has made hugely significant music exploring that experience and she (to date) has not. Of course, wider questions of cultural silence, evasion, passing, in the context of disability, music, and the industry, are also discussed where relevant and illuminating. Also, by way of discussing my choice of artists, I should say that I have been gently guided by my publisher to remember one particular meaning of "popular" in popular music, and to focus more on relatively well-known, transatlantic musicians—those with a public profile—rather than, say, some of the more quirky, marginal, cult, or grassroots figures I might have had a stronger personal preference for. I do see the need for readers to have recognizable examples or easy access to them. I have sought to strike a balance here. Of course, where the presence of disability might be a contributing factor in understanding the very *un*popularity of a pop or rock artist or band, then such are discussed. In particular, though, there are energetic grassroots disability arts movements in which live music sounds centrally—the organisation and musical aesthetics of which are informed by various DIY practices (McKay 1998), that may seem underplayed here, even in chapter 5 where the do appear (see, for instance,

Fig. 5. Physically disabled street musician, Glasgow, 2009. Author's collection.

Brown 2008; Cameron 2009; Elflein 2009; Calvert 2010), though I would argue that this is not necessarily the case elsewhere in my work (Moser and McKay 2005; McKay 2009b; McKay and Higham 2011).

The chapters that follow are structured in most cases around specific issues or questions originating from popular music: the singing voice (chapter 2), the performing body (chapter 3), hearing and listening to music (chapter 4), and the popular music industry (chapter 5). The exception is chapter 1, focused on a case study that is both chronologically and medically specific—that of the late polio generations and their use of popular music. Important artists (important in the context of disability) appear and reappear in different chapters. Young, for instance, is a polio survivor, who could sing with a falsetto voice, who was in early career a kind of performing epileptic, and in mid-career made music for the disabled, and has campaigned with his family about disability, and he recurs throughout, really. This tells us that many disabled artists have multiple strategies, if—and we will see that that is a very big if—they have been fortunate enough to sustain a lengthy pop or rock career. Some important questions for pop and rock, for cultures of disability, are explored across different chapters. Popular music as a *dis*abling rather than enabling cultural practice, for instance, is discussed in the context of rock-music-induced hearing loss in chapter 4 and in terms of the industry's wasteful, even fatal, lifestyle of excess and risk in chapter 5. As I write again later, *pop crips. It really can.* The *un*popularity of some pop when it gets too cripped keeps coming back, periodically through the book sounding the lamentable limits of audience or industry acceptability and inclusiveness toward the disabled.

*Hallo to you out there in Normal Land.* Yeah, and to all you crips. On a Sunday morning in October 2008, when I ought really to have been completing the introduction for the disability special issue of *Popular Music,* I was instead flicking through the Sunday newspaper over a late breakfast, trying to avoid the finance pages. I picked up one of the free magazines, the *Observer Music Monthly,* and read an interview with polio survivor and epileptic Neil "Shakey" Young, which included a photograph of him with polio survivor Joni Mitchell; I glanced at a short photo feature on rock 'n' roll suicide Kurt Cobain and at another on 1980s Smiths–era Morrissey; I read an article on the thirty-year career of visually impaired Malian couple Amadou and Mariam, in which they talked about how "music gave us the strength to overcome the blindness" (quoted in Adams 2008, 53); I read a review of a new Robert Wyatt album, which included a photograph of Wyatt smoking a cigarette in his wheelchair, and a review of a Hank Williams compilation; skimmed an article that mentioned polio survivor Ian Dury's album *Do It Yourself*, and another in which Wyatt was referenced again. All this in one unthemed magazine. While I thought I was not doing my research on popular music and disability, here I was doing it all the same. The point is one that disability studies has taught us compellingly: the moment we begin to look for, to discuss disability (in popular music), we find it everywhere. Whether in its focus on bodies perfect and deviant alike, the romantic appeal in rock lyrics and lives to tropes of suffering or cognitive impairment, its damaged or what I call *mal canto* voices, its continuing status as expressive vehicle for emotional autobiography (from artists and audience members), its intermittent fetishing of enfreakment, its industrial carelessness and destructive appetites, or in the place of pop repertoires in music therapy or disability arts and advocacy, in fact, pop is a profoundly dismodern cultural formation and practice (Davis 2002). My hope (be bolder! My burning aim) is that *Shakin' All Over* opens new ground in the process of illustrating, understanding, and interrogating that important Sunday morning observation.

## CHAPTER 1

# "Crippled with Nerves"

## Polio Survivors in Popular Music

> Even I used to sing, when I was on crutches—because I had the
> polio thing, which I'm sure we'll get to eventually—I would take
> the crutch, like a guitar, stand in front of the mirror, and think I
> was Elvis.
>
> —Saxophonist Dave Liebman, remembering his 1950s
>   childhood (quoted in Kirchner 2011)

WE ARE HERE ALREADY, in polio land. This first chapter is the most historically situated of the book, as well as in some ways the most medically restricted. But it is also intended as something of an overview, to give a sense of the scope of how disability figures in popular music and rock, and it opens some key areas and artists for further discussion later. It focuses largely on the rock-and-roll generation of polio survivors: children and young people from the late 1940s to the early 1950s who contracted poliomyelitis ("infantile paralysis") during summer epidemics in the last few years before reliable vaccinations were widely available (in the West). As Liebman has observed, of his own experience, aged three, in 1949, "I'm the last of the last to get polio" (2012, 7). In using polio as the focusing device I am aware that I may seem to be privileging the medical condition and its consequent disabilities over the people, the artists concerned, and their cultural products. But I am interested in the historical specificity of the disease in the postwar West. The introduction of the vaccines that successfully eradicated polio within a few years made that generation dramatically the last (in the West), while the chronological coincidence of the rise of pop culture would lead in a decade or two to a remarkable generation of pop and rock musicians who had been shadowed by "the crippler," as polio was known colloquially in the United States.[1] I discuss these, and go on to look at the work of Ian Dury (1942–2000), who was for some years the highest profile and most outspoken visibly physically disabled pop artist in Britain. This made Dury "one of society's ultimate 'not me' figures" in the cultural context of the wannabe pop world, of course, but he is of special interest due to his songs around the topic of disability, his inventive and provocative "narratives of corporeal/cultural difference," in Rosemarie Garland Thomson's terms (1997, 41, 16).

Through the twentieth century, increasing public awareness of polio outbreaks (epidemics in New York in 1916, Los Angeles in 1934, Berlin in 1947, Copenhagen in 1952) caused periodic panic among local populations. As Marc Shell writes in *Polio and its Aftermath,* "For seventy years, polio traumatized the world. . . . An American president suffered from its paralyzing effects. So did sixty million other people worldwide. Even when polio did not kill its victims outright, it often crippled them for life. The survivors were the visible reminder of polio's ever-increasing power to slay, maim, and deform. . . . No one knew what caused the disease, and there was no cure" (2005a, 1). But, according to Tony Gould in *A Summer Plague,* "everything to do with polio in Britain, not least the disease itself, was on a minor scale" (1995, 161). This changed with the epidemic of 1947, in which 7,776 people contracted the disease. Over the following decade some 58,000 were affected, around 4,000 of whom died, and of the survivors 35,000 were left with a degree of paralysis (Balls 2000, 32–33).[2] One medical student working in a London hospital during one outbreak in the 1950s, when hospital staff were themselves coming down with the disease, described this plague-like situation as "absolutely bloody terrifying" (quoted in Gould 1995, 162). At this time, the 1950s being the high point of the "polio *zeitgeist*" (Gould 1995, 219), the Salk vaccine was available in Britain for young people (by injection), though not yet widely used. (It would be superseded within a few years by the Sabin vaccine, dispensed nationwide to schoolchildren on sugar cubes.) Some early vaccinations malfunctioned, and infected the patient with the disease. Such an iatrogenic family disaster is what happened to 1960s folk singer Donovan as a boy in Scotland, as he explains in his autobiography.

In the disruption following the Second World War, three epidemics hit [Glasgow]: scarlet fever, diphtheria, and polio. The children were hardest hit.

The vaccines were too strong, and I was actually given the polio disease this way. So my right leg began to show signs of "wasting." An operation was performed, cutting the Achilles tendon in the foot, and I wore an ugly leg brace for some time after. It was a long boot made of a hard substance that I wore only at night to give the little leg support. Removing the device would tear the hairs and hurt so much that I cried each morning, painful for my mammy and daddy to watch. (Leitch 2005, 3)

Polio is a highly contagious viral disease that can attack the body's nervous system. Transmitted by fecally contaminated food and water, in temperate climates it can be a seasonal disease—therefore, summer swimming in pools and lakes was a childhood activity feared and discouraged by many parents. Also, polio is primarily a disease affecting children. Its characteristic operation is that by attacking nerve cells the virus permanently paralyses the activated muscles. So, while Ian Dury in the early 1970s would write and sing a halting love song, "Crippled with Nerves": a highlight of his band's live set (released as a single in 1975), the title phrase itself was both resonant and neurologically informed: Dury was indeed crippled with (by) his nerves, and the audience saw him perform the singing of that. Or, as Canadian singer-songwriter and polio survivor Joni Mitchell has put it:

Polio is the disease that eats muscles. If it eats the muscle of your heart, it kills you; if it eats the muscles that control the flexing of your lungs, you end up in an iron lung; if it eats the muscle of your leg, it withers, or of your arm, it withers. In my case it ate muscles in my back—the same thing happened with Neil Young. I had to learn to stand [again], and then to walk. (quoted in Matteo, n.d.)

A key early figure here is the 1930s and 1940s music, radio, and film star Connie Boswell, originally of the Boswell Sisters. Boswell fascinates for her crossover solo success in the early 1940s in the visual culture of film, of course, but also for her position as a disabled female popular performer in a predominantly ablist culture and society. Boswell occupied a "unique position as the only visibly disabled 'A-list' female popular entertainer for most of the twentieth century" (Stras 2009, 298)—which also indicates the extent to which we may consider popular musical disabilities so primarily as male phenomena: pop and rock offer masculine prerogatives, as much of this book illustrates. In many of her film scenes, viewers see Boswell sitting on a piano, sitting on a chair near a radio (source of music), using her very

Fig. 6. Connie Boswell of the Boswell Sisters, publicity card 1938/44. Author's collection.

active arms and hands as physical manifestation of the melody or lyric, employing regular cutting to or splicing of shots of moving bodies—dancers, a cat—which add visual momentum to her corporeal static-ness. On stage singing live, she could be sitting in an elaborate (disguised wheel)chair, and be pulled by stagehands in the wings and maneuvered to center stage, or she would be apparently standing ready for the audience and the song, curtains opening to reveal her already in position. In these instances an adapted barstool would be used, hidden beneath a voluminous stage dress. Historically, from the theatrical dance tradition of ballet, "postural uprightness and verticality were imbued with connotations of nobility and moral conduct": "the emphasis placed on carriage . . . was predicated on a belief in the self-representational potential of the body" (Smith 2005, 77, 76). Yet for Boswell, chaired, or for many of the limping polios, pop stars, and rockers, there have needed to be different self-representational possibilities.

A notable number of other children and young people who would go on to make their mark in various music fields were struck by "the crippler." Table 1 is an incomplete list, but it has value because it illustrates the numbers involved, as well as the geographical locations—and global shifts, as both shifts in music production and vaccination programs impacted—and musical distribution.

As noted, this medical-musical cluster can be partly explained by the concurrence of polio epidemics with the childhood years of an early pop and rock generation, dramatized—or made poignant—by virtue of the fact that many of these young people were among the last ever to contract the disease (in the West[3]). So, broadly speaking, while those who contracted polio in the 1940s and 1950s on this list were in Tony Gould's phrase "born too soon" (1995, 188) in the sense that they were too young to benefit from the imminent introduction of the vaccines, they were also born at just the right time to feel the beat of the rock and pop worlds of youth music, the counterculture, and beyond. (As discussed in the introduction, there is a wider coincidence of polio occurrence and mass communications technologies in the twentieth century.) I look at this claim, and at ways in which they would find in the *youthquake*'s new sonicities and performative practices opportunities to make sense of their own disabled bodies, to accommodate their childhood "changes" (Neil Young), to revisit from adulthood their "dreams of [being] paralysed" (Steve Harley), to sing their medicalized autobiographies: "If they're caring for me why do they boot me and punch me?" (Ian Dury). The validity of such a connection is interrogated in fig. 7.

TABLE 1.1. Popular Musicians Who Contracted Polio

| Name | Music, Location | Polio Contracted |
|------|-----------------|------------------|
| Connie Boswell | singer, actress (USA) | c. 1910 |
| Dinah Shore | singer, actress (USA) | 1918 |
| Brownie McGhee | blues singer and guitarist (USA) | c. 1919 |
| Horace Parlan | jazz pianist (USA) | 1931 |
| Doc Pomus | rock and roll songwriter (USA) | 1931 |
| Carl Perkins | bebop pianist (USA) | c. 1930s |
| CeDell Davis | blues slide guitarist (USA) | c. 1936 |
| Michael Flanders | music hall/radio singer (UK) | 1943 |
| Ray Peterson | pop singer (USA) | c. 1940s |
| Walter Jackson | soul singer (USA) | 1940s |
| Judy Collins | folk singer (USA) | 1948 |
| David Sanborn | jazz saxophonist (USA) | 1948 |
| Ian Dury | rock singer (UK) | 1949 |
| Donovan | folk singer (UK) | 1949 |
| Dave Liebman | jazz saxophonist (USA) | 1949 |
| Neil Young | rock guitarist and singer (Canada) | 1951 |
| Joni Mitchell | singer-songwriter (Canada) | 1951 |
| Charlie Haden | jazz bassist (USA) | c. 1952 |
| Gene Simmons | rock musician (Israeli-born) | c. 1952 |
| Steve Harley | rock and pop singer (UK) | 1953 |
| Israel Vibration | reggae vocal trio/duo (Jamaica) | 1950s–60s |
| Staff Benda Bilili | street band (Congo) | c. 1960s–80s |

To historicize a little further though we need also to recognize the medical situations of some countries in the developing world, and acknowledge that the most recent polio and pop expressions are not from the successfully vaccinated West but from less developed areas of the world. In this way polio, even in what we hope is its terminal narrative moment, is *still* able to demarcate the privilege of access to advanced health services, including vaccinations. So Jamaican reggae and African guitar-based dance music from the Democratic Republic of the Congo constitute the later musical manifestations by polio survivors.

There are important considerations concerning the weakened physical body's capacity to make music for the instrumentalists among these polio survivors—especially for those from blues, jazz, and jazz-tinged musics who valorized instrumental technique as a route to musical individuality.[4] For instance, Joni Mitchell has explained her unusual guitar chord technique, and hence characteristic acoustic sound, as the result of her attenuated muscularity: "My left hand is somewhat clumsy because of polio. I had

Fig. 7. Walter Jackson single advertisement, 1966. © Ace Records Ltd., London. Used with permission.

to simplify the shapes of the left hand, but I craved chordal movement that I couldn't get out of standard tuning without an extremely articulate left hand" (quoted in Houston 2000). What we can view as Mitchell's cripping of technique was bold indeed: she drew on the blues of the past and helped shape the rock of her present by also delving into jazz.

*introducing* **CARL PERKINS**

MODERN JAZZ SERIES

DTL-211

With LEROY VINNEGAR, *Bass* And LAWRENCE MARABLE, *Drums*

WAY CROSS TOWN
YOU DON'T KNOW WHAT LOVE IS
THE LADY IS A TRAMP
MARBLEHEAD

WOODYN YOU
WESTSIDE
JUST FRIENDS

IT COULD HAPPEN TO YOU
WHY DO I CARE
LILACS IN THE RAIN
CARL'S BLUES

Here is Carl Perkins. The newest and freshest of the Modern Jazz pianists with the most unique technique of them all. Since childhood, Carl has employed his left hand in a backward position while playing the piano, suspending his left arm over the keys and using his elbow to play additional bass notes. This, combined with his highly imaginative ideas, gives him a dynamic and exciting new sound.

In this album of original and standard tunes, Carl plays the principal types of music on the Jazz scene and proves that he is the master of blues, ballads and up-tempo rhythms. Credit should also be given to Leroy Vinnegar and Lawrence Marable who provide perfect backing and exciting moments of solo artistry.

Carl Perkins was born in Indianapolis on August 16, 1928 and began his professional musical career with Tiny Bradshaw's band in 1948. He moved to the West Coast a year later and with the exception of 2 years in the Armed Services, has worked with his trio and other top Jazz men in Los Angeles. A favorite of most Jazz men, Perkins has played with Miles Davis, Max Roach, Dizzy Gillespie, Illinois Jacquet, Stuff Smith, Clifford Brown, Frank Morgan and Dexter Gordon.

**BEST SELLING 33-1/3 12 INCH LONG PLAYING ALBUMS**

**JAZZ**

DEXTER BLOWS HOT AND COOL
Dexter Gordon's Jazz Stars
Silver Plated • Don't Worry About Me •
Blowing for Dootsie • I Hear Music

INTRODUCING CARL PERKINS
Progressive Piano Stylings
Carl Perkins and Trio

BUDDY'S BEST
THE BUDDY COLLETTE QUINTET
Soft Touch • It's You • My Funny
Valentine • The Cute Monster and Others

EXPLORING THE FUTURE
The Curtis Counce Quintet
So Nice • Angel Eyes • Into the Orbit
and Others

**ROCK 'N' ROLL**

BEST VOCAL GROUPS IN ROCK 'N' ROLL
—12 Hit Songs
The Cuff Links • Penguins • Medallions •
Pipes • Meadowlarks • Birds • Souvenirs
• Romancers • Calvanes

THE COOL COOL PENGUINS
Do Not Pretend • Sweet Love • Lover
or Fool • Cold Heart and Others

ROCK 'N' ROLL VS. RHYTHM 'N' BLUES
Roy Milton and Chuck Higgins
Reeling and Rocking • The Itch • Tanky
Honk and Others

HIT VOCAL GROUPS
The Medallions, The Penguins, the Cuff
Links
Speedin' • My Pretty Baby • Be Mine or
Be a Fool • So Tough • It's Too Late
Now and Others

**SPIRITUAL AND GOSPEL**

SPIRITUAL MOMENTS
The Famous Lillian Randolph Singers
17 of the World's Best Loved Spirituals

BEST GOSPEL SINGERS
Zion Travelers, Soul Revivers, etc.
12 All-Time Gospel Hits

**POPULAR**

DANCE PARTY
Peppy Prince Orchestra
Ghost of a Chance • Solitude •
I Cried For You • Diane and Others

**COMEDY**

THE FUN TICKLERS
Hilarious humor by the world's greatest
comics, including Redd Foxx, Allen Drew,
Don Bexley and Dave Turner

If Not Available at Your Dealer Order Direct—*Send for Free Catalog*
DOOTO RECORDS AND TAPES • 800 WEST 1st STREET • LOS ANGELES, CA 90012

Fig. 8. Back cover of 1956 LP, *Introducing . . . Carl Perkins* album, showing his "crab"-like left-hand position and technique. © Ace Records Ltd., London. Used with permission.

In the beginning, I built on the repertoire of the open major tunings that the old black blues guys came up with. It was only three or four. The simplest one was D modal (D A D G D B); Neil Young uses that a lot. And then open D (D G D G B D), with the fifth string removed, which is all Keith Richards uses. . . . Then going between them I started to get more "modern" chords. (quoted in Bego 2005, 29–30)

Mitchell's was a strategy of adaptation, and the resultant music was not heard as an expression of limitation—rather, it was prized by her, her fellow musicians, and her fans as the articulation of an individual voice: "good thing I couldn't [play standard technique] because it came out original" (quoted in Bego 2005, 29). It is estimated that there are "at least 35 unique tuning" innovated by Mitchell in her guitar playing, as well as many minor variations on these (O'Brien 2001, 209). In later life, due to post–polio syndrome causing her further muscular atrophy, Mitchell sought out different guitars on which to continue playing her different tunings. These specially constructed guitars were particularly lightweight, shaped to her body contour, to reduce stress on her back and left arm (see Hecht 2003, 72); intriguingly, bearing in mind Mitchell's folk singer-songwriter origins and the historic controversy around Bob Dylan's electric turn in the 1960s, each was an electric not an acoustic instrument. An added benefit in live performances was that the electric guitar, linked to a computer, could access all of her alternate tunings instantly (O'Brien 2001, 263). Elsewhere, polio forced the blues guitarist CeDell Davis to "rethink" his approach to his instrument, and Davis has remained a controversial figure in the blues tradition in part because of his unorthodox musicality. According to blues writer Robert Palmer, who also produced Davis's 1990s recordings:

[Davis explained:] "I was right-handed, but I couldn't use my right hand, so I had to turn the guitar around; I play left-handed now. But I still needed something to slide with, and my mother had these knives, a set of silverware, and I kinda swiped one of 'em."

This was the beginning of a guitar style that is utterly unique, in or out of blues. The knife-handle on the strings produces uneven pressure, which results in a welter of metal-stress harmonic transients and a singular tonal plasticity. Some people who hear CeDell's playing for the first time think it's out of tune, but it would be more accurate to say he plays in an alternative tuning. (Palmer 2004)

Whether "utterly unique," "out of tune," or employing an "alternative tuning," we begin to glimpse within music an adaptive technique which may be
both common across polio survivors more widely *and* the very route away
from the commonplace toward the individual.

The West Coast modern jazz pianist Carl Perkins, whose left arm had
residual paralysis from childhood polio, played with this arm parallel to the
keyboard, and was known as "the crab" for his sideways-on technique.
("*Crab-walk* became a common term used by doctors in the 1950s to describe the way that their polio patients moved": Shell 2005a, 146.) As fig. 3
shows, the back-cover photograph on his only album as leader, *Introducing . . . Carl Perkins,* clearly displays Perkins's physically adapted playing
position (Perkins 1956). The sleeve note explains that this approach to the
instrument has given him "the most unique technique of them all. . . . [By]
suspending his left arm over the keys and using his elbow to play additional
bass notes [he has] a dynamic and exciting new sound" (Perkins 1956). Arguably, with the compensatory introduction of the elbow as part of the
playing body, Perkins's physical incapacity has effectively extended instrumental range. Like another modern jazz pianist, Horace Parlan, Perkins
challenges the totality of the assumption that, "to claim the title *pianist,* one
must have two functioning hands" (Lerner 2006, 75; emphasis in original)—
and more, that these should be "fully, often fabulously, able hands" (Lubet
2011, 54). Parlan recovered from childhood polio but with his *right* hand
and the right side of his body partially paralyzed. This would normally have
a greater impact on piano technique than a restricted left hand, such as
Perkins's, particularly in jazz, where a bassist was usually also present: many
bassists expect a lighter touch from the left hand of a pianist when they are
playing together, to avoid the muddiness of two sets of bass notes. It was
recommended by his childhood doctor that Parlan take up the piano as a
form of physiotherapy. Parlan learned to compensate in his piano playing
by using his left hand (which usually plays bass notes and chordal accompaniment) also for mid-range melodic phrasing and soloing. This helped him
find the kind of alternate individual voice so prized in jazz instrumental-
ism, as explained admiringly by the English jazz critic Leonard Feather in
his 1960 sleeve notes for Parlan's first Blue Note album.

> The fourth and fifth fingers of the right hand are not used at all. The second and
> middle fingers, and sometimes the thumb, are used to complete voicings of
> chords that are basically supplied by the left hand. Occasionally, too, the left

hand is used exclusively in single-note lines. Incredible as it may seem, along with all of this, the left hand does a normal job of comping in its regular register. (quoted in Wimmer, n.d.)

In fact, Alex Lubet has recently reviewed Parlan's playing, and revises Feather's old but enduring description of his right-hand impairment and technique: in Lubet's view, "index and pinky" fingers are used only—and no thumb—"these appear to be largely immobile, but positioned such that Parlan can maneuver them like xylophone mallets . . . [and] he is able to play all-important octaves" with them too (Lubet 2011, 52). Alto saxophonist David Sanborn contracted polio at the age of three in 1948—it dangerously affecting his breathing. He was confined to respiratory treatment (the "iron lung") for a period, and subsequently took up a wind instrument for the purpose of physical therapy (see Sanborn, n.d.). That such polio survivors—professional musicians with disabilities—are jazzers is not lost on Lubet, who sees the jazz cultural system—as opposed to the Western classical tradition—as, even "if no utopia, provid[ing] expressive latitudes sufficient to accommodate the embodied variations of technique and style" of such instrumental players. Both Parlan and Sanborn were encouraged to take up their instruments in childhood as an element of their physiotherapy and recovery; as Marc Shell has noted, "for some polios, more than for most other people, performing music is a supremely athletic challenge" (2005a, 220). For each, it is arguable that the successful musical career came about *because rather than in spite of* the childhood disease, musicality originating as a therapeutic response to the residual symptoms of the medical condition. And this took place in the music of jazz, "whose essence is *the embrace of difference*" (Lubet 2011, 65; emphasis added).

In March 1962, one of the earliest popular music interventions around polio was made, with the broadcast on BBC Radio's Home Service of Ewan MacColl, Peggy Seeger, and Charles Parker's "radio ballads."[5] Entitled *The Body Blow*, this was the fifth in their innovative series of eight documentaries that combined the sound effects of actualité, the original voices of interviewees recorded in situ, and specially composed folk music by MacColl and Seeger. Subjects of the radio ballads included the working class (train drivers, road builders, fishermen, miners), but also some identity groups at the margins of society (the new teenagers, travelers, and, in *The Body Blow*, a group of adult polio survivors). Producer Parker explained that he was presenting "the intensely personal experience of a group of polio sufferers, with the intention of purging the healthy person's somewhat atavistic fears of the grievously deformed or disabled" (quoted in Cox 2008, 122). If the outward aim of the program was focused on changing the perceptions of the audience toward people with disabilities, the core purpose of the radio ballads in general was to present the authentic voice of the subject. (All five musicians donated their recording royalties for *The Body Blow* to the Polio Research Fund: Cox 2008, 123.) *The Body Blow* had an intriguing further result. One of the interviewees, Dutchy Holland, was literally part of the program's restorative project; his capacity to speak depended entirely on the phase of his mechanical ventilator ("he could only speak on the 'inspiration' phase of the iron lung's breath": Cox 2008, 122). But through the recording and editing of Holland's voice, the program presented an enabled communication. As the disembodied voice of the radio program narrator explains approvingly and comfortingly to the listening audience, to Holland's "machine-chopped speech, the tape recorder, with the editing it makes possible, can restore wholeness" (MacColl et al. 1999). That's some media program, to be capable of "restoring wholeness."[6]

Although criticized at the time and more recently (see Cox 2008, 126–27, 193–95; Harker 2007, 170–71), the actual music in this radio ballad has some moments of wonderful effect—notably, in the section "Can't Breathe," which juxtaposes the sound and rhythm of the iron lung with a pared-down instrumentation featuring English concertina (an instrument, of course, in which the sounds are produced by mechanical wind manipulation), and MacColl and Seeger's contrasting voices singing lyrics in unison about "your friendly machine." The machine's rhythm sets the tempo for the song, while also faintly and pathetically evoking the sound of waves breaking on a beach; the concertina is played so tentatively that its introductory solo notes sound vulnerable, shaky, about to give way. The lyrics admittedly do veer uncertainly between precise well-expressed detail and sentimentality or melodrama, even in the same verse.

> Steel and plastic deputy for lungs
> Does your breathing for you night and day.
> This small machine, you shield, your sword and butler,
> Holds death at bay. (MacColl et al. 1999)

Discussing *The Body Blow* with Peter Cox in 2007, Peggy Seeger's view of her own contribution was that "the problem is the singing is too sweet—[it evokes] self pity; it should have been factual singing—this is soppy sing-ing. . . . [but] I love the tunes" (personal correspondence with Cox, 2008).

So far, then, for the likes of Dury, Steve Harley, Young, and Mitchell, their common experiences were twofold: childhood polio in the late 1940s or early 1950s—disease and medicalization—and then growing up as teen-agers and young people through the sonic boom of the counterculture. The '40s and '50s shaped (misshaped) them; the '60s shaped them again. A cul-tural cluster like this polio-pop one is also explicable by foregrounding the solitariness and introspection of much treatment of the disease—separated from peers and family, polio children would draw on the artistic compensa-tion of the isolate.[7] Here, we can identify one of the creative opportunities that can be—that has been—carved out of what Ato Quayson calls the "car-ceral economy of medicalization" (2007, 52). Tony Gould, the English writer of *A Summer Plague: Polio and its Survivors,* explains that studying for a degree in English literature was only a possibility for him *after* polio, which he contracted at the age of twenty: university was "a place where—BP—I never imagined I would be going. . . . The switch to a cerebral life was di-rectly attributable to polio" (1995, 312). Joni Mitchell has spoken of her "childhood illnesses that developed a solitude and a deepening and fostered 'artisticness'. . . . I think that the creative process was an urgency then, that it was a survival instinct" (quoted in Mattteo, n.d.). Of her yearlong polio rehabilitation from the age of nine she has concluded that "convalescence in bed develops a strong inner life as a young child" (quoted in Bego 2005, 20). The 1970s English pop singer Harley spent three-and-a-half childhood years in hospital: "I wasn't hit badly [by polio], but it changed my life. . . . For a long time my life was in a bedside cabinet and it was a notebook and pen, all words, words, words. . . . I am solitary as a result" (quoted in Cooper 2005, 48). His long-term impairment consists of atrophied right-leg mus-cles, related limping gait, and chronic uncertainty of balance. In the 1980s he came out of semi-retirement to accept the lead role in a new Andrew Lloyd Webber musical, *The Phantom of the Opera,* in which he would play and sing a disfigured hero. He was replaced after extensive rehearsals but before opening night with the suggestion that "the legacy of his polio . . . caused doubts about his ability with the physical rigours of the part" (Coo-per 2005, 48). Although I argue later that Harley's lyrics, his music, and his voice all bear traces of the experience of disability, it was only in 2005—thirty years after his hits—that he actually sang explicitly of his own childhood polio experience, in a slow heavy rock song called "The Last Feast," which he has described as "a primal scream . . . . remember[ing] pain beyond description after the [corrective] surgery" (quoted in Cooper 2005, 48). In fact, the direct lyrical reference is largely confined to the chorus, in which the childhood memory of polio-induced paralysis is compared and contrasted with his current desired state of religious grace.

Sweet angels, open my eyes
I been dreaming I've been paralysed
Sweet angels, open my eyes
I been dreaming I'm in paradise. (Cockney Rebel 2005)

For some of the singers identified here, periods of treatment—and, in particular, stretches of residential rehabilitation, which could effectively mean years of childhood institutionalization—did also at least present the opportunity for entertaining with the voice. After all, the polio ward held a pretty captive audience. 1960s pop singer Ray Peterson first began singing as a boy when he was undergoing treatment at President Franklin D. Roosevelt's famous Warm Springs hydrotherapeutic center in Georgia. Joni Mitchell's youthful singing was rather more protest-oriented.

I guess I really started singing when I had polio. . . . They said I might not walk again and that I would not be able to go home for Christmas. I wouldn't go for it. So I started to sing Christmas carols, and I used to sing them real loud. When the nurse came into the room I would sing louder. (quoted in Crowe 1979)

Danny Goodley has written of the fact that, "despite these effects of institutionalisation . . . constraints have the paradoxical effect of *promoting resistance*" (2003, 116; emphasis added). In Canada in 1951, both Mitchell (aged nine years) and Neil Young (aged five) contracted the virus; Mitchell has said that "Neil and I have a lot in common: Canadian; Scorpios; polio in the same epidemic, struck the same parts of our body" (quoted in McDonough 2002, 96). In Young's case, as his father wrote at the time, overnight the child "moved like a mechanical man, jerkily, holding his head in a tense position" (quoted in Rutty 1988, 8–9). Home after a short period of hospital isolation, the boy told his father "Polio is the worst cold there is" (quoted in Rutty 1988, 15). Young's polio impairment consists of "a slight limp evident when he walks" (Rutty 1988, 25, n92), and he elaborates:

Polio fucked up my body a little bit. The left-hand side got a little screwed. Feels different from the right. If I close my eyes, my left side, I really don't know where it is—but over the years I've discovered that almost one hundred per cent for sure it's gonna be very close to my right side . . . probably to the left. (quoted in McDonough 2002, 46)

In Christopher J. Rutty's view, the 1970 Young song "Helpless" contains his childhood memories of the experience of the disease. The song focuses on the moment, location, and aftermath—both immediate and long-term—of the boy's contraction of the virus—and possibly also of the girl's, if we bear in mind a famous performance of "Helpless" such as Young's in *The Last Waltz* film of the star-studded 1976 concert organized by The Band. Here, Joni Mitchell features on backing vocals; the two Canadian polios on the same stage singing the same song about a shared past (Scorsese 1978). (Mitchell's intriguing reference of disability culture is occasionally seen elsewhere, in, for example, the framed self-portrait she used as the cover for her 1994 album *Turbulent Indigo,* where she presents herself as Vincent van Gogh, complete with bandaged ear.) We are in a very specific geographical and temporal place: "a town in north Ontario," remembering the singer's own childhood: "All my changes were there" (Young 1970). The song title is also a kind of single word chorus, *and* is repeated in groups of four by backing singers, including the fade-out at the song's end. Such a repeated state of *helpless*ness captures the family moment, which is one of disease, uncertainty, dread, as well as perhaps some social shame, since, as Young sings, "The chains are locked and tied across the door." Standard procedure by medical authorities to polio outbreaks in Canada and elsewhere (see Shell 2005a, 32–34) meant that Young would be isolated in hospital, while his family were subject to quarantine at home, his father remembering: "I was the only one . . . allowed out . . . , and only to buy groceries. The white quarantine sign greeted me every time I returned to the house . . . the words on the sign 'Poliomyelitis. Infantile Paralysis'" (quoted in Rutty 1988, 10).[8] The high tremolo of both Young's voice and the guitar, and the melancholic fall of the voice at the end of most lines, contribute to the pathos of the situation described. Alongside the lyrics, Young's falsetto-style vocal delivery also takes the listener back to a boy's childhood—a point we will return to in chapter 2's discussion of disabled voices.

In the case of reggae group Israel Vibration, the fact of institutionaliza-

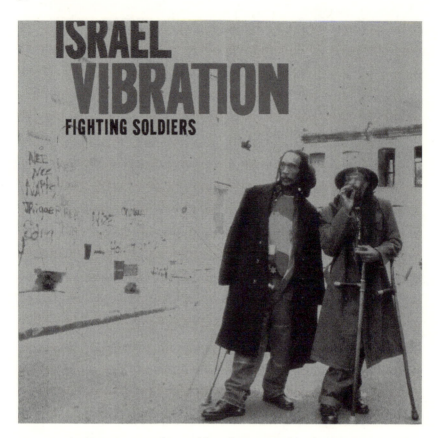

Fig. 9. Israel Vibration 2002 *Fighting Soldiers* album cover: "they hold the metal crutches like rifles . . . a mix of gangster and 'fighting' polio survivor." © Nocturne Records, Paris.

tion was formative for the group: separation from the majority effected a stronger minority identity, since the three original members met and began to sing with each other while they were long-term residents at the Mona Rehabilitation Centre, near Kingston, Jamaica. The three young men had several points in common: a passion for the close harmony reggae singing popular at the time, an interest in Rastafarianism, and the experiences of polio and institutionalization. Their first public performance was at the Theological College next door to the center in 1974. When they left the center, some other Rastafarians rejected them, seeing their impairments as a punitive sign from God (see *Riverfront Times* 1996). When performing live onstage the singers are able to stand and move around by use of their crutches, while on the cover photography of their 2002 album, *Fighting Soldiers,* they pose with their walking aids on a rundown street. In one image, they hold the metal crutches like rifles and point them at the viewer—a mix of gangster and "fighting" polio survivor. Occasionally, Israel Vibration sing songs that resonate with their experience of impairment, while even the reggae accompaniment, with its characteristic and insistent offbeat rhythm and chords, seems suddenly more fitting for musicians with mobility difficulties, where a lilt is no longer so far removed from a limp. Indeed, Israel Vibration invite us to consider reggae music per se as a music of disability, precisely because of its *alla zoppa* characteristics.[9] Song titles like "Tippy Tippy Toes" and "Level Every Angle" emphasize the visual and sonic narrative of disability. It is not difficult to hear the latter as extending the fairly standard post–civil rights and post–Bob Marley rhetoric of one-love reggae into a kind of disability rights context. So "Level Every Angle" becomes at least in part Israel Vibration's plea for public spaces and design to consider the access requirements of mobility restricted people, as they sing:

> Some people are blessed while others are cursed . . .
> From every angle things should be level
> And everything would be all right. (Israel Vibration 2002)

While being eradicated in much of the world with the introduction of successful national vaccination programs from the 1950s on, polio would still be an active disease in the Caribbean, in some parts of Africa, and elsewhere. There are a number of polio survivors in Staff Benda Bilili—a group of disabled street musicians from Kinshasa—in the Democratic Republic of the Congo (see fig. 31). The sleeve notes to their 2009 debut album, *Très Très Fort,* explain that the band "are like nothing you have ever *seen* or *heard* before"—laid bare is the visual appeal of the disabled body in pop. The notes continue by describing and explaining:

> Four singer/guitarists, sitting on tricycles and occasionally dancing on the floor of the stage, arms raised in joyful supplication, are the core of the band, backed by a younger, all-acoustic rhythm section pounding out tight beats. . . . Benda Bilili means "look beyond appearances"—literally: *put forward what is hidden.* (Staff Benda Bilili 2009, first emphases added)

Look beyond appearances: the band's name is effectively a disability activism slogan. One of their key songs is entitled (on the English-language release) "Polio," and its lyrics deal directly with the personal experience of living with polio and are a call to action, like a public information announcement, urging people to have the polio vaccination:

> I was born as a strong man but polio crippled me
> Look at me today, I'm screwed onto my tricycle. . . .
> Parents, please go to the vaccination centre
> Get your babies vaccinated against polio. (Staff Benda Bilili 2009)

This lyric is quite unlike any of the other rock and pop ones we have looked at about disability caused by polio, for the reason that it is written and sung in a social context where polio is still an active virus, a real health threat. Dancing to a pop song with a lyric that sings "Get your babies vaccinated" makes a direct and powerful message—arguably made more so by virtue of being sung by polio-disabled musicians.

## Ian Dury: "Hallo to you out there in Normal Land"

> Cole Porter . . . fell off his horse and never wrote another decent song. You'd think it would be the other way round, wouldn't you?
>
> —Ian Dury (quoted in Birch 2010, 200)

> The stereotype of the "flawed" artist remains as strong as ever within western culture. Post-punk singer Ian Curtis, of the cult rock band Joy Division, for example, owed some of his reputation for tragic extremism to his epilepsy. But while impairment may on occasion be said to add to the appeal or the insight of a particular artistic figure, it is important to remember that many artists with accredited impairments have denied or ignored this aspect of their lives. Others have reacted in a personal rather than a political way. Contemporary examples include musicians Ray Charles, Jacqueline du Pré, Evelyn Glennie, Stevie Wonder, Hank Williams and Ian Dury.
>
> —Colin Barnes (2003, 7–8)

I want to take issue with the last named by Colin Barnes here. It is my argument that in fact Ian Dury—that "flaw of the jungle"—produced a remarkable and sustained body of work that explored issues of disability, in both personal and social contexts, institutionalization, and, to an extent, the pop cultural tradition of disability. He also, with the single "Spasticus Autisticus" (1981), produced one of the outstanding protest songs about the place of disabled people in what he called "normal land."[10] Jim Drury makes the passing observation that, as Dury's career developed, "he began singing more frequently about life as a disabled person" (2003, 95), but such a trajectory is, I think, extremely unusual for pop and rock musicians. It is arguable that, in this book, only Neil Young has a comparable cripworthy portfolio. And we can see that Dury himself recognized the place of autobiography and suffering in songwriting because of his wonderfully sharp comment about Cole Porter; in Dury's perception, as in his life, songs would *improve* after falling off the horse, because then there is experience to draw on.

The music business could be nervous about pop engaging directly with disability, though. One of Dury's managers, Peter Jenner, sensed that his disabled body was a significant turnoff for the major record companies. In fact, in his pre-punk career, Dury had once been judged "unsuitable for stardom" by CBS's A&R department (Muirhead 1983, 17), while even the professional chaotics at the punk–era Stiff Records could be nervous about telling the truth about one of their biggest stars. Dury's decision to appear in the video for the chart-topping single "Hit Me With Your Rhythm Stick" in 1979 *without* a jacket—hence displaying his withered arm—what the video's producer understood as Dury's act of "com[ing] out about his disability"—sparked a panic at the record company (see Balls 2000, 203). He sang on "Spasticus" that "You can read my body but you'll never read my books," yet the texts he produced, his song lyrics, were a compelling counterpoint to a straightforward, or inescapable, reading of his body. Sometimes, his body *was* his book, as he wrote autobiographical and observational lyrics about disability, and then performed those stories on stage. The artist and sometimes Dury bandsman Humphrey Ocean has described the impact of Dury's arrival somewhere: "His body became part of the room, and the dynamic changed" (quoted in Birch 2010, 79).

In the summer of 1949, aged seven years, Dury contracted polio in an open-air municipal swimming pool in Southend. He spent the next eighteen months in Black Notley Hospital, Essex, in a ward full of seriously ill and disabled children, and then transferred for three-and-a-half years to the residential Chailey Heritage Craft School and Hospital in Sussex, de-

Fig. 10. Stiff Records package tour poster, 1977, Dury far right: "the most scandalous and hilarious anti-hero to have emerged in the year of punk." Author's collection.

scribed by its founder Grace Kimmins in 1903 in the language of the time as "the public school of crippledom," located in an old workhouse building, with origins in the Victorian Guild of the Brave Poor Things (Borsay 2005, 108; see also Balls 2000, 35–36). Some of Dury's songs from the height of his success draw directly on his own autopathography—in particular, those five childhood years of institutionalization.

By the 1950s Chailey was a National Health Service residential school and hospital for children with disabilities, and severe deformities, based around an austere ethos of fostering independence—the success of which Dury did acknowledge in later life: "Chailey made me strong physically and mentally," he said in 1999 (quoted in Balls 2000, 43). Combined with this, though, was some stark discipline, which, in Dury's memory, segued into institutional violence—between children and by caregivers. On top of this, Dury recalled sexual abuse: "A lot of the staff were pervs. No buggery, but a lot of enforced wanking" (quoted in Balls 2000, 36). What is confirmed in his experience from the 1950s is a longer-lasting practice of physical and psychological abuse within British residential special schools, as Anne Borsay has outlined.

> Some special schools were brutal with harsh discipline and living conditions reminiscent of the workhouse. . . . [They] failed to react appropriately to their pupils' emotional responses, shaming them into the repression of feelings about impairment and family separation. . . . The significance of disability was also denied. Schools made strenuous efforts at "normalization" by experimenting with new aids and appliances. Their staff mocked the academic abilities of pupils and their capacity for personal care. (2005, 114)

Others, more critical still from disability studies and activism, have thought of such strategies and institutions of separatism as the "disability gulag" (Harriet McBryde Johnson, cited in Siebers 2008, 158)—which "represents control as care and protection and describes forced confinement as voluntary placement" (see Siebers 2008, 158–59)—or as "eugenic locations" (Snyder and Mitchell 2006, 4).

In his music, Dury was powerfully critical too. It is highly likely that his most compelling and harrowing song about the institutionalization of disabled people, "Hey, Hey, Take Me Away," from the 1980 album, ironically titled *Laughter,* draws on his experiences of life at Chailey. I suggest also that the song title and repeated phrase in Dury's song—a one-line chorus, a plea—is a jokey reference to the 1966 summer novelty hit by Napoleon XIV about mental breakdown and the lunatic asylum: "They're Coming to Take Me Away, Ha-Haaa!," which is also echoed in each song's lyrics' dactylic rhythm. But Dury's "take me away" is an act of liberation rather than confinement: he wants to be taken away *from* the place rather than being taken *to* it.

> Hey, hey, take me away
> I hate waking up in this place
> There's nutters in here who whistle and cheer
> When they're watching a one-legged race
> And a one-legged prefect gets me in bed
> Makes me play with his dick
> One-legged horn and he's shouting the odds
> Driving me bloody well sick. (Dury 1980)

Dury's opening vocal scream and Davey Payne's saxophone harmonics are reprised from earlier songs like "Dance of the Screamers" for the supply of emotional intensity and disturbance, but there is so much more in this one short (under two-and-a-half minutes) song—as well as a clear distanciation from other disabled people ("I hate waking up in this place"). Lyrically, co-writer Mickey Gallagher remembers it from the recording sessions as "the song that shocked everybody" (quoted in Drury 2003, 120). It covers masturbation, adventures of escape, sexual abuse, physical violence by caregivers, physical violence between children, the fear of and disgust at the disabled body or mind, self-loathing, suicide, the yearning to be "normal". . . . Dury's delivery moves between spoken word, angry and rushed shouting and swearing, and a pathetic sobbing that is sometimes a whisper. Gallagher heard in this crying Dury's familiar "best acting voice, which he probably developed as a boy in those institutions, to get people on his side" (quoted in Drury 2003, 122). The editing of the voice tracks is extraordinary and sometimes brutal, and contributes powerfully to the song's confusion, discomfort, and fright: one can hear the joins, sense the edifice, feel the effort needed to hold it together. Some of Dury's words are spliced out halfway through, odd sentences make no sense, he runs out of time toward the end as the prerecorded music runs away from him, he misses a cue and speeds his words both to catch up and to fit the remaining bars. In its reflexivity the recording process is laid bare, of course, but more importantly the listener is disrupted and disturbed. Such "formal deviation" within the finished product of a pop song is noteworthy, not least as "formal deviations, which are dealt with harshly in real life when manifested as bodily deformities, may be prized within art; . . . in musical forms, the 'deformations' are often the most highly valued" (Straus 2011, 113).

Dury presented a cluster of masculine identities—the mid-twentieth-century music hall cheeky cockney à la Max Wall (a comedian renowned for his visually excessive walking) or Max Miller, the elder punk dandy, the bohemian art school jazz buff, the frank raconteur of disability, for instance. His first biographer Richard Balls described his 1977 performances as offering a stage persona and costume that ranged from Bill Sykes to the Pearly King to Tommy Cooper (2000, 177). With asper gusto he embraced one of the key roles available to some people with disabilities since the king's fool of the Middle Ages: "to display the underside of society" (Stiker 1997, 70). There was also in Dury's writing an approach to sexuality (and not necessarily solely heterosexuality) that told stories ranging from tongue-tied fancying to tongue-twisting sexual acts. Even in gender terms Dury recognized himself to be not quite "straight"—the lace glove onstage, songs like "Su(e) perman's Big Sister." (It is worth here considering the cracks in the constructions of masculinity in Dury's work with the more overt cultural exploration of gender and sexuality in the poems of American polio survivor Mark O'Brien: "O'Brien's representation of disability collapses gender stereotypes based on the able body", but also "uses disability to confuse gender categories with sexual ones for the purpose of rejecting the stereotypical asexuality of disabled people": Siebers 2008, 172, 173.) The socialist writer David Widgery, who was himself a polio survivor, has explained: "That's why I found Ian Dury so emancipated. Suddenly there was this sex symbol who had a limp" (quoted in Gould 1995, 250). From another perspective, a problem with Dury as a cultural representative of disabled people may have been his dirty-old-man-in-a-mac persona—that in a way he confirmed for what he called the "walkie-talkies," the inhabitants of "normal-land," and what other disability activists have called the TABs (temporarily able-bodied), something distasteful, dangerous, deviant, sexually threatening within, even inherent to, people with disabilities.[11] Yet, is it possible that Dury instead confirms the acute observation made by Tobin Siebers in his discussion of O'Brien that "It is only by appearing oversexed that the disabled man appears to be sexed at all" (2008, 175)?

Some musical and subcultural movements created new cultural spaces and corporeal possibilities (see Church 2006 for a discussion of the 1960s hippie "freak" identity in the context of disability). Notably, the shocking enfreakment of punk rock was embodied in the staring, semi-hunchbacked Sex Pistols singer Johnny Rotten (both eye and spine permanently affected by childhood meningitis,[12] while his pseudonymous surname was in reference to the poor state of his teeth). Jon Savage (another pseudonym) has documented how, at an early gig in 1976, Rotten improvised a song introduction:

> Right!
> Here we go now
> *A sociology lecture*
> A bit of psychology
> *A bit of neurology*
> A bit of fuckology
> No fun! (quoted in Savage 1991, 156; emphasis added)

Versions of the body would figure centrally in the work of the Sex Pistols, from the band's name to the title of their one album, *Never Mind the Bollocks,* which contained a song called "Bodies," in which Rotten tells us repeatedly that "I'm not an animal" (Sex Pistols 1977). As already mentioned in the introduction, the dwarf was a freakish visual presence in the punk iconography of boutique and film alike, while bands with names like the Epileptics (UK), Disability, or the Cripples (both U.S.) were briefly popular. Subhumans was another punk band name: two significant bands—one in Canada; the other in Britain. The punk audience's style of anti-dancing, the pogo, and its preferred practice of greeting bands onstage by spitting or "gobbing" at them, signal corporeal nonconformity or excess. Dick Hebdige describes some of the features of punk that manifested themselves during and after the "freak disorder" of 1976, including dance that consisted of "twitches of the head and hands or more extravagant lurches," as well as "the ECT hairstyles" (1979, 24, 109, 121). According to Marc Bayard, "the early days of American hardcore' punk were populated by 'freaks and misfits'" (1999, 6). My own punk experience was partly informed by my own body, my own autopathography, as I rediscovered recently when I dug out an old piece of writing about the subject.

### BODIES

I'm learning a new way of walking too, there really is that in punk, a sort of spastic lope I'm quite good at. . . . Childhood memories of blood tests and biopsies in hospitals north and south of the border, and lying next to the Scottish boys in their iron lungs. *Let's see those legs, young man. Trip up a lot, you say?* I never knew my suspected dystrophic muscles would ever actually come in useful. If something like that can be a bonus, punk's the subculture for *mee-ah!* (McKay, n.d.a; italics in original)

To what extent did the punk aesthetic of the later 1970s make it possible for someone like Dury to find mainstream success? One of the clutch of blazing reviews of the groundbreaking Stiff Records package tour of 1977 described Dury as "the most scandalous and hilarious anti-hero to have emerged in the year of punk." In another, BBC Radio 1 DJ Annie Nightingale saw Dury as embodying the shift in rock music that punk was claiming: "Rock's latest hero is the very antithesis of the stereotype, flamboyant, aggressive sex symbol. Dury is 35 and still semi-crippled by polio which struck him at the age of seven. The walking stick he uses on stage is no theatrical prop" (quoted in Balls 2000, 183, 182–83). Yet it is important that we recognize that Dury's career predated punk. His founding band Kilburn and the High Roads (1971–76, with various lineups) relied heavily through the pub rock scene of those times on a visual distinctiveness predicated on freakery. (Intriguingly, it was around this time that, in Britain, the Union of the Physically Impaired Against Segregation (UPIAS) was articulating its radical social position in the influential manifesto *The Fundamental Principles of Disability* (see Barnes 2003). The analysis and action plan identified here would be important in the construction of the social model of disability.) As *New Musical Express* neatly encapsulated it in 1975, the Kilburns were

> composed almost entirely of demobbed cripples in chip-stained Dannimacs and vulcanised slip-ons. They all had short hair—badly cut and partially grown out like ex-cons. They had a bass player . . . who was nearly seven feet tall, a black drummer who had to be lowered manually onto his drum stool[,] and a lead singer with a stiff leg, a face like Gene Vincent, and a withered hand encased in a black glove. (quoted in Drury 2003, 15)

"Solidarity in marginality" (Stiker 1997, 60)? Later Kilburns members recognized the arresting visuality of their own freak show or circus troupe aesthetic—mandating not the gaze but the stare, in Thomson's distinction (see Thomson 2000). The band were, in the phrasing of Snyder and Mitchell, from a different sociohistorical context, but making the same point that this was culturally "unusual," "a convention of cripples . . . an array of disabled characters occupying a shared social space" (2006, 46, 45; see fig. 13). When "midget" (Dury's word) bassist Charlie Sinclair joined, he experienced what Dury called the "certain outcast thing" the band embodied and presented as their show.

> People would just stand and stare. They would just crowd around the stage and gawp most of the time. It was probably quite a frightening thing for some people. At the time it was all glam rock, but there was none of that with us. It was just a bunch of guys you would see on a park bench with a can of Super Lager or something. It really did look like 'care in the community' some days. It was disturbing visually. (all three quotations in Balls 2000, 119)

The "black drummer who had to be lowered manually onto his drum stool," David Rohoman, told me the following in 2010.

> Those successful years proved to me that if you have the determination, the drive, then you can achieve almost anything. Who dictates what the norm is? And being with Ian [Dury] in Kilburn and the High Roads, just made that feeling even stronger. That band was an intimidating and powerful collection of very unusual people, disabled, freakish, frightening I suppose for some of the audience. There was Ian at the front, me behind the drums, short little Charlie [Sinclair], great big tall Humphrey [Ocean], and on sax, yes, Davey Payne who you never quite knew what was going to happen with, always a bit of edge. [Laughs] No one else but Ian could have gotten that sort of bunch of musicians, those characters, to play together. It says a lot about his I suppose man management, not necessarily what you usually think of with Ian. He chose each person not only for their musical ability or inability, but as though he was making a painting, a mosaic. (McKay 2010b)

Some pop disabilities are among those which, like the freak shows of nineteenth-century America, could offer "a counternarrative of peculiarity as eminence" (Thomson 1997, 17), in which "enfreakment" could mean authenticity, authority, even status. Also, though, unlike other more contemporary popular manifestations of the relocated "freak show" (see Thomson 1996, part 6), the Kilburns seemed to pose an actual threat to audiences. As both Sinclair and Rohoman acknowledge, they were perceived as "frightening" and as "disturbing," and that was the audience reaction they aimed for.

The uncompromising visual image and attitudinal stance were key aspects of the Kilburns's stage practice, which both anticipated and then would speak to the punk generation about to be waiting in the wings.

Seeing Dury onstage with the Kilburns in the early 1970s, reviewers frequently compared his pose to that of the then recently deceased American rock-and-roll singer Gene Vincent, as well as noting his use of the microphone "as if it was some form of surgical apparatus" (*Time Out*)—"Either he was propping the mike stand up or it was keeping him upright" (*Melody Maker*) (see Balls 2000, 105–6). Of course, Dury would also pay homage to Vincent in his songs—in particular, 1977's "Sweet Gene Vincent." Vincent's performances of disability in black leathers and flaunted limp (from at least two road traffic accidents) were central to his British stage and television acts. In 1955, prior to his pop success, Vincent had been knocked off his motorbike in the United States, resulting in a permanent and visible limp, as well as a requirement to wear a steel brace to protect the seriously damaged left leg. The leg would be further damaged in another road traffic accident, along with a fractured collar bone, following a gig in England in 1960 (during which his tour companion the singer Eddie Cochran was killed). Following a backstage collapse the next year during another UK tour, Vincent would be reported in the music press flying back to the United States "mentally and physically broken" (Heslam 1992, 97). But his December 1959 British debut was reported in the *New Musical Express* thus: "In spite of an old leg injury which has left him slightly lame, Vincent performs miracles with the mike stand. . . . Add a peculiar half-crouching stance, and his act . . . was [as] exciting to watch as it was to hear" (quoted in Heslam 1992, 75). In the 1960s, British pop television producer Jack Good famously instructed Vincent to exaggerate his disability for the camera with the words: "Limp, you bugger, limp!" (quoted in Birch 2010, 86)—to be physically disabled onstage was now insufficient; the defect had to be ostentatiously performed before the camera to ensure that viewers at home would catch it. Dury talked in 1973 about Vincent's impact on him as a young fan in the 1950s and 1960s.

> Gene Vincent got to me more than anybody; he was in a special little category because he was what I wanted to be as a singer. *I didn't know he was crippled at the time, so that didn't have anything to do with it.* It was his head, the shape of his head, because it was opposite from mine. . . . It was his thinness, his wastedness. (quoted in Balls 2000, 54; emphasis added)

This remark dates from before he has written "Sweet Gene Vincent"—the lyrics of which acknowledge Vincent's physical frailty and disability ("lazy skin and ashtray eyes . . . But your leg still hurts")—a song Dury wrote in the company of a cardboard cutout of Vincent he kept in his flat. Yet even here Dury the pop fan is evaluating and articulating his musical enthusiasms within a corporeal framework. It is Vincent's body, the way it moves and is held in performance, as well as the "sad Virginia whisper" of his voice, that matters to Dury, and that he wants to emulate (Dury 1977).

So, it is arguable that Dury and the Kilburns's pre-punk performative strategy influenced the punk aesthetic of imperfection, rather than Dury's success being explained by the sonic, visual, and corporeal shift that punk may, or claimed to, have caused. At the final Kilburns concert of their fractious career, in London in 1976, one of the support acts was the Sex Pistols. Dury recognized with some concern in Johnny Rotten's clothing, bodily performance, and vocal delivery his own act, by a younger singer for a new generation of audience. He turned to the Sex Pistols' manager, Malcolm McLaren, and said "What's all that about, Malcolm? He's copying me, isn't he?" (quoted in Balls 2000, 143). The extraordinary contumacious body of young punk Rotten was drawing on the same of old punk Dury, but then Dury had been doing it for years with the Kilburns anyway, and also drawing on the imperfect rock-and-roll body of his own youthful idol in Gene Vincent. Compellingly, there is a strand of disabled cultural identity running through and connecting these three musical figures, these three generations, these three rock rebel front men, with Dury at the center of it.

Dury's 1980 song "I Want to be Straight" is usually understood as his own response to, even rewriting of, the early hit "Sex & Drugs & Rock & Roll," which was generally seen as an anthemic celebration of the hedonistic pop and rock lifestyle (though its lyrics suggest otherwise, offering a more knowingly critical position: "Keep your silly ways, throw them out the window"). But "I Want to be Straight" is more complex—possibly moving outside a heterosexual frame ("straight" as in not bent or queer), as well as "straight" in the obvious meaning of *not* hedonistically narcotized: "I want to be straight / I'm sick and tired of taking drugs and staying up late," he sings, after all. But from its very title as well as its deliberately pop-corny introduction, in which the band members introduce themselves to the listener in turn by first name, the song offers us a paean to orthodoxy perhaps, but more interestingly, a paean to orthotics. When the notoriously or legendarily "edgy" saxophonist Davey Payne (from the Kilburn days) an-nounces "My name . . . is David" he does so in his best (worst) disabled voice, for example, sounding like he has cerebral palsy. As a result of the historical development of orthopedics and orthotic technologies, "straightening out physically and straightening up behaviorally are put in the same semantic field, a normative one" (Stiker 1997, 115). Concluding the spoken introduction, bandleader Dury says "and I'm Ian, and—guess what?— OI!—I want to be straight," with the word "straight" landing on the first beat of the propulsive rhythm of the bulk of the song. It's his "guess what?" interjection here that interests me. Easily, of course, it refers the listener back to "Sex & Drugs" of three years before, and shows the change in the Dury persona that will surprise them. But should we be so very surprised at this disabled man who wants to be straight, who wants to confirm, who wants to conform? In *Polio and its Aftermath,* Marc Shell writes:

> Polio's asymmetrical freezing of various muscles made for deformities so visually disturbing that the science or art of orthopedics owes its development to "making the crooked straight" in the age of the polio epidemics. . . . Orthopedists explicitly promised parents that their surgeries would make their polio children more attractive. Tens of thousands of untreated polios were called deformed, misshapen, or hunchbacked. Even the "fixed grimace" face of bulbar polios came up for consideration. Polios who could not afford surgeries often earned their living in the freak shows. (Shell 2005a, 15)

Dury's performances influenced other performers outside music too. Actor Anthony Sher recalled his startling design of costume for the 1984 Royal Shakespeare Company production of *Richard III*: "a cross between a pirate and a slug, all in slimy black, wearing an ear-ring, hair spiked punkishly (modelled on Ian Dury who has polio), the crutches twisted and gnarled. The nightmare creature is there" (1985, 156). Thus Dury's corporeality, exaggerated, dehumanized, made more monstrous, affected wider cultural consciousness.

Let us turn now to "Spasticus Autisticus," Dury's controversial 1981 single. As a global consciousness-raising exercise, the United Nations declared 1981 the International Year of Disabled Persons. Recorded in the Bahamas (without his usual backing band, the Blockheads, but with leading reggae musicians Sly Dunbar and Robbie Shakespeare) the song, and the single (his first for his new, more commercial label, Polydor), "Spasticus Autisticus" was Dury's public response to a public gesture. In this song there is, I think, an extraordinarily powerful—not only within the context of the pop world—"narrative of corporeal otherness . . . [presenting] the disabled figure's potential for challeng[e]" (Thomson 1997, 16). In fact, his motivation for the song, and his understanding of his own position as a public figure of disability, were complex. One idea was to "get a band together who were either recruited from mental hospitals or recruited from really savagely disabled places" (Dury, quoted in Polydor 1981). Instead, he explained, he wrote a "war-cry."

> The Year of Our Disabled Lord 1981 I was getting lots of requests. I turned them all down. We had this thing called the 'polio folio', and we used to put them in there. . . . Instead I wrote this tune called "Spasticus Autisticus." I said, I'm going to put a band down the road for the year of the disabled; I'll be Spastic and they can be the Autistics. I have [my band named the] Blockheads and that means they're autistic anyway. And my mate goes, "No—Spasticus Autisticus, the [rebel] slave." Great, I'm Spartacus. So I wrote this tune. . . . [I]t wasn't allowed to be played anywhere and people got offended by it—everybody except the spastics. (quoted in Gould 1995, 253)

As he notes, the politics of self-naming is evident in the flaunted stupidity of calling his backing band the Blockheads (after one of his song titles), though before settling on that name he was considering "Cripple, Nigger, Yid, Chink & Dead Fish. Easier to say than Dozy, Beaky, Mick & Wotsit, innit?" (quoted in Balls 2000, 185). As a grammar-school boy, after Chailey, Dury was bullied and nicknamed "Spastic Joe," and forced to wear the school's uniform shorts (which displayed his heavy iron leg caliper) for the first year. He was regularly beaten by school prefects, until they complained to the headmaster (according to Dury, probably with some embellishment): "Look, he doesn't feel pain, he's got polio. We can't beat it out of him, so can we mind-fuck him instead please?" (quoted in Birch 2010, 40–41). One possible title for his first solo album, before choosing *New Boots and Panties!!* was *The Mad Spastic* (Birch 2010, 174). Of course, "Spasticus" was also a cultural effort at what Brendan Gleeson has termed "the reappropriation and revalorisation by disabled people of abject terms for impairment" (1999, 136). This is the strategy of reappropriation as employed elsewhere, for example, by Nancy Mairs, who has written that people

> wince at the word "cripple". . . . Perhaps I want them to wince. I want them to see me as a tough customer, one to whom the fates/gods/viruses have not been

kind, but who can face the brutal truth of her existence squarely. As a cripple, I swagger. (quoted in Thomson 1997, 25)

We have seen that Dury was happy to use language and even to produce music that could make people "wince," not least (though not only) when he wrote songs about disability. Having said that, it is noteworthy that the lyrics of "Spasticus" are not sprinkled with the swear words so common elsewhere in Dury's oeuvre; much of their power comes from their startling simplicity and childlike structure and rhyme, as here describing bodily imperfection and malfunction or mobility difficulties.

> I widdle
> when I piddle
> 'cos my middle
> is a riddle. . . .
> I'm knobbled
> on the cobbles
> 'cos I hobble
> when I wobble. (Dury 1981)

Yet the BBC did indeed ban the song (in fact, the corporation had previously banned the 1977 Dury single "Sex & Drugs & Rock & Roll," so he did have a track record of controversy, which perhaps undermined his stated serious intent with "Spasticus"), though only until a 6:00 p.m. watershed—a decision that itself irked Dury. His record label subsequently sought to strike a defiant, as well as sophisticated, note regarding the record's failure to chart, releasing a statement that said: "Just as nobody bans handicapped people—just makes it difficult for them to function as normal people—so 'Spasticus Autisticus' was not banned, it was just made impossible to function" (quoted in Balls 2000, 240). There were also protests about the song from the primary British charitable organization responsible for the support and care of people with cerebral palsy, then known as the Spastics Society. Rather than a musical act of self-empowerment and the reclamation of abject terminology by a high-profile disabled artist, the Spastics Society heard a controversial singer confirming by aggressive repetition in the song's chorus the common playground insult.[13] On an Australian tour in 1982, the authorities in Brisbane threatened to have Dury arrested if he played "Spasticus" live; of course he did it anyway. It is notable that a major part of the afterlife of "Spasticus" has been in the context of its (partial) censorship: in the 1990s, it appeared variously on a CD included with an *Index on Censorship* special edition entitled The Book of Banned Music (1998), and on a Channel 4 television documentary on the top-ten banned records in popular music history. We might think that the removal of "Spasticus" from the "polio (or disability) folio" to be stored in the censorship file was one more act of making it "impossible to function." Yet the drama can be replayed, without loss of power. The 2010 biopic of Dury, *Sex & Drugs & Rock & Roll,* has a central narrative strand around that song, understanding it as a keystone to Dury's life and musical career (Whitehouse 2010). The 2010 musical play based around Dury's songs, *Reasons to be Cheerful,* was produced by Graeae, Britain's leading theater company for people with disabilities (Graeae 2010). Graeae reprised their performance of the song in a powerful and moving way before a televised global audience during the 2012 London Paralympic Games' opening ceremony. The packed stadium crowd and singers together shouting "I'm Spasticus!" with images of banners held aloft saying the same on-screen was a tremendous crip-pop-media moment in contemporary British culture, televised live not by the BBC but by Channel 4.

Fig. 11. Graeae Theatre Company narrate and celebrate disability and popular music history in their 2010 musical of Ian Dury songs, *Reasons to be Cheerful.* Nadia Albina and John Kelly © Photographer Patrick Baldwin. Used with permission of Graeae Theatre.

As his first single since leaving the independent Stiff Records for the major label Polydor, it was a provocative, or even perversely self-destructive, choice. In fact, we can, and should, go further—to release it as a single (let alone that it was on a new label, and with a new band) was an extraordinary, and brave, if also frankly career-shattering move on Dury's part.[14] A Sly and Robbie-backed Jamaican dance-rhythm pop song about spastics, released as a single, with a political message and a powerful and discomforting accusation? The press release accompanying the single contains a section entitled "No handicap," and locates the song firmly within Dury's childhood experience, in a section headed "About Polio" (Polydor 1981). Yet in other ways it is the song that most departs from polio and from Dury's medical-musical autobiography toward a much more general and encompassing position—the song's hero's name is, after all, Spasticus *Autisticus,* and Dury had no personal experience of autism. This widening out is clear from the propagandizing text included on the picture sleeve, in which Spasticus, who is a radical and righteous Psychomodo—to link polio cockney rebels Dury and Steve Harley (see also ch. 2)—explains his purpose.

I COME AMONG YOV AS AN EXAMPLE
SENT BY MY TRIBE TO PORTRAY THEM
AS THEY ARE, AS BEAVTIFVLLY AS I AM, IN ALL MY GLORY . . .
THE EXTREME MEMBERS OF MY TRIBE ARE KILLED AT BIRTH.
WITHOVT THE AID OF OTHERS MY TRIBE CAN ONLY CRAWL
S    L    O    W    L    Y
HALLO TO YOV OVT THERE IN NORMAL LAND
WE TOO ARE DETERMINED TO BE FREE. (Dury 1981; typography in
   original)

The unconventional typography is a textual mark of strangeness from this foreign "tribe" of the disabled, while there is a shift in voice from first-person singular to what Siebers calls "the political first-person plural" as the piece progresses (2008, 65). Dury, via Spasticus, articulates here the point made a year later in the original 1982 publication of *A History of Disability* by Henri-Jacques Stiker. In the context of a normal, accepted, and even expected response to severe pre- and postnatal disability, what should be displayed is the desire to kill. We should not hide from the fact that major disability, especially mental, generates such an urge to make it disappear that it must be called by its name. In embryonic form the desire to kill, to see dead, is extended to all those who are stricken. (Stiker 1997, 8)

Stiker continues: "Let's not have any illusions." As Tobin Siebers (himself a polio survivor) also puts it, in his sketch of what he terms the ideology of ability in *Disability Theory,* "It is better to be dead than disabled" (2008, 10). Well, Dury, in pop, before either of these academic writers had articulated their views, already had no illusions. When we consider Dury's doubled text (song lyric and sleeve lyric) the extraordinary thing is not that "Spasticus Autisticus" failed in the single charts, but really more that it was ever released as a single.

To conclude, with the song "Spasticus Autisticus," the polio and pop generation I have charted and discussed moves most powerfully and demandingly outside its own cultural and corporeal concerns to challenge and to populate a wider, more ambitious territory—the entirety of Normal Land. Critics confirm for us the power involved, as popular music and its media's *infectious* nature extends the discourse of disability through "the polio thing," as saxophonist Dave Liebman has termed it. In a 1962 review of the radio ballad *The Body Blow,* the *Sunday Telegraph* caught the neuromuscular condition: "I doubt whether a listener with full attention on this program can avoid sympathetic agitation in his own muscles. At a playback for the press last week we all had trouble breathing" (quoted in Cox 2008, 126). An extraordinary 1973 review of the Kilburns actually articulated the impact of the band's rhythms on the audience in terms that can be understood within impairment, within corporeal defect: "Dancing to the Kilburns is like being on the verge of shitting your pants and enjoying it! You can't stand still so you jerk around uncomfortably for a while, then you develop a system of easy flowing constant motions to keep your bowels from evacuating" (quoted in Drury 2003, 16). And we too will return to and develop our discussion of many of these polio musicians throughout the book, for they have played pivotal and influential roles in (re)shaping pop and rock music culture around disability. How should we though preliminarily read that generation's cultural work overall? It is in part an achievement, the familiar and comforting disability narrative of overcoming, which draws on isolation or instrumental training as therapy as routes toward expression.

Here we have seen that songs of childhood memory are not innocent or idyllic, but painful, scar(r)ed, and angry. Nor is overcoming always comforting, and the rejection of victimhood here is sometimes uncompromisingly stated. It is a performance, which capitalises on popular music's intermittent capacity to value images of deviancy or enfreakment, and raises important questions about the musical body, the singing voice and lyric, their damage, and pop history itself. Here, related subcultural styles and attitudes can contribute acceptability and access. It is too a political act—of advocacy, consciousness-raising, or campaigning. The music may be part of pop, but it needs to be acknowledged that it can seem quite *un*popular (a notion we will return to): CeDell Davis with his "out of tune" guitar-playing; Dury with his single that was banned and that bombed, for instance. My aim has been to uncover and explore the polio and pop generation, and to show how the work of Ian Dury sits at the impressive heart of it. That most public of his songs about disability, "Spasticus Autisticus," closes with a number of male and female, normal and impaired voices proclaiming each in turn "*I'm* Spasticus!"[15] I have argued that the song is directed outwards, to the inhabitants of Normal Land, as a piece of cultural advocacy. But it is also directed inwards, in its closing collective gesture of self-identification and self-empowerment. To achieve both, in a single pop song, makes it in my view a compelling challenge to what Marc Shell (2005a) has termed the "the paralysis of culture" that surrounds polio survivors—makes it instead a culture from paralysis.

## CHAPTER 2

# *Vox crippus*

## Voicing the Disabled Body

> I shall . . . judge a [vocal] performance . . . according to the image
> of the body (the figure) given me.
>
> —Roland Barthes, "The Grain of the Voice" (1977, 299)

> There's a lot more to singing than just opening your mouth. It's a
> very physical act, and the power and control you need to hold a
> note, to protect your voice, to growl, to shout, even to sing very
> softly all depend on a finely balanced interplay between your vocal
> cords and the lungs, the diaphragm, and the muscles of the chest,
> abdomen, and back. . . .
>
> —Teddy Pendergrass, *Truly Blessed* (1998, 232)

I KNOW, the chapter title is Dog Latin. We'll chase that tale later. In this
chapter I explore ways in which the voice has sung the disabled body in pop
and rock. Simon Frith has pointed out that "singers use non-verbal as well
as verbal devices to make their points—emphases, sighs, hesitations,
changes of tone; lyrics involve pleas, sneers and commands as well as state-
ments and messages and stories. . . . It's not just what they sing, but the way
they sing it that determines what a singer means to us and how we are
placed, as an audience, in relationship to them" (1989, 90). It's not just the
relational meaning of singer and audience either, but also—particularly,
one might argue, in the context of consumption of recorded rather than live
performed music, when the voice is present and the body absent—a meaning of the body itself. According to Frith, "the voice as direct expression of

54

the body . . . is as important for the way we listen as for the way we interpret what we hear." Although we do not necessarily have guitars or keyboards or drums, what we *do* have in common with our singers is that "we have bodies too, throats and stomachs and lungs" are usually included (Frith 1996, 192). And we like to sing along in some form—in accompaniment, in sympathy, in tribute, or in karaoke. We do this even when we are seemingly not capable of it; it is a participatory pop pleasure. Thus can singer and fan bodies combine, in vocal harmony (even if out of tune). The body is integral even in the terminology of singing—we speak popularly of a "head voice" or "chest voice," for example. The sung voice presents in its pure and perfect—and, as we will see/hear, impure and imperfect—sonicity a corporeal identity and hermeneutic.

There is almost always a voice in pop and rock, and "idiosyncratic vocal stylisations are a principal characteristic of popular music styles across most genres" (Wise 2007, 6). Popular music culture is "a song form; words are a reason why people buy records; instrumental hits remain unusual—to paraphrase Marilyn Monroe in *Seven Year Itch,* you can always tell classical music: 'it's got no vocals!'" (Frith 1989, 90). In fact, there is a critical imbrication here, and one that work on disability and popular music can help unpack. It is not only that popular music has lyric—it is also that popular music has a *voice,* and is able to powerfully manifest a body in relation to that voice. There is a shift point in the same sentence, from Frith's focus on *words* to Monroe's on *vocals.* Nor should we overlook the power of the singing voice itself; after all, of every musical practice, "human vocal music—singing— . . . should be most prone to evoke strong emotional feelings in the listener" (Scherer 1995, 242). In what follows I am exploring the correlation between the singing voice and the body of the singer, arguing that there is a claimed sincerity or authenticity within the performance that makes it one that is not (only) an act. While pop and rock fans are adept at recognizing the performative modes and gestures of their preferred artists—the self-conscious reinvention of a Bowie or Madonna or Britney, for instance—there is also a way in which, when we hear the pop voice, "we hear singers as *personally* expressive"; for fans, "it is in real, material, singing voices that the 'real' person is to be heard" (Frith 1996, 186, 185; emphasis in original). Billie Holiday expressed this in her spoken introduction to the wonderful late televised recording of "Fine and Mellow" in December 1957, when she nods in gentle appreciation at Lester Young's tenor solo—the musical articulation of a life, near its very end, played slowly and with absolute distillation in twelve bars—Prez died in early 1958; Lady Day the following year—each far too young: "Anything I-I *do* sing it's-it's part of my life" (Holiday 1957). It is my argument that the singers we will look at in this chapter have an autopathographic impulse or trace that sounds through the voice—and even when manipulated or technologized the human singing voice resonates (with) the body, perhaps arguably then most of all.

In the context of disability, music offers "advantages of working with a nonverbal medium. Music can represent mental states directly, including those classified as illnesses or disabilities, without the mediation of language" (Lerner and Straus 2006a, 8). Debatably an aspect of that nonverbal medium that extends it beyond the purely instrumental can be the sound of the singing voice itself: not what the voice sings necessarily or only, but what it sounds like, and how it is heard.[1] So, while Lerner and Straus emphasize the voice's representation of *mental* states, we are concerned here with *vox corpus*—that is, primarily how the voice's nonverbal sounds relate to a body. More specifically, of course, the critical question is how the voice's nonverbal sounds relate to a disabled body. Roland Barthes's continuingly suggestive short essay "The Grain of the Voice" (first published in 1972, and translated into English in 1977) has been influential in popular music analysis of the voice/body relation, though it may need cripping. For instance, Barthes writes provocatively of the lungs as "a stupid organ (lights for cats!), swells but gets no erection" (1977, 296), which, in its assumption both of the lungs as healthy and functioning, *and* worthy of dismissal, does present and confirm Tobin Siebers's ideology of ability. Lennard J. Davis maps the kinds of poststructuralist theorizations of the body the work of Barthes was so pivotal to, in which

> the body is seen as a site for *jouissance,* a native ground of pleasure. . . . The nightmare of that body is one that is deformed, maimed, mutilated, broken, diseased. . . . Rather than face this ragged image, the critics turn to the fluids of sexuality, the gloss of lubrication, the glossary of the body as text, the heteroglossia of the intertext, the glossolalia of the schizophrenic. But almost never the body of the differently abled. (quoted in Siebers 2008, 59)

But let us here be generous to Barthes, for he may be able to help us, as he puts it, "to listen to my relation with the body of the man or woman singing" (Barthes 1977, 299), and he is in fact in that same essay (did he not live in contradiction without shame?) a great embracer of the imperfect in music and voice. (Others are unconvinced. For Tim Wise, "Barthes's 'grain' is in fact simply a metaphor, moreover unworkable as an instrument of analysis in that *the corporeality of the voice is a given*": 2007, 7; emphasis added.) The imperfect is valorized through the theory of the grain, which can take us to the critical sonic space of vocal cripping. If, as Barthes posits, "the 'grain' is the body in the voice as it sings, the hand as it writes, the limb as it performs" (1977, 299), our question should be how does the grain of the singing voice sound or signify a dysfunctioning body or hand, or the lack of a limb? Does it sound different? Can it, at least theoretically, *not* sound different? Neil Young (who should know) has observed of popular music that "There have always been a lot of weird voices"—and he continues: "How 'bout Ray Peterson? . . . Now there's a weird voice" (quoted in McDonough 2002, 98). Peterson, like Young himself, survived childhood polio, and we are beginning to see that the question of the "weirdness" of the voice is also a question of the "weirdness" of the body. It is not only that the singing voice can transmit a sense or type of body in pop and rock, which we might, after Barthes, want to continue calling a or the "grain"—it is that, for disabled singers, there is a regular, unbreakable relation with or presentation of the body, and the voice of such a body is understood in the context of that body. As a singer, in what ways does one sound like a crip? How does the voice "sing a song of difference," as Laurie Stras has put it (2009)?

Two aspects of the popular sung voice are of interest to me within disability popular music, and constitute the heart of this chapter. So I am answering Barthes's own question, asked of himself, of us: "am I hearing voices within the voice?" (1977, 296). And my answer is, yes, I am (too) hearing voices within the voice. First is a discussion of the place and meanings of the falsetto voice within a disability context—can we say that, for disabled singers, this false voice tells a corporeal truth, or a series of truths? Within this I include the partial, often uncool vocal high that is the yodel. Also in a falsetto context I consider the manipulated voice, the place of what, as we have seen, the narrator of the 1962 polio BBC radio ballad *The Body Blow* calls "machine-chopped speech" (MacColl et al. 1999) in pop and rock. Here, recording equipment can be a form of assistive technology, *en*abling the communication of singing, and the studio may become the creative space or tool of overcoming. Following that, I look at the sounds of damage, at what I call the damaged voice and the damaged grammar of related lyrics. I have a new musical phrase to describe such music: not *bel* but *mal canto*. While the falsetto focuses on the voice alone, the sounds of damage explores the voice in relation to the words (which can be non-words) sung. How have such singers managed to, well, *sing*,[2] and how has the popular music industry—sometimes more specifically its several remarkable though not always profitable branches of *un*popular music—accommodated such voices? Here, the inclusion and performance of speech disfluencies in song—¡tic—TIC—st-stutter!—are perhaps the clearest vocal marker of disability, though interestingly they are not that common in the pop or rock repertoire. (And they transmit feebly to the written page.) These facts may be related, suggesting that the more obvious the display of disability is in the context of the voice, the less popular the music sung; such a position will be discussed. In identifying these two areas for critical discussion, I should acknowledge two further points. Firstly, these are not always separate voicings, but are techniques that can combine and overlap in individual singers' oeuvres. Secondly, each of these singing voices—falsetto, yodeling, technologically manipulated, damaged or disfluent—has an extensive wider practice outside disability music. My argument is not (necessarily) that, say, the use of falsetto is per se always a vocal manifestation of the singer's disability; it is rather that, by their use of falsetto, a notable number of disabled singers invite us to reevaluate and extend the meanings of that vocal technique. As all fans know, from Dylan onwards, pop and rock are replete with damaged voices, and celebrate that fact as part of the culture—"Say it in broken English," sang Marianne Faithfull in her striking new broken voice on her eponymous comeback album in 1979, following a decade lost to drug abuse and the street. But again, if the singing body is disabled, how should we read its damaged voice, which may too be singing damaged words?

## Voicing the Disabled Body in Pop: Falsetto

> Falsetto seems profoundly perverse: a freakish sideshow: the place where voice goes wrong.
>
> —Wayne Koestenbaum, *The Queen's Throat* (1993, 164)

> . . . the best non-voice in the business.
>
> —Honor Wyatt, on the singing voice of her son Robert (quoted in King 1994, n.p.)

To pick the question up again, in what circumstances can a "non-voice" be the musical sound of, if not a nonbody—that's just too deficit-oriented, too negative, and is, besides, an impossible state for a singer (except through technological manipulation)—then at least a different-featured or different-functioning kind of body? The first form of voice I want to consider is that commonly employed by someone like Robert Wyatt—a drummer who became a man with paraplegia and a wheelchair user *and altogether more of a singer*[3] following an accident in 1973: falsetto. And let me be very clear: I am well aware that the falsetto has been employed and understood in popular music as a signifier of high emotion, or of camp or queerness, of sexual desire and pleasure, and that this practice occurs in a range of pop genres. But my point is to extend the critical figuration of falsetto in recognition of its place also within disability voicing by some artists. I am not (or not yet, possibly) saying all falsetto is crip; I am saying that falsetto's range of meanings is extendable, and I am offering a new way of thinking about its sounds and practices.

Wyatt's is an intriguing case. As his mother, Honor, put it, "I remember somebody describing his voice saying it was the best non-voice in the business," and she went on to articulate its impact in corporeal terms: "it sort of gets you in the solar plexus, his voice" (quoted in King 1994, n.p.). Notwithstanding maternal pride, there is something important in each of these observations—the voice that is not a voice, which has an impact on the listener's body. In the somewhat ambivalent view of Wyatt junior, the voice is

> a very difficult instrument to play, if you've only got my technique anyway. . . . I can't listen to singers the way I listen to other musicians—I get really embarrassed when singers start doing funny things with their voice that clearly they wouldn't do in the normal course of your average telephone conversation. In a way I find it a limitation, I'm only comfortable singing fairly close to speech patterns. (Wyatt, quoted in King 1994, n.p.)

Yet while hugging speech patterns in his vocal delivery—and more, pursuing an ostentatious Englishness (that is, non-transatlanticism) in his singing accent from his earliest days in the 1960s with the Wilde Flowers and Soft Machine on—there remains the question of Wyatt's falsetto. For a man to sound thus is surely "doing funny things with the voice" and a delivery not normally heard in a telephone conversation, after all. So I have in mind the falsetto voices employed by disabled male singers like Wyatt, and polio survivor, epileptic, father of disabled children and active fundraiser for disability groups Neil Young, or the visually impaired indigenous Australian singer Geoffrey Gurrumul Yunupingu, or of Curtis Mayfield in his later quadriplegic years, as well as the very particular form of head voice that is heard in the yodeling of Hank Williams. I consider them as sonic signifiers of vulnerability and sensitivity, which are themselves in turn characteristics frequently connected by fans, other musicians, and music journalists, as well as by these artists' marketing people, to their perception of the artists' disability-related pain or suffering or sincerity. But that high voice of the falsetto also has something profound to sound in the context of the emasculation, feminization or infantilization of the disabled adult male body, and we need to review these processes or states too.[4] While, as Rosemary Garland Thomson has summarized, "the non-normate status accorded disability feminizes *all* disabled figures" (1997, 9; emphasis added), our focus is on the way the sung voice of some disabled male musicians channels or embodies those processes.

As we have noted of the name, the falsetto is a false voice—diminutive of *falso,* Italian—the production of the tone of which is, in the words of *The Oxford Companion to Music,* "an unnatural effect" (Ward 1970, 344). It is usually associated with a male voice singing higher than its normal register (for example, to imitate a female voice); thus the deceitful trick at the heart of the falsetto—its central lie—is a confounding of gender expectations, as a man sings like a woman or a girl, or potentially a boy. Yet this can be nuanced: "If this is confusing to gender normatives, it is because the male is taught restraint. Thus he must move beyond his 'real' voice to his 'false' one to express real emotion" (Miller 2003). Frequently, then, if something is declared false something else must be true—and the drama of the falsetto does seem to push us to a binary, as we will see again. I wonder if in disability it is possible to argue that the falsetto seems to present a truth, to sound a body truth. Truth claims are dangerous things, so, to qualify: "'truth' is a matter of sound conventions, which vary from [pop] genre to genre" (Frith 1996, 197). What are the sound conventions of falsetto for singers with disabilities? Not merely "unnatural," falsetto is also commonly described in classical music and opera discourse as artificial, superficial, thin, colorless, peculiar, limited (all recurring adjectives in dictionary and encyclopedia entries and search-engine responses). In pop and rock, though, the falsetto has developed alternative values, particularly in certain preferred genres. (Frith's observation that "there have been few falsetto rappers so far" (1996, 195) may still bear legitimacy, and indicates how versions of masculinity remain musically constructed, limited.) So the appearance of male falsetto in Western popular music readily connotes high emotion, queerness or camp-ness in musical styles from soul to disco—and, in his writing about queering the voices of opera, Wayne Koestenbaum confesses to fearing and hearing the falsetto as the "voice of the bogeyman, voice of the unregenerate fag; voice of horror and loss and castration" (1993, 165)—while rock's "fascination with high–register male vocalists" may indeed transmit "a sense of transgression . . . of the bondage of social norms and conventions," as Ken McLeod has argued (2001, 190). Yet for Edward D. Miller vocal "style is not *ipso facto* a way to confess to *a wayward or freakish masculinity. The use of the falsetto in the recordings of male soul/r 'n' b performers does not reveal identity. Rather it expresses longing; the falsetto displays a dramatic tenderness"* (Miller 2003; emphasis added). Overall, in pop and rock, what we can say with confidence is that "the semantics certainly oscillate. The aggressive metal falsetto contrasts dramatically with its folk counterpart where . . . it shows vulnerability . . . [while i]n soul . . . falsetto singing, sighing and shrieking are used to express moments of extreme joy or grief" (Bernays 2010).

Further, the very particular falsetto form of introducing a high register into a normal vocal line that is the *yodel* has its own significance within disability discourse. The yodel involves a leap or break between registers, and Tim Wise identifies three types (only one of which is the *yodel-aydel-oo* figure, though all uses of the very term are recognized as "highly charged with negative associations"; that is, profoundly uncool: 2007, 57). Because it moves between two registers, the yodel is a binary form, and its non-legato delivery distances it from the classical world. "Its binary nature gives it especial interest," writes Wise.

> as a moment when change is perceived: it jumps. This phenomenon must be a key to its semiotic potential, particularly considering the difference of effect between smooth connectedness and sudden jerks. . . . Smooth carries suggestions of sophistication and poise, easy grace among the social elite. . . . It is no wonder that classical techniques, in their valorisation of smoothness, have found no place for such register-breaking effects, since the snap in the voice signals something working against the valued concealment: the gauche break in the voice of the awkward pubescent . . . or the losing of one's cool in the sob . . . or the uncouth hillbilly boisterously proclaiming his identity. Smooth means never losing the esteemed control, whereas . . . [t]he unhidden crack in the voice becomes a clear boundary. (2007, 56)

We can also glimpse here in the jerk, snap, break, or crack of the voice, as it reaches or strains to a high, to another way of singing—even losing control—an awkward, potentially (and potentially knowingly) unattractive difference. If a voice technique jerks or cracks, how often is it because its body is jerky or cracking?

"Wayward or freakish masculinities" are commonplace in disability studies, because disability is assumed in what Ian Dury calls "normal land" to enfreak or diminish manhood. Such refiguration of gender and sexuality through disability is seen in the most everyday of situations, as Tobin Siebers reminds us, in his cripping of Lacan: "More often than not accessible toilets are unisex. There are no Ladies and Gentlemen among the disabled because the ideology of ability conceives of people with disabilities as ungendered and asexual" (Siebers 2008, 168). Moreover the exclusion is mutual: ladies and gentlemen are not allowed to use the special accessible toilets. For Lenore Manderson and Susan Peake, "since masculinity is defined as able-bodied and active, the disabled man is an oxymoron." On the impact on men of adventitious disability, they continue:

> Becoming disabled for a man means to "cross the fence" and take on the stigmatizing constructs of the masculine body made feminine and soft. In contrast, being feminine and disabled are consistent and synergistic; the traditional notions of woman and disability converge, reflected in the ascription of characteristics such as innocence, vulnerability, sexual passivity or asexuality, dependency, and objectification. For many, disability may include incontinence, placing disabled men even closer to the feminine, leaking body with its indeterminate borders. (2005, 233–34)

It should not surprise us then that the unnatural and indeterminate voice of the falsetto is one musical technique employed to sound the reconfiguring experience of gender identification of the disabled male singer: "We hear women as better able than men to articulate emotion because femininity is defined in emotional terms. . . . By the same token, the intimate male voice is unmasculine, unnatural. In pop this is registered by the recurrent use of the falsetto" (Frith 1989, 90–91). Though, as we have seen, the falsetto is a voice of queer and camp in opera and disco alike, there is not so much evidence of it in queer-*crippery,* despite the persistent emasculation of disability. (Bruce Palmer, one of Neil Young's bandmates in mid-1960s California, invited him to join his band despite the fact that Young could, in Palmer's view, "only . . . sing like a fag": quoted in McDonough 2002, 138.) Perhaps, as we will look at in chapter 4, there may be a fragment of queer-cripping high sound in the hyperemotional sobbing of someone like 1950s singer Johnnie Ray. Indeed, Ray identified the (disabled) jazz singer Jimmy Scott (1925–) as one influence on his style—"Scott was an early, influential progenitor of a tradition of high-voiced male singing in American, and especially African American, popular music" (Lubet 2011, 62). Scott's own disability, caused by the hereditary condition Kallmann syndrome, which disrupts sexual maturation, meant that within the largely heteronormative, often even hypermasculine world of jazz, he has been regarded "as a boy, a woman, a 'fag,' and even, jokingly, a lesbian" (Lubet 2011, 62).

Frith has noted of the male high voice in pop and rock that "the more strained the note, the more sincere the singer" (1996, 195). Via Neil Young, or indeed Wyatt, a potentially different, more partial and vulnerable, relation between the male body and voice is sounded. Thom Yorke hears in Young's "soft vibrato," for instance, a man "singing in that register, in that *frail* way" (quoted in Cooper 2008, 19; emphasis added). This quieter falsetto is employed and understood as the sound of "sensitivity" (Young's word: quoted in Cooper 2008, 21), introspection, sincerity.[5] The sleeve notes to Yunupingu's 2008 album *Gurrumul* link his voice to his disability, but also tell us that the very voice itself signifies: "Blind since birth, . . . *he tells stories through* his songs and *his angelic and unique voice*" (Yunupingu 2008; emphasis added). Accompanied by acoustic guitar, double bass, and high vocal harmonies, Gurrumul's falsetto must work doubly hard to transmit sensitivity for a wider audience because most of his song lyrics are in Australian First Nations languages such as Gumatj and Gälpu. In Wise's view, the introduction of a high voice into a song can suggest "frailty or loss of control," and "because it often occurs in singers presenting a sensitive nature (for example, Joni Mitchell . . . ), we tend to hear this break as indicative of the fragile personality near the breaking point" (2007, 44). Jack Nitzche, who began his long relationship with Young as one of his producers in the 1960s, recalled trying to address Young's early self-doubt; to persuade him that his voice had an attractive and expressive quality: "That strange thing in his voice—all that quivering and shaking, like you think the guy might have a nervous breakdown in front of your eyes? I told him that was appealing. I said, 'You sound *different*'" (quoted in McDonough 2002, 219; emphasis in original). Since Young, on account of his epileptic fitting in his twenties, did actually frequently neurologically break down in front of people (including, as we will see, onstage), there is a homology between fragile voice and body—each quivering and shaking, uncertain and liable to break down, in Shakey's songs. "The aneurysm, polio, epilepsy—all those things are just part of the landscape" he said in 2006, recovering at the time from an aneurysm and related complications (quoted in Birnbach 2006), and we may observe that the high voice, the Young falsetto, is the sound of that personal and pathological landscape.

In some uses of the head or high voice, there is produced a mood of "disturbed fragility, and the technique suggests perhaps even the breaking voice of a pubescent youth" (Wise 2007, 48). In general, this high voice can be understood as the voice of the child, but for disabled singers it can also be heard as a vocal representation of the infantilization of the disabled male. In Young's early work the falsetto is frequently employed, and indeed it would go on to become characteristic of his singing. As his biographer Jimmy McDonough has sharply observed, "Young's surname is to the point" (2002, 12), while a 1968 song from his Buffalo Springfield period captures this, in high voice and eponymous lyric alike: "I am a child." As we have seen, in his 1970 polio song "Helpless," the high tremolo of both Young's voice and the guitar, and the melancholic fall of the voice at the end of most lines, are components of the song's meaning, and pathos. Alongside the lyrics, Young's falsetto-style vocal delivery also takes the listener back to his boyhood, to a crisis moment in it. Rickie Lee Jones says that Young's voice is "Hesitant, whiny, masculine and feminine . . . [the sound of] what it's like to be a teenager . . . [when y]ou are saying goodbye to childhood" (quoted in McDonough 2002, 15), but in fact that sung voice does not say goodbye to childhood—he stays Young until he is old. What is noteworthy here is the way that, for all its familiarity, within a crip reading of "Helpless" Young is sounding out for us the point that the voice is not yet broken, but the body may already be.

And the body is broken in all sorts of ways. Of course, incontinence is also a feature of childhood—the baby or toddler's "leaking body"—and we can extend Manderson and Peake's oxymoronic reading of "disabled man" to include the state of childhood. Talking about his relationship with his partner, Alfreda Benge, Robert Wyatt has framed it in the context of his adventitious disability: "we had a couple of years together before I was paraplegic . . . [when] she had spent all that time trying to avoid having a baby and she ends up with this incontinent giant" (quoted in Johnson 1997). The metaphor of infantilization Wyatt employs about himself here is an ambivalent one, and not only because he feels himself to be both baby and giant. Wyatt later came to reference his pre-accident identity and musical career as that of "my adolescent self, the drummer biped" (quoted in King 1994, n.p.). This is a view confirmed by his biographer Michael King, who introduces his book as a chronicle of "two remarkable and remarkably different careers. It's a division laid between the folly of youth and the responsibility of maturity and delivered through a debilitating accident" (King 1994, n.p.). We can see that in these latter instances Wyatt's disability does not include the experience of infantilization but is in fact a—*the*, even—life moment of maturizing. Yet we are still left with that "non-voice" that sings—the Wyattesque paradox of the unnatural falsetto sticking "fairly close to speech patterns."

There is another falsettist in popular music whose later work makes us think again about the place of the high voice in disability culture. The African-American soul singer Curtis Mayfield (1942–1999) had major success in the 1960s and 1970s both with the vocal group the Impressions and as a solo artist. Mayfield was a singer, songwriter, guitarist, producer, notably successful black independent music industry businessman, and a social activist. His songs were characterized by gospel sounds and dance beats, soul harmonies and catchy melodies, his own deceptively light funky guitar playing, and his fragile-sounding falsetto. In 1990, a workplace accident—he was performing onstage during a concert in New York—resulted in a severe spinal-cord injury that left him in a quadriplegic state, paralyzed from the neck down. Asked in an interview in 1994 if he could still sing, Mayfield replied: "Not in the manner as you once knew me. I'm strongest lying down like this. I don't have a diaphragm anymore. So when I sit up I lose my voice. I have no strength, no volume, no falsetto range, and I tire very fast" (quoted in Burns 2003, 214–15). Yet Mayfield returned in 1996 with a new album of songs, *New World Order*, which heavily featured his characteristic falsetto delivery. How was this achieved? In large part, via technological manipulation of his recorded voice in the studio.

Of course, the most famous technologically facilitated disabled voice is not from music at all, but from the mediated presence of a star thinker, Professor Stephen Hawking, whose retro-styled metallic robotisms sound the intellectual cyborg of the day, contrasting starkly or unnervingly with the visual image of a bent, crushed wasting of his chaired body. But in pop and rock other manipulated voices have been possible, and this is one of the cultural realms where we may take issue with Siebers's observation that "there are no survivors" (2008, 7). For one thing, in pop it is recognized as a good career move to die young, for sales spike postmortem, of rereleased and unreleased material. The hyperdisability of death (is that the case, or is death another experiential category altogether?) means no body, but the sung voice as spectral presence, a purer and more free-floating musical signifier than ever, remains. And the industry has innovated ghoulishly: new recordings—fragments of songs, previous rejects, with a new band or backing track, even a vocal duet of a living and a dead artist, spliced to life with an electric shock or an electronic charge in the studio—are offered as original works. Holograms of the famous dead are introduced in "live" concerts, performing again with other musicians (see Harlow and Gillespie 2012).

For Mayfield the vocalist, the challenge was twofold: to be able to sing once more at an acceptable level of quality over the duration of an entire song, and to be able to sing his falsetto. The first was achieved by bringing the studio equipment to him, in his bedroom at home, and arranging his body so that it was most physically capable of producing vocal lines for capture by the equipment. In one account, "he was suspended by harness to give gravitational power to his voice, just to find breath to complete a musical phrase or two" (Curtis Mayfield website). Another account elaborates on this: he "developed a technique that enabled him to record a few lines at a time, which could be edited in the studio later. He discovered a way of getting gravity to help his lungs do the work in the studio and it was this way that Curtis evolved the system of singing, lying down at a slant (sometimes flat) on the studio floor" (Burns 2003, 229). Line by line, songs were composed and vocals painstakingly recorded, which various guest producers and musicians worked up elsewhere. As for the falsetto, the most intriguing point is that it continued at all, since he was in fact now physically incapable of reaching that range that had made him famous. He could no longer move on up. Post-accident, his voice tracks were recorded at the lower pitches and slower speeds which he could now achieve, and then handed to an engineer. As his biographer Peter Burns explains, "he recorded his voice at a slower and lower level than in the past and the results were sped up for the falsetto sections" (Burns 2003, 229). In this way, Mayfield's voice was manipulated to retain the pre-accident sound of sensitivity and sincerity. Many of the reviews of *New World Order* were full of wonderment at the disabled overcoming—though for Ray Pence, the album is about "Mayfield's resistance to portrayal as a victim" (2008, 12)—the very representation of Mayfield's disability Pence has found most common in the music press. But in such a positivistic social-model reading as Pence's what can be overlooked is consideration of, as Mayfield sings on "Here but I'm Gone," "what my mind erased" (Mayfield 1996)—the set of deficits that is hinted at in several of the absence- or negative-oriented lyrics Mayfield sings. It is almost impossible to listen to this album on some level without a heuristic impulse to bring in the knowledge of the material condition—the physical arrangement, the health context—of its production. Although there is no overt reference in lyric, music, or album artwork and text to his disability, in sung lyrics like "How did I get so far gone? / Where do I belong? / . . . I still feel as if I'm here but I'm gone," or "Sometimes I'm up and sometimes I'm down / It's like one way in and no way out," or even the album's opening line: "Darkness no longer," an autopathographic narrative is being both tentatively and compellingly presented to the listener. A review by Michael E. Ross in *Salon* focused on Mayfield's voice: "while evocative, [it] has always been a thin, seemingly fragile wraith of an instrument. You'd think such an accident would make breathing difficult, much less singing. But, no—Mayfield's voice . . . is as expressive as ever, its feints and inflections still there but with a new maturity and foundation" (Ross 1996). Via the assistive technologies of the recording studio, the disabled Curtis Mayfield's falsetto, that false voice, was reconstituted to tell in music a profound body truth. His own personal new world order, as a man with quadriplegia, linked, rather than broke, with his past as a pop star. Mayfield's thin high voice from that extraordinary—in everyday and Garland Thomsonian terms—1996 album stands not (only) as the means of delivery, the source of energy of a narrative of overcoming to inspire struggling people (such as those others, alongside the singer himself, with disabilities), or as giving pleasure because it alleviates the fears of the able-bodied. It is also a powerful statement of musical creativity, and, as much as "Move on up" or any of Mayfield's other anthems of the civil rights movement, *in its very thinness and its highness*, is a strong and deep reinscription of cultural identity and social solidarity.

We conclude this discussion of the high male voice by looking at the weirdest falsetto, sort of, in pop and rock—the one in the yodel. The use in yodel of the register shift to including the falsetto is identified as a moment in the song where difference is signified.

> The break in the voice is made for some kind of *expression of emotion or significance*. The point in the overall musical stream at which this break happens is

DURING A RECENT PERSONAL APPEARANCE

Fig. 12. "Wasted legend, cowboy crip . . . notorious yodeler": Hank Williams MGM publicity image, *c.* 1950 © Wikimedia.

crucial to the passage's affect: it is a point where something *different* happens. This "difference" distinguishes such a moment from one in which, for example, there is a simple change of pitch, or where a rhythm is intoned at a constant pitch: the difference is a change of vocal register that is particularly arresting, even startling. (Wise 2007, 32; emphases in original).

The introduction of the falsetto in a normal range vocal line mid-word is classified by Wise in his typology of yodeling, and he writes that such falsetto "word-breaking can be taken as a sonic analogue for the breaking heart or for a fall" (Wise 2007, 44). *Fallsetto*—the singing voice that sounds the failing, falling body; as the voice goes up, the body goes tumbling down; as the voice fluctuates between normal and high register, so may the body waver and control lapse. Such a reading is embodied in the corpus of work (he recorded sixty-six songs, of which fifty were self-written, and thirty-seven made the Billboard charts: Hemphill 2005, 170) of 1950s country singer and songwriter Hank Williams who, among many other things, from wasted legend to cowboy crip, was a notorious yodeler. Williams's spina bifida occulta, though generally the least serious of the types of spina bifida birth defect, would give him constant back pain in his short adult years. The reference he makes (shortly) to *two* deformed vertebrae suggests that his spina bifida occulta was the type more likely to lead to complications. His hectic and excessive lifestyle in the early 1950s—constant touring, alcoholism, narcotic consumption, poor diet, failed back surgery, regular enforced stays in sanatoriums, and, toward the end, wearing an orthotic "chrome-and-leather back brace" while suffering from chest pains, near impotence, and incontinence (he was twenty-nine years old when he died) (Hemphill 2005, 148, 169)—did nothing to alleviate and feasibly aggravated his condition. Hank's bucket had a lot of holes in it. Even when he got a break, it's possible to read a critical medical irony into it, as George Lipsitz has done.

> Unable to afford medical treatment as a child, . . . [Williams] remained suspicious of physicians later in life and secured one of his greatest professional triumphs singing as part of a travelling caravan sponsored by Hadacol, a "quack" medicine that promised to cure arthritis, ulcers, asthma, tuberculosis, epilepsy, paralytic strokes, high and low blood pressure, and gallstones. (1994, 24)

The single on release at the time of his death in 1952 or 1953 (late New Year's Eve or early New Year's Day) was "I'll Never Get Out of This World Alive," which includes a surprisingly (bearing in mind the title) witty lyric that manages to sneak in the observation that, actually, "nothing's ever gonna be all right." On record, Williams's musical accompaniment usually included the Hawaiian steel guitar, placed high up in the recording mix so it could be heard on radio and jukeboxes, with its "sliding whine that . . . [was] the perfect complement to, and a virtual echo of, the tortured voice." Indeed, the counterpoint of the steel guitar made it "the most important element in Hank's accompaniment, a delicate echo of his mournful cry" (Hemphill 2005, 31, 97). Williams's regular use of the yodel in his recordings includes him in seeming satiric self-referential mode on "Howlin' at the Moon" (1951). Here he is in the character of a lovesick howling dog, with an inhuman howl, trying, as the lyric puts it, "to quit my doggish ways." (Williams was, after all, as he sang elsewhere, a man not born but "hatched.") We can hear in the opening line of "Howlin'" not just a nod to the "doggish" narrative to come, nor only too an acknowledgement of the ravages of his excessive and chaotic current personal lifestyle—but also the recognition of the experience of his own corporeality, born with spina bifida: "I know there's never been a man in the awful *shape* I'm in." Later on in his career, as he missed or messed up shows with greater frequency, he recorded an apology for fans and listeners in which he presented his autopathography: "I had two ruptured discs in my back. The first and second vertebra was no good . . . deformed when I was a child, or wore out or something." On another occasion, he harangued his booing audience, offering to show them the surgery scars on his back as evidence that he really was suffering (Hemphill 2005, 149, 153). The upper-register howl at the ends of verses on "Howlin'" also concludes the song itself, and is—as befits the falsetto—the unnatural, dehumanized, sound of deformity, one more "non-voice" in the high crip realm.

While of course "there are many falsetto voices in pop music that may not provoke . . . castration anxieties" (Miller 2003), nonetheless, the falsetto is a vocal device that is notably employed by some male disabled singers, and which is understood as a sonic signification of sincerity and emotion (falsetto as truth); the expression of suffering, pain, and sensitivity (including the *falsetto*); the voicing of vulnerability (the physical effort to make and hold the note); and the emasculation of the disabled man (it is the sound of his feminization or infantilization, or queering). Koestenbaum provocates that falsetto is the song of "a freakish sideshow: the place where voice goes wrong"; it is "breath that took the wrong exit out of the body" (1993, 164,

169). For us, it is breath of the dysfunctioning body. It moves across musical genres and generations alike—Thurston Moore of Sonic Youth has said that "Neil [Young]'s the real thing; he's Hank Williams" (quoted in McDonough 2002, 18)—in such cases we can say that the false voice is employed to sing a body truth. Such a straining or forcing to a higher register as here also begins to move toward Laurie Stras's notion of the "damaged voice" (2006, 179–83); this is a post–Barthesian reading of the "grain" that would develop Barthes's privileging of the imperfect in the body-voice relationship into the context of the disabled body in pop. And it is to that that we now turn.

## *Mal canto,* Damage and Disfluency: Voicing the Disabled Body

> [There is] a more powerful consequence of hearing damage in a voice—it connects the listener inescapably with the body of the performer, and the emotion in the performance is communicated as a testimony of personal experience.
>
> —Laurie Stras (2006, 176)

> My awareness within the record of "Spasticus" wasn't a shared awareness amongst "walkie-talkies," so I obviously knew there was a risk that I was going to alienate a lot of people and they were going to get the hump with me, [saying] "What's this fucking spazzer doing moaning?" Well I wasn't moaning, I was actually doing the opposite of moaning. I was yelling.
>
> —Ian Dury (quoted in Drury 2003, 131)

For Stras, the damaged voice is "a marker of corporeal impairment" (2006, 176); for Ian Dury, in his elected English of the "fucking spazzer" (spastic), it is telling that the "opposite of moaning" in music is not, say, singing, but "yelling." I want to turn now away from the freakish falsetto to consider other ways in which disabled singers have used their voices to sound their embodied difference; in my Dog Latin (howlin' like Hank), *vox crippus* remains the topic.

A damaged voice is one that is injured, that has been caused detriment by hurt. But damaged is also, etymologically, to be subject to damnation, to be condemned (all three from the Latin, *damnum,* loss). We are quickly not so very far from Henri-Jacques Stiker's initial commentary in *A History of Disability* on the Bible, in which "Defect is linked to sin" (1997, 27). A judgment is inscribed in the language of damage—as a result of which those who are damaged are in the same linguistic moment damned, condemned. Yet, in the powerful perversity of pop, as with other cultures that valorize the freakin' unusual, to be damaged is potentially to be raised, (pop) idolized, not damned. As Stras puts it:

> The damaged voice continues to be accepted, even preferred, in many genres within popular music, to the point of optimum levels of damages appearing suitable for different types of singing: the gravel-voice of the rock singer is not interchangeable with the subtle hoarseness of the jazz vocalist. . . . [D]amage here seems to be linked with concepts of authority, authenticity, and integrity. (Stras 2006, 174)

According to the critical advocacy of Petra Kuppers, "disability, culturally linked to invisibility and the 'ugly,' needs reperforming, reclaiming, remapping if it is to appear in the registers of the beautiful" (2002, 191). If there is a sonic equivalent to the visualities of "ugliness" then its reperformance or reclamation in a popular music context is the terrain of those with damaged voices, who may be challenging the aesthetic norms of pop by singing the body ugly, or at least the body different. While the voice of the *bel canto* tradition may be about masking its physicality and effort in a legato display[6]—and the voice of the auto-tune generation about employing technology to manipulate or repair the manifold stray notes of live pop singing, "flattened out *into perfection*" in Barthes's phrase, ripped from context (1977, 299; emphasis in original)—the voice of what I am calling *mal canto* is capable of speaking to us in the sung language of pop about the experience of the disabled body. So "what is disabling in one repertoire is positively enabling in the other" (Stras 2009, 317). We can hear other "non-voices," Mrs Wyatt, to go with other sorts of nonbodies. Again I emphasize, as in the introduction to this chapter, that I am not making a universal claim: not all damaged voices are necessarily the essential embodiment of a damaged corporeality.[7] But enough of them do posit such a relation to demand our critical attention, and in such a project we once more crip pop.

The English polio survivor and singer Ian Dury had a remarkable voice for the delivery of his own remarkable lyrics. In Dury's most successful band, the Blockheads, Mickey Gallagher was his keyboard player, songwriting partner and sometime health facilitator—the kind of intriguing mix of creative and practical roles that demonstrates the necessary complexity of a collaborative relationship with a disabled artist. Gallagher has articulated what would become Dury's characteristic vocal dialectic: "He couldn't really sing, but he had . . . the great verbal" (quoted in Birch 2010, 178). His lyrics were complex and witty, with sources from popular culture and Cockney rhyming slang, delivered in a deep imperfect voice of advanced Barthesian granularity. In a live setting he often sang out of tune, while "yelling" or screaming became established features of his vocal and lyrical repertoire. Musical movement and vocalized pain combine and are signaled in the title of a song like "Dance of the Screamers" (Dury 1979). The lyrics show him consciously speaking on behalf of and as one of "the screamers"—people with disabilities, imperfections, the marginalized and misunderstood: the kind of people who are doubly cursed, because they "went and missed the end bit" of the show, "but we never quite caught the bus"—and addressing the prejudices of the normals. The lengthy fading coda of Dury's vocal screams, plus the upper-register free-form harmonics of Davey Payne's distorted saxophone, takes Dury towards what one of his musicians described as an "unbearable" sonic territory. This pop made even the musicians in the studio "wince," for it was "painful," "horrible," and indeed even "deafen[ing]," which, as we will see in chapter 4 on music-induced hearing loss, ranks as a degree-zero achievement for a musical culture. His screams cracked a mic (see Drury 2003, 94–96). Underpinning a lyric and vocal performance like "Dance of the Screamers" is Dury's childhood memory of intensive physiotherapy—part of his early treatment for the neuromuscular damage caused by his polio—at Black Notley residential hospital: "It was called the screaming ward and you could hear people screaming on the way there, and it was you when you was there, and you could hear the others on the way back" (quoted in Gould 1995, 231). The socialist writer and polio survivor David Widgery described the painful sessions of electrotherapy on his leg as "real Nazi-time" (quoted in Gould 1995, 247). Dury's screaming music is not just about the pain of treatment or childhood unhappiness and homesickness, nor only a sonic metaphorization of disabled marginality. It is also an uncompromising voicing of the experience, the reality of pain, on a pop record. And, as Tobin Siebers reminds us, "pain is not a friend to humanity. It is not a secret resource for political change. It is not a well of delight for the individual. Theories that encourage these interpretations are not only unrealistic about pain; they contribute to the ideology of ability" (2008, 64). In "Dance of the Screamers" Dury sought to represent in music what Siebers calls the "raw . . . real-

Fig. 13. A London-centric "cultural coarseness"? "People would just stand and stare": publicity postcard of Ian Dury's early 1970s band, Kilburn and the High Roads, Charlie Sinclair left, Dury second left, Dave Payne far right. Thanks to Mike Weaver.

ity" of pain via an extreme, primal, and non-verbal use of his voice—his lyrical dexterity jettisoned for once. For Chaz Jankel, who wrote the deliberately contrasting light jazz-funk musical accompaniment, the song's meaning was clear enough: "I think that for some disabled people the only way they can express themselves is through screaming and dancing. The lyric is saying that for some people screaming is their only way of getting the point of view heard. That is what rock 'n' roll is all about. It's a different form of screaming for attention." While the link between the mode of articulation of disability and that of pop is perhaps glibly stated, the legitimacy of the position is nonetheless confirmed by Gallagher, who saw the Blockheads's audience changing as the musical repertoire developed: "A lot of people who had experienced those things that Ian sang about started coming to our gigs and came backstage for autographs. You'd hear people saying, 'He's writing about me'" (both quoted in Drury 2003, 95).

As he hobbled round stage and studio, not infrequently falling over, in spite of the constant company of a minder/carer, Dury sang with asper gusto, and performed with his voice while aware of the impact of the look of his body. Dury articulated in an early interview from 1973 something about performativity as a tactic he employed while effectively institutionalized for over three years at Chailey Heritage School.

> Being in that place is one of the reasons I talk the way I talk. Before that I talked not quite BBC. A third of the kids there were funny in the head as well as being disabled. . . . The situation was that from within you got very strong, but also you got *coarsened*. . . . There was a lot of behaviour that just don't happen in the outside world. Later you pretend to be arty about it but when I was there, I was just there, it was real. Thinkin' about it now, I realise it was fuckin' heavy. It was like a hospital in one way, like a school in another way, and like a prison in another way. (quoted in Balls 2000, 40; emphasis added)

Here is evidence of the blurring of performative strategies between being disabled and constructing a persona that would be attractive on stage, as in life—the *über*-Cockney working-class banter of the self-styled "Upminster kid" or *Lord Upminster*, as Dury song and album titles put it (from a middle-class grammar-school boy). It was the "coarsened" Dury that offered to the world his shocking (even in the punk context of 1977) short unaccompanied spoken introduction—rhythmic, like a tabu count-in—to the song "Plaistow Patricia," from *New Boots and Panties!!*: "Arseholes, bastards, fucking cunts and pricks" (Dury 1977). One childhood friend of Dury's recalled his surprise on hearing Dury's speech in later years: "I could never understand where he acquired his cockney accent, because when I was with him, he spoke like me, fairly well in fact" (quoted in Birch 2010, 114). Humphrey Ocean, artist and short-term bassist in Kilburn and the High Roads, has linked Dury's mode of speaking with his disability: as he limped uncertainly, so also he "veered giddily between middle class and working class" (quoted in Birch 2010, 79). There is a direct connection in all of this between voice and body, between the singing (of disability) and the disability itself. His early 1970s accompanist, Steve Nugent, recognized this too: "The accent he presented to the world was pretty far removed from the one he grew up with. All that 'gor blimey' stuff was laid on with a trowel. A lot of it came from the fact that he felt he had to struggle out of being institutionalized and being physically marked out as somebody who was different" (quoted in Drury 2003, 123).

Intriguingly, like Dury, the other English polio survivor and pop singer of the 1970s, Steve Harley, was also a faux East Ender in vocal delivery and image. After all, Harley's band was called Cockney Rebel—the implication being that he was both those things, a Cockney (born in the East End of London) and a rebel. Harley was a highly successful front man, singer, and lyricist who, I argue, did voice through sound and word a different kind of identity. Could cultural "coarseness" (Dury's term) be a compensatory catch—a way of linguistically toughening out for these performing polios? It's one of the male routes open to the talking crip. Harley's and especially Dury's asper—or, more accurately, asperated—voice and delivery signify a persona, and a strategy. Rosemarie Garland Thomson has reminded us that

> To be granted fully human status by normates, disabled people must learn to manage relationships from the beginning. In other words, disabled people must use charm, intimidation, ardour, deference, humour or entertainment to relieve nondisabled people of their discomfort. Those of us with disabilities are supplicants and minstrels. (Thomson 1997, 13)

If we follow the Dury template strictly, we must acknowledge that those of us with disabilities are wind-up and fuck-off merchants, too—the kinds of performers who may "use excess and destabilisation in order to move beyond the difference-denying polite frameworks of asinine sameness" (Kuppers 2003, 47; see also for other musical examples Cameron 2009).[8] Steve Harley's repertoire included a vocal delivery and lyrics and musical arrangements that drew on tics, pauses, an occasional stutter, masses of mispronunciations, nursery nonsenses. He limped on to stage to the accompaniment of pop music that could be rhythmically unusual, driven by a percussive center that was more than slightly off-beat. Hit songs like "Judy Teen" and "Mr Soft"—each a top-ten single in the British charts in 1974— were peopled by eccentric characters, and voiced with stutters and echoes, but their rhythms are notable too, for the punctuated or broken stops and silences, and most of all their *alla zoppa* stepfulness. At his commercial peak in the mid-1970s, after glam and before punk rock, Harley presented an image of pomp and disturbance with albums like *The Psychomodo* and *The Human Menagerie,* playing the poppy madman and decadent, singing songs of suicide and "mild schizophrenia," as he sang on "The Psychomodo" (Cockney Rebel 1974). Although he told me that he did not consciously explore any personal sense of disability during the songs of the peak Cockney Rebel years (personal interview, 2005), it is possible to trace some such

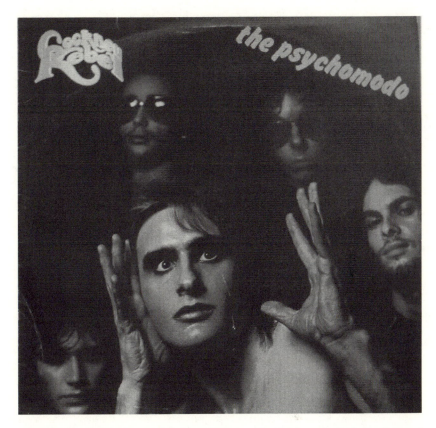

Fig. 14. Self-styled Cockney rebel Steve Harley as *The Psychomodo:* "a fictive figure of combined cognitive and physical impairment," on the 1974 album front cover. EMI Records, London.

recurring interest, even from the modest freakery of the album titles alone. 1974's *The Psychomodo* presents a fictive figure of combined cognitive and physical impairment—a conflation of the psychotic Quasimodo, who is mad and hunchbacked. Judging by the front cover, which shows a bare-shouldered, wide-eyed Harley with a tear rolling down his cheek, fans were invited to identify the body of Harley himself with the doubly disabled Psychomodo character. In the chorus of the album's title song, the lyric sheet gives, in damaged grammar: "Oh! We was so hung up and wasted/ Oh! We was so physically devastated" (Cockney Rebel 1974). That both Harley and Dury should seek to re-voice themselves as Cockney is partly a reflection of the attitudinality of rock during these years to be authentic, situated, street-wise, urban, British rather than transatlantic, of course. But this cultural rebranding also clearly connects disability with a class position (working class)—an uncomplicated confirmation of the view that to be disabled is to have a social placing that is lower rather than upper.[9]

In a deconstructive reading of opera, Andrew Oster identifies in the bel canto tradition of melisma a "destructive effect": "vocal melismata . . . destroyed language by splitting words and by separating syllable from syllable" (Oster 2006, 164). So opera—and later, soul—singers have performed and displayed their vocal technique by stretching words through scalar exercises; beauty at the expense of meaning, in Oster's reading. But the deviant potential of *mal canto* too produces a voice in which semantic and syntactical order can be as disrupted as the disabled mind or body of the singer. In the recording studio the effect of semantic and syntactical disruption to represent disability is achievable very simply. For instance, Napoleon XIV's 1966 hit novelty song "They're Coming to Take Me Away, Ha-Haaa!" is a comedic representation of mental illness. The B-side of the original forty-five-rpm single features a song entitled "!aaah-ah ,yawa em ekat ot gnimoc er'yehT," by the artist called noelopaN VIX; it is the same song played backwards, with the same title spelled backwards, by the same artist, whose name is also spelled backwards. It is a banal musical reference to madness—yes, a facile confirmation of the notion that "madness manifests itself in entirely observable ways," as Nicola Spelman has written of the A-side (2009, 123), as well as the ultimate low budget B-side. But I wonder whether this aurally and textually reversed B-side also does debatably sound and spell out the disruptive potential of cognitive impairment, sort of, in a pop single. In its very unlistenability, is it a radical piece of popular music? Half a single, back-to-front, the B-side, for those who have "flipped their lids," as the song lyric puts it? (Perhaps that should be "sdil rieht deppilf"?) Reversing the recording—most strikingly with the vocal line—and putting that out as or on the record, subverts the listener's pop pleasure (while I am not sure that it contributes another listening pleasure, as pop innovation often does); my suggestion is that it can also be a way of sonically representing disability, particularly those forms with a symptom of cognitive confusion, as well as a means of producing the sense of bewilderment or ignorance felt by many of the able-bodied in the presence of those who sound severely linguistically disabled. In the middle section of Robert Wyatt's mildly impenetrable "Little Red Riding Hood Hit the Road" (hitting the road being

precisely what Wyatt had done the year before its release, of course, in falling out of an upper-story window, resulting in a serious spinal-cord injury),
the recorded lyrics that have just been sung are repeated in the song—but
the recording is now played in reverse (Wyatt 1974).[10] We hear the voice
articulating but cannot make out the words; it has indeed become a kind of
"non-voice." (Unlike noelopaN VIX's B-side song title, Wyatt's reversed lyrics are not spelled out.) The song segues into the next, "Alifib," which opens
with Wyatt's rhythmic breathing—a regular sigh like a man doing his physical exercises, or his rehabilitative physiotherapy. The breathing continues
audibly through much of the song, setting the rhythm and tempo, until a
largely free section of bass clarinet and tenor saxophone breaks in. Wyatt
introduces one of his most famous lyrics, a sort of infantile stultiloquence.

No nit not
Nit no not
Nit nit folly bololey (Wyatt 1974),

a lyric he returns to later in the song, in spoken voice, struggling to enunciate it, and sounding cross, with himself or someone else (perhaps his partner, Alfreda, whose voice in turn enters the song at the end, as a counterpoint to Wyatt's experimentalism and expression, asking with grounded
curiosity, "And what's a bololey when it's a folly?"). The sung language and
the singing voice in these two songs from *Rock Bottom* moves through four
distinct approaches in the space of a few minutes: the Wyatt vocal recording
is played backwards; there are no words, only a Beckettesque breathing
from Wyatt; a childlike nonsense lyric is offered by Wyatt in a frail delivery
with pared down backing; and then the female voice of (maternal) common
sense presents the carer's counterpoint. All of these voices communicate
too of disability, in a language of damage, partiality, incomprehension.

  We have been moving in this discussion of *mal canto* in disability pop
toward speech disfluencies in the singing voice, whether real or studio produced. As I wrote earlier, speech disfluencies may be the clearest marker of
disability in the pop and rock vocal repertoire. To conjecture for a moment,
that they are relatively uncommon—I have had to search with some effort
for my examples—may be a result of the early decision of the vocally disfluent wannabe muso to not be the front-line singer, but the drummer, keyboard player, turntablist, say. Not stage front with voice and mic and spot,
but at the side with an instrument. Though with our knowledge from other

examples through this book of the *productive* relation between disability and music, between medical intervention, treatment, physiotherapy, and creatively inspired cultural expression, we should be wary of making such observations. After all, as Andrew Oster reminds us:

> As in aphasia, oral apraxia, and other neurological speech defects, the symptoms of stuttering can be lessened through recourse to music, via pitch or rhythm exercises. . . . Stutterers who lapse into repetition or delay (i.e., *block*) on certain spoken words have been shown to gain fluency when they sing the same words . . . the act of singing proves effective in overcoming stuttering. Music, and specifically *song, facilitates fluency.* (2006, 158; second emphasis added)

Emblematic here is the case of American country singer and songwriter Mel Tillis, who made a career in large part from the dynamic facilitative shift from spoken disfluency to sung fluency, including performing that shift on stage as he moved between inter-song comedic p-p-patter (often narratives about stuttering) and musical lyric. He had a casual neurological explanation: "you know, music comes from one side of your brain and your speech from the other side" (quoted in Clark 2002). Tillis released an album in 1975 entitled *M-M-Mel,* called his female backing group the Stutterettes, wrote an autobiography entitled *Stuttering Boy,* and has a website that instructs viewers to click the button to get "To the N-N-Next Page!" (Mel Tillis website, n.d.). He frequently observed that his stutter (one of the stories is that it was the result of a childhood bout of malaria) was the root of and route to his success, and felt comfortable enough late in his highly profitable country career to accept the public role of honorary chairman for the Stuttering Foundation of America. He never stuttered in song. In one of those intriguing crip crossovers that I have found to be surprisingly common in researching disability in popular music, as a songwriter Tillis's biggest early hit was "Ruby, Don't Take Your Love to Town," first in 1967 for Johnny Darrell and then again only two years later for Kenny Rogers and First Edition. It is a song of disability experience, narrating from his first-person perspective the emasculated and desexualized transformation of the unnamed military veteran returned home from "that crazy Asian war," and its impact on the domestic sphere where he is now trapped and from which Ruby, his wife, escapes nightly for sexual fulfillment. He is diminished and she is dissatisfied, since, after all, "It's hard to love a man whose legs are bent and paralyzed." Indeed, the vet cannot even manage the soldier's trained solution—killing the object: "*If I could move* I'd get my gun and put her in the ground" (First Edition, 1969; emphasis added). In the 1969 First Edition version, Rogers's repressed vocal delivery adds tremendously to the drama, and the dropping out of the guitars for a percussive break near the end ("the slamming of the door") strips it even further down, bare. We cannot and should not ignore the fact that this extraordinarily popular and (genderedly problematically) powerful song of male disability, twice a hit during the time of the Vietnam War, of course, was written by a disabled man—a man used to negotiating the mockery and rejection that followed his stutter, his every word. (Tillis even claimed he was himself rejected for military service in the early 1950s—from the proud duty of his "patriotic chore," as Ruby's veteran puts it—with the explanation that "the Air Force doesn't need any stuttering pilots" (quoted in Clark 2002).)

Further, in a popular music form like rap—which is focused on the rhythmic articulations of the spoken voice—the stutterer is not always absent. For the British rapper and spoken word poet Scroobius Pip "growing up with a stutter has helped me, because it developed my vocabulary from a young age. I'd know certain words I'd stutter on, and as I was speaking I'd be thinking half a sentence ahead, needing to replace that word with another. It's a great little tool, because it allows you to have two streams of consciousness going on at once" (quoted in Howard 2008). The speech-therapy technique of replacement words (for the speaker to avoid those known to cause blocking) has functioned in Pip's case to facilitate his rapping career—a small other instance of the way in which, in popular music as in culture and society more widely, disability can enable. Yet although the stutterer is not absent in Pip's music, the stutter is, at least in recordings, though "Live, it can be a problem. If I know a song too well, I have to drag myself back" (quoted in Howard 2008).

Perhaps the relatively scarcity of speech disfluencies in vocal music is less to do with the producer than the consumer—a sign of audience distaste for such an audible lack of capacity. To conclude this section and the chapter, let us pursue the disfluency line a little further, with particular reference to the sonic display of inarticulation in the sung voice as both a symptom and a trope of disability. Because it is a "deviation from accepted norms of verbal syntax," *stuttering* in the vocal line of a song "may . . . be seen as an alternate, impaired melisma" (Oster 2006, 165). As a form of delivery in pop and rock, although a relatively unusual one, it is also the voice foregrounding its own communicative potential and lack. The stutter is the sounding

of the voice's deficit, which introduces the drama (often comedy) of unut-
terability into the song. The sonic quality of the stuttering voice connote an
incapacity, while the blocked lyric, the specific word the voice is trying to
enunciate, also captures and repeats the struggle and failure involved. In
Daniel Goldmark's view:

> songs about such disabilities feature these people in the midst of their impair-
> ment, showing how it affects them. . . . Songs about stuttering thus differ from
> other disability songs, not only because the impairment is not physically obvi-
> ous but also because the impairment in other circumstances would be an im-
> pediment to performing, not its raison d'être. (2006, 92–93)

As we see often in the multiple world of disability, speech disfluencies can
be linked to other disabilities. For example, "a disproportionately high
number of polios stutter. The fact is not surprising from the merely etymological viewpoint. The cognate terms *stumble* and *stutter* mean the same
thing" (Shell 2005a, 211; see also Shell 2005b, 33). It is in fact the case that
*stumble* and *stammer* have the same etymological root, which suggests the
very kind of connection between (disabled) voice and body this chapter has
aimed to develop and interrogate.

Although "disabilities in general do not abound in Tin Pan Alley songs"
of the 1930s and 1940s, Goldmark does show the extent to which the speech
disfluency of the stutter is employed in lyric and vocal performance with
some frequency, as one of the minor tropes of novelty songs. Titles show the
subject: "K-K-K-Katy," "Lil-Lil-Lillian," or "Stuttering Song," "Sammy Stam-
mers." The people stuttering in these songs—singer, or character sung
about—are always male (though one seeks some kind of balance, being
called "The Boy Who Stuttered and the Girl Who Lisped"), "perhaps re-
flecting the roughly four-to-one ratio of men to women who stutter" (Goldmark 2006, 92). Songs of this period helped to fix the characteristics of
stuttering in the popular consciousness: "vocal blocks and interruptions
combined with socially constructed stereotypes such as social ineptness or
gawkiness, and secondary physical symptoms, such as spitting and whis-
tling" (Goldmark 2006, 103). In such songs then

> derision about stuttering centers on gender . . . , amounting to a disempowering
> or figurative emasculation of the men who have such an impairment. These
> songs, written at a time when the concept of masculinity was shifting radically,

plainly reflect the confusion and paranoia about what was appropriately manly. (Goldmark 2006, 103)

The comedic possibilities of the stutter would not be lost on subsequent generations of pop musicians: "Stutter Rap" by Morris Minor and the Majors was a 1988 parody of the Beastie Boys, a response to the then new form of rap music's vocal delivery, and a hit single centered on speech disfluency as a comic trope in popular music. Goldmark finds that Tin Pan Alley songs "practically all situate stuttering in the context of romantic love. . . . Stuttering complicates finding or pursuing a mate" (93–94). Sometimes the musical accompaniment also stutters—or rather the rhythm of the melody follows the repeated blocked syllable of the lyric. Ian Dury's late song of unrequited love for the girl in the sandwich counter, "Geraldine" (1998), follows the Tin Pan Alley tradition on both counts here. It ends with Dury repeating a series of sixteen "stutters" as he seeks to say her name: "G-G-G-G-G-G-G-G-G-G-G-G-G-Geraldine," with the band rhythmically accompanying him.[11]

The 1974 chart-topping single "You Ain't Seen Nothing Yet," by Canadian rock band Bachman-Turner Overdrive, is replete with stuttering in the chorus, which increases as the song progresses, and has a certain curiosity in the context of inarticulate heterosexual masculinity.[12] Although the lyrics tell in first-person narrative of the uncertain love life of the male singer (Randy Bachman)/character, in fact the chorus, which is where the blocking occurs, is, in strict diegesis, spoken by the female lover, the "devil woman"; it is *she* who is laying down the challenge of sexual experience and confidence, who in fact "cures" him of his lovesickness with her potent allure and all-round good medicine, and *he* who "ain't seen nothing yet." How can it be her stuttering, though? In the world of lovesick stutterdom, strong and successful sexual women "with big brown eyes" are not the disabled. We must understand the stutter as his, a result of his reporting her speech, which, in its brazen sexual confidence causes him to, well, freak out. "She said I needed educating," Bachman ad libs in the coda; intriguingly, her initial act of education is his disarticulation, itself initiated by the damaged grammar of the double negative ("ain't seen nothing"). The unstuttering electric guitar power chords that are introduced in each vocally stuttering chorus (contrasting with the strummed folk-rock guitar of the verses) add a touch of certainty and security to the song, reconstituting the masculinist position and counteracting the doubt the sexually active female has induced in the male singer. By the very end he is agreeing, enthusiastically: "I know I ain't seen nothing yet."

We need also to consider the absolute cry-call of contumacious youth that was The Who's single "My Generation" (1965), possibly the best-known stuttering song in rock history—and "still the best known song in the [Who's] entire catalogue" (Chris Charlesworth, quoted in Wilkerson 2009, 51)—one which may well in fact have been an influence on Bachman-Turner Overdrive's song. In "My Generation," the notorious stutter from male lead singer Roger Daltrey moves into a different realm altogether, and not only because the blocking happens in almost every line of the song, apart from the chorus. The stutter is not located within a lyric narrative of romantic love and wooing or sexual desire, nor does it function comedically. Rather, masculine anger, generational contumacy, and class-based inarticulacy are voiced in a musical performance of disability. An earlier single released by the band that year had been, after all, "I Can't Explain," with its plain lyric of inarticulacy—"My Generation" develops this importantly, because both lyric and delivery, word and voice, present the struggle of signification. Here we would do well to remember Simon Frith's observation of the popular music singer that "the voice is the sound of the body in a direct sense. Certain physical experiences, particularly extreme feelings, are given vocal sounds beyond our conscious control; . . . what one might call *inarticulate articulacy*" (1996, 192; emphasis added). The place of the stutter in The Who's "My Generation" is a prime pop instance of inarticulate articulacy.

> Why don't you all fffffade away
> Don't try and dig what we all s-s-say
> I'm not to trying to cause a big s-s-sensation
> I'm just talkin' 'bout my g-g-g-generation. (The Who, 1965)

The (non)communicative aspect—and its desire to speak only to some and explicitly not to others—is emphasized by the lyrics as well as the delivery, in which the stutters are extended in each repeated verse. In all its contradictoriness, Daltrey's subject is "talkin' 'bout my g-g-g-generation," even as he instructs older people not to "try and d-dig what we all s-s-s-s-s-say" (and here, the second time he sings this verse, the voice moves out of time with the music on the repeated "s" of "say"). The blues-influenced call-and-response structure maintains the closed communication—youth talking to youth, excluding the "old" (whose only activity in the lyric is, of course, to die)—while the song almost musically disintegrates in its coda. I asked one 1960s "Generation" fan, who had seen The Who perform in their earliest days in London, about the song, and was told that *everyone* in the audience then received and understood the line "Why don't you all ffffffade away," in which Daltrey stumbles and pauses on the letter "f," struggling to enunciate it, let alone the entire word, as really saying "Why don't you all ffffffuck off." Over decades, narratives accrete around classic songs: so the stuttering lyrics are a vocal sign of youthful inarticulacy when faced with the miscomprehension of the older generation, while for others they are the sound of a narcotized British subculture (Mods on speed). There was sufficient anxiety around Daltrey's vocal delivery for the BBC initially to ban the single on release for fear that "Daltrey's stuttering [was] an insult to those suffering from the affliction" (it still reached number two in the British charts, selling 300,000 copies: Wilkerson 2009, 51). The stutter in each of these rock cases—Bachman and Daltrey—is a vocal performance of disability: each singer did not have a speech disfluency in his real life. Like most speech disfluencies in pop and rock vocals—like many performed disabilities, too, of course—these are controlled displays of the out-of-control body, since the very act of vocal delivery in such songs of stuttering generally includes the fact that the stutter stops on cue (for instance, at the end of a chorus) and normal utterance returns. While for Goldmark this means that in the end the disability is "routinized, ignored, and effectively made invisible" (2006, 103), I think we should conclude that via stutterance as utterance disabled pop is capable of both hiding and laying bare the experience or symptom of disability.

In the context of popular music and disability, can we disembody the voice? In this chapter my answers are extremely clear: no and yes. No, we cannot disembody the voice: the disabled body sounds the corporeal and cognitive experience and knowledge of its own disability through its strained, damaged or disfluent voice, in *mal canto* style. There is a continuity between the peculiar sounds of the voice and the peculiarities of the singer's disabled body or mind, and his or her—mostly his—lived experience of that. The damaged voice allows us to "recognize bodily dysfunction sublinguistically" (Stras 2006, 183). Reflexively, the very voice tells the autopathography, and its sung words are the support act. And, yes, we can disembody the voice: by the use of recording technology, the relation between body and voice can be fractured, or at least attenuated. (Of course, in the very act of recording or transmitting the voice there is a displacement of the body, but our interest is in a less common removal.) The disabled voice is manipulated by technology in order to reconstitute a whole and functioning body. As Curtis Mayfield puts it, in one of the very best of those extraordinary late quadriplegic recordings, "I'm here but I'm gone" (2006).

## CHAPTER 3

# Corpus crippus

## Performing Disability in Pop and Rock

Melos: Greek for "limb", hence "melody."
—Bruce Chatwin, *The Songlines* (1987, 228)

IN THIS CHAPTER we look at ways in which other pop and rock musicians have performed and articulated—or been defined by (not least by me)—their visible physical disabilities and symptoms. Unsurprisingly, in society more widely "quantitative studies support the theoretical and qualitative work that suggests that physical disability has a negative impact on body image" (Taleporos and McCabe 2002, 974), but what are the implications of that for cultural workers in a creative industry in which body image is both a transactional and expressive category? Rosemarie Garland Thomson explains the operation of the ocularcentric pleasure of the performed text: "the visibly disabled performance artist generates the dynamic of staring, the arrested attentiveness that registers difference on the part of the viewer. In the social context of an ableist society, the disabled body summons the stare, and the stare mandates the story" (Thomson 2000, 335). We will narrate and critically discuss some of these stories, and we will complicate others. There is particular reference to ways in which some successful musicians with a pop profile negotiated their public transformation, as a result of adventitious disability, to a stigmatised identity, an embracing of what Erving Goffman has termed "undesired differentness" (quoted in Siebers 2008, 102). What happens to the star in pop's corporeal culture when his (usually) TAB-ness ends, he is no longer "severely able-bodied" (Paul Long-

87

more, quoted in Thomson 2005, 33), no longer a "walkie-talkie" (Ian Dury)?[1] Terry Rowden has described "disability as a simultaneously individualizing and deindividualizing corporeal state" (2009, 127, n27), and we will look at the cases of some musicians who have transitioned in public between individual and the newly disabled *de*individual. We will also look at a key experience within the neurodiverse, across two generations of stars and musics, with particular reference to the neurocognitive medical state of epilepsy and the role of some of its more dramatic and frightening symptoms in the onstage performance of rock. Of course, in any discussion of performing the body we should acknowledge the special, the extraordinary roles of the disabled here: as Carrie Sandahl and Philip Auslander remind us, "the notion that disability is a kind of performance is to people with disabilities not a theoretical abstraction, but lived experience" (2005, 2).

It is a familiar point that popular music is one of those contemporary cultural zones in which the body signifies centrally. A short range of examples illustrates this: the overtly sexualized body of the performer from Elvis Presley to Britney Spears or Lady Gaga (especially when meated); the dancing body of fans, from hot jazz to disco to, iconically, electronic dance music—but also the "anti-dancing" of subculturalists like 1950s trad jazz fans or 1970s punks; the mediated pop body of music video; the transformed body (Cher once asked an audience "How'd ya like my new ass?"); the primitivized black body (Josephine Baker); the genderly or sexually ambivalent body (early David Bowie, Annie Lennox with facial hair in male impersonation); the disfigured or taboo—sometimes by tattoo—body; the theorized body of pop. Frequently there is a discourse of perfection in the presented pop body, but not always. As the transformed or ambivalent or taboo bodies just cited may suggest, sometimes there is the attraction or spectacle of what we can term the imperfect, damaged or—in Thompson's influential reclamatory word—the extraordinary body. This body in performance seeks to break the connection Petra Kuppers sees in her link of "invalidate, *invalid*": what we find in some pop is that it offers a validating space for the invalid—or, more accurately, that pop's cultural workers, some of the disabled ones, have sought to carve out within it such a space of validation. (We know too that other disabled musicians have sought to "pass," and other nondisabled musicians have sought the cachet of disability.) While recognizing that this is too neat and swift a reversal, it probably is the case that I am as interested in the fits as in what Kuppers calls the "non-fits

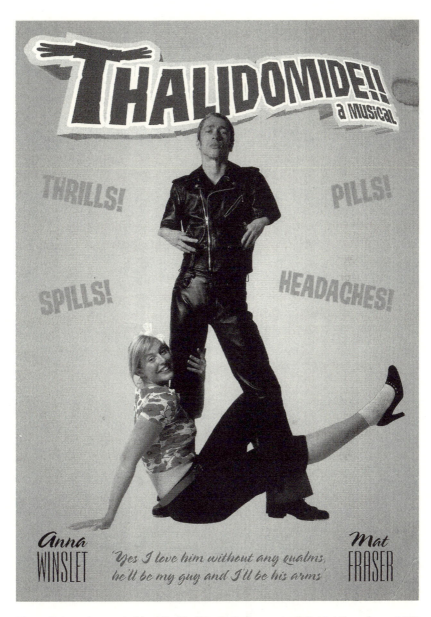

Fig. 15. In popular music "the [disabled] body figures centrally": Mat Fraser's 2006 UK touring show *Thalidomide!! A Musical:* "He'll be my guy and I'll be his arms." Author's collection.

between knowledges" (2003, 8). And actually, in this chapter I am interested in fitting, too—the place of the neurological seizure in performance.

I am not arguing that pop is unique in music as the most body-centered and disability-oriented—indeed, Andrew Oster makes the case for opera as the "prime locus for the study of human disability. The sheer corporeality of opera's medium, fraught with singers' blaring vocal chords, heaving chests, and exaggerated body gestures, lays bare the human body's physicality and vulnerability as in no other performed genre of music" (2006, 157). Also, opera draws on a historic tradition of corporeal difference—Francesco Cavalli's mid-seventeenth-century character Demo, from *Il Giasone*—that century's most popular opera—is "a hunchback dwarf." Who stutters (Oster 2006, 158). But pop and rock are too drawn to the freak show, and there is also in some popular music forms the physical display of effort, as Simon Frith has pointed out: "rock performers are expected to revel in their own physicality too, to strain and sweat and collapse with tiredness" (1996, 124), and the almost invariably amplified nature of that music contributes further impact and exaggerates effect. Most importantly though, the bodily multiforms of pop and rock are commonly predicated on a discourse of authenticity: we want and expect the singer, say, to be less a disabled character (such as Demo) than a disabled person, whose performativity of disability on stage, screen, or record—expressed for example through body, sung lyric, voice—we are willing to overlook in our desire for a version of the real. Popular musicians are used to thinking of their own bodies, which might range between the form of taking care of their voices, or (as we will see in greater detail in chapter 5) fulfilling the hedonistic appetites the industry has allowed, or encouraged, or demanded them to develop. Singers especially, the (usually, but not exclusively) front *men,* have also an actorial perspective, in the sense that they become adept at understanding and manipulating how audiences respond to their bodies. Theirs is a persistent, professional performativity, using the term "broadly to refer to the processes of self-presentation, impression management, and the theatricalities of everyday life," as Lenore Manderson and Susan Peake put it (2005, 231), but also more narrowly in the showbiz pop understanding. In this chapter we look at the real and the performing bodies of our disabled stars, which are always different from one another—aware and stared at—and always inescapably the same.

Some other versions of the real in disability pop, it seems, we do not desire—and in particular we do not want female pop singers in wheelchairs.

Fig. 16. Kata Kolbert, "Live Your Life," 1987 self-released single: "I couldn't be a singer in a wheelchair on my own terms." Author's collection.

In *She-Bop II*, Lucy O'Brien outlines the efforts of one such to make it in the industry in the 1980s in Britain.

> A bright girl with multi-coloured hair extensions called Kata Kolbert tried to break through. Her debut single 'Live your life' on her own Nevermore label had cool song-writing and soft vocals that invited comparison with Nico and Kate Bush. The only drawback was that, restricted to a wheelchair with severe arthritis, Kolbert was unable to promote it in the acceptable way. *Her wheelchair was not sexy.* While trucking her demo tape around record companies, she was met with both uncomfortable comments and blank rejection. "I couldn't be a

singer in a wheelchair in my own terms," she said. "They wanted me to be a brave struggling cripple in a nice long dress." . . . An active member of the disability arts movement in Britain, Kolbert was frustrated with her polished pop being restricted to the disability circuit. (O'Brien 2002, 245; emphasis added)

Never heard of her? Precisely. In her relative obscurity and pop failure, despite what O'Brien sees as her high promise, Kata Kolbert stands, sits as a symbol of the enduring masculinist imperative of the pop industry and media, the gatekeepers of which help a few disabled men up the steps to the golden stage, but try to keep the women off, or in the wings or the shadows, or (like Connie Boswell, who remains the one extraordinary exception) with their disability veiled. The press release for "Live Your Life" situates Kolbert's story within the pop industry, in an awkward mixture of accusatory and plaintive:

> * Kata Kolbert has her first single out now. This is it. . . . She is wheelchair bound with arthritis, and was turned down by all the major record companies because of this, DESPITE her opera trained voice. She formed Nevermore to put out her own records. . . .
> * Kata cannot play live more than once a month. It's taken her eight years to get this far. She does not have the money for a concerted publicity campaign. All she asks is for a chance to be heard.
> * Is that too much to ask? (Kolbert 1987)

If the feminist English novelist Virginia Woolf—still writing on one side of the Atlantic when Boswell was beginning to sing solo on the other—could declare in the early twentieth century that she could not tell "the truth about my own experiences as a body" (followed by a universalizing addendum: "I doubt that any woman has solved it yet": Woolf 1931, 144), it is the case in popular music even in the early twenty-first century that we still can only tell (some of) the truth about men's disabled bodies. How surprised should we be at such exclusions and silences? Even (*even*?) academics cannot hide their distaste for or discomfort with certain corporeal categories, as the cripping of, for instance, theoretical lacunae lays bare. Disability scholars have argued that "recent body theory has never confronted the disabled body. . . . Disability is as much a nightmare for the discourse of theory as for ableist society" (Siebers 2008, 58). Susan Wendell agrees: "In most postmodern cultural theorizing about the body, there is no recognition of—and, as far as I can see, no room for recognizing—the hard physical realities that are faced by people with disabilities" (quoted in Siebers 2008, 82). Kolbert may not have made it on to the leading British charts television program of her times, *Top of the Pops*—though, as we will see, that could be a mixed achievement for a wheelchair user—but surely she is due more than the odd melancholy paragraph in popular music studies such as O'Brien's or mine, a shade in a skirt in a chair to confirm the gender and disability limits of the industry. . . .

## Adventitious Disability: Male Stars and the Public Negotiation and Mediation of Becoming Disabled

> According to his doctors, he will probably be able to sing, but it's unlikely that he will ever walk again, which means that he probably won't perform. If he sang from a wheelchair, it wouldn't be the same.
>
> —Music journalist Dennis Hunt reporting Teddy Pendergrass's condition, 1982 (quoted in Pendergrass 1998, 231)

> . . . being confined to a wheelchair ensured no use of foot pedals [at the piano], compounding the difficulties that Wyatt faced. After all, what is a drummer without a kit or a band? In Wyatt's case, the answer would seem to be an intriguing performer.
>
> —Steve Lake, reviewing Robert Wyatt in concert, 1974 (quoted in King 1994, n.p.)

I do focus on the male experience in this chapter—men's disabled bodies are the privileged subject of pop and rock, and they can be granted access to its pantheon, or to its minor award ceremonies, depending on the star's level of success. This may be particularly so in masculinist-oriented popular musical areas such as rock and jazz, more so than other pops. As explained, my focus first is on those pop and rock figures who have lived a public transformation, through adventitious disability while in their pop career. Of course, the very fact that the physically disabled pop stars who are, say, wheelchair users have been predominantly adventitiously so, as a result of accident or severe medical condition, is a telling indication of the *limits* of pop as an inclusive zone for the differently configured and able. We have already discussed the place of the sung voice as a feminising or infantilising signifier of disabled male musicians, but here the solid, fragile stage presence of the body itself is central, because "body perception and satisfaction with one's bodily capabilities are usually *negatively impacted* by [for example] spinal cord injury" or other catastrophic physical event (Taleporos and McCabe 2002, 974; emphasis added). Lenore Manderson and Susan Peake describe how "people lose their autonomy and hence adulthood with insults to the physical body." They continue:

> Changes to bodily functions, for instance, place the individual in a position analogous to childhood; needing assistance with feeding, bathing, toileting, and dressing, the individual [now] inhabits a social location that is presexual, and, to an extent, pre-engendered. (2005, 232)

We will explore the actualities of such claims by considering the experiences of a group of male singers, each of whom became disabled while a pop star of some degree. I am not only interested in their degree of "detachment [and] . . . estrangement from an ableist music business that prefers 'artists [who are] exceptionally physically attractive by normate standards' and where 'prominent figures with visible disabilities are virtually unknown'" (Pence 2008, 15), but also, and equally, their degree of engagement and continuity with their earlier work. Importantly, this includes the mediation of their transformation, which is one of the key features that sets such public figures apart, and by mediation I am referring to their representation in or absence from the music press, television, video, auto/biographical writings, and so on. Our subjects are the African-American musicians Teddy Pendergrass and Curtis Mayfield, and the British musicians Robert Wyatt, and, to a lesser extent, Edwyn Collins. Drawing on some men's experiences of adventitious disability, Manderson and Peake have noted that, post-accident, "individuals need to adapt to their losses and develop new ways of performance to give life new, or to recover old, meanings" (2005, 232). How were these singers' damaged masculine bodies received by the public, presented in the media, and how did their performances change, as well as continue?

At the height of his success throughout the 1970s, African-American soul singer Teddy Pendergrass (1950–2010) had been, first, lead singer with Harold Melvin and the Blue Notes, and then a solo artist whose debut album in 1977 went platinum. One of his performative strategies was his women-only concerts, at which he presented a powerful black masculine heterosexuality for female audiences, singing in a characteristically power-ful deep voice a repertoire of late-night seductive and romantic soul music. In a car accident in 1982, aged thirty-one, Pendergrass suffered a serious spinal-cord injury, resulting in paraplegia. As a pop star, he had to negotiate the consequences of his changed life condition and corporeal capacity in public: "While other patients went through their daily routines and had their bad moments under the shade of anonymity, I could not hide from being Teddy Pendergrass, the Entertainer. . . . While I was in rehab, on more than one occasion total strangers would tiptoe into my room at night and flick on the light, just to see if the man sleeping in the bed really was 'the' Teddy Pendergrass" (Pendergrass 1998, 223, 234). In his autobiography, Pen-dergrass recounts how a particularly insensitive newspaper article about him some months after his accident both pierced and provoked him. Enti-tled "Vacancy: In Search of the New Pendergrass," and written by music journalist Dennis Hunt (though Hunt is notably not named by Pendergrass in his text), it read more like an obituary than a feature. In Hunt's words, Pendergrass

> was the cool, macho man with just a hint of sensitivity, exuding a kind of animal sexuality that seemed to turn on many females. Since the late seventies, he has been the number-one black male singer-sex symbol. . . . According to his doc-tors, he will probably be able to sing, but it's unlikely that he will ever walk again, which means that he probably won't perform. If he sang from a wheel-chair, it wouldn't be the same. His accident left a void. Who's going to be the next Teddy Pendergrass? (quoted in Pendergrass 1998, 230–31)

Pendergrass remembers how his "spirit collapsed" on reading those words: "If I sang from a wheelchair, it 'wouldn't be the same.' What the hell did that mean? I was stunned, enraged, hurt, devastated. To say this added insult to injury—literally—doesn't even start to describe how diminished, worthless, and inhuman those words made me feel" (1998, 231). Pendergrass was able to draw some strength in transition from other disabled black male musi-cians, including Johnnie Wilder of 1970s disco band Heatwave, himself a man with quadriplegia following a 1979 car accident. It was important for Pendergrass to see that, "despite what had happened to him, . . . Johnnie had continued to write and record his music" (Pendergrass 1998, 253), not least because there were those in the music press doubting precisely that Pendergrass would himself be capable of carrying on. In due course, Stevie Wonder suggested to Pendergrass the title of a new album, but more, too: "I also found talking to Stevie inspiring in a way I didn't appreciate as much before my accident. In addition to everything else we had in common, there was now a disability. Only he, Johnnie Wilder, and a few other people could understand the challenge of appearing and sounding confident when in fact you feel vulnerable, even helpless" (Pendergrass 1998, 258–59).

As we have already seen, the 1990 near-fatal workplace accident and resultant severe spinal-cord injury that happened to Curtis Mayfield (1942–1999) left the African-American singer, songwriter, guitarist, producer, and independent music-industry businessman in a quadriplegic state—paralyzed from the neck down. In his analysis of the media coverage and music industry response to Mayfield's accident and disability, Ray Pence found a common view among journalists that

> Mayfield had lost his music-making abilities along with his physical mobility. They saw quadriplegia as an end to his career, despite Mayfield's statements to the contrary, and changed the subject to his previous triumphs and his future legacy. When [the 1996 album] New World Order proved that Mayfield was living and working in the present, its release often became a story of overcoming disability instead of another chapter in Mayfield's long story of working hard to make music no matter what the circumstances. (2008, 13)

For example, Pence discusses a 1993 Rolling Stone feature "that undercut its valuable overview of Mayfield's career by portraying his impairment as victimization. A full-page picture of Mayfield in bed [taken from a] high angle perspective underscores Mayfield's immobility and the photographer/spectator's figurative and literal power *over* him. At first glance, *Mayfield looks like he belongs in a morgue, not a recording studio*" (2008, 11; second emphasis added). Mediations such as these of Pendergrass and Mayfield indicate the difficulty musicians dealing with the onset of serious disability have with their own trade press, especially, it would appear, in the context of musicians who are brazen enough to want to carry on in popular music despite their newly damaged bodies.[2]

The impact of the spinal-cord injury on Teddy Pendergrass's vocal capacity was notable: "there was no denying it: My singing was different now; things didn't come as easily as they did before . . . the injury had paralyzed

Fig. 17. Teddy Pendergrass's comeback gig after his accident, Live Aid 1985, Philadelphia: "it's not how you fall down, it's how you get up." MTV. © Live Aid / MTV.

the muscles that support the voice" (Pendergrass 1998, 279, 232). Yet Pendergrass's comeback gig was as high profile as it was possible to be. In 1985, forty months after his accident, he was invited to perform as part of the Live Aid concert in his hometown of Philadelphia. This was the culminating event in a campaign by popular musicians to raise funds to combat famine in parts of Africa. His manager, Shep Gordon, arranged it—the same man who had said to Pendergrass a year after his accident: "Teddy, it's not how you fall down, it's how you get up" (quoted in Pendergrass 2002), and Pendergrass took the opportunity. A stadium-sized crowd in the United States, a parallel event in London, at Wembley Stadium, and a satellite-linked live televised broadcast for a huge global audience of the twin concerts. It was really an astonishingly brave return to live singing, as he said in a later television interview, the big smile on his face an acknowledgement of the retrospective realization of the size of the challenge he had set himself: "in front of ninety thousand people, and millions of people around the world, I decided to find out what was going to happen"; that is, what sort of reaction he would now elicit from a live audience, and even whether he could actually sing again professionally (Pendergrass 2002). He was anxious about the audience perception of the before-and-afterness of it all, and about the vocal and physical performance: "Would an audience hear and see *me*, Teddy Pendergrass the singer, or would they see that poor disabled guy who used to be Teddy Pendergrass? I played out every imaginable scenario, from my being unable to control my chair to missing notes" (Pendergrass 1998, 271; emphasis in original). In the summer heat of the day, backstage he was allocated an air-conditioned trailer—but no ramp had been supplied so he could access it. One condition of his accident was that he was no longer able to regulate his body temperature, and so he was in danger of overheating. He was understandably nervous—having been persuaded by his children up to the night before the concert not to withdraw—and he was feeling self-conscious about the weight he had put on since the accident. The Live Aid film of Pendergrass's single song that momentous day, the 1970 Diana Ross hit ballad "Reach out and Touch (Somebody's Hand)," with the song's writers Nick Ashford and Valerie Simpson, is rather moving, because Pendergrass himself is clearly so very moved to be onstage in front of an audience.[3] In fact, after his reception by the crowd as he has carefully maneuvered himself in his powered wheelchair to his mark on the stage, he quietly cries center stage before he begins to sing. The film footage shows an aerial shot of the massive stadium crowd, and then focuses one of the large stadium screens in close-up on Pendergrass's face as he wipes away the tears and the crowd erupts. The band vamps for a short while Pendergrass composes himself. When he says to the audience, "I want you to know I feel your love," it sounds not like a crowd-pleasing showbiz statement but a heartfelt recognition of support and validation: pop helping its own. The first note he sings is a little flat, and elicits a grimace from Pendergrass, but he soon tunes in. The choice of song resonated doubly: it was "the right message for the event, and the right message for me" (Pendergrass 1998, 271). The song title and lyric concern a physical act—a body touching another body—which was, of course, one of the simple acts Pendergrass could no longer very easily do. As he writes in *Truly Blessed:*

> Rolling offstage to a deafening ovation, I felt like a new man. I could do it. Within minutes, I was in the back of a limousine, with the air conditioner blasting and bags of ice packed under my arms and all over my chest to cool me down. I was exhausted. But it was all worth it. (Pendergrass 1998, 272)

Medical complications, including effectively an entire year back in hospital in 1986–87, combined with a return to regular alcohol and narcotic use, dented this initial optimism, so that a couple of years later, Pendergrass could think "Live Aid wasn't about what I could do; now it was about what I couldn't. . . . And that productive, fulfilling life with disability I'd heard so much about, *well, where the fuck was that?*" (Pendergrass 1998, 286; emphasis in original). In a 2007 interview, he talked about a lost decade, how time changed in his life after the accident: time "lingered at first. I would say the first ten years it was slow" (Pendergrass 2007).

Yet as he continued, even if falteringly, his return to recording and performing, the Pendergrass black music repertoire of late-night love songs, smoothly produced soul classics, light dance numbers, was maintained as before. He explained in 2002 that "I kind of want to let people know, and understand, that I'm still who I am, I just ride [in a wheelchair], I don't walk—I ride. . . . I never wanted to conceal or hide that, or be ashamed of it, and I figured if there was a problem it was other people's problem, not my problem" (Pendergrass 2002). He speaks of continuity with his pre-accident self and music—so the song remained the same—but also of an openness and frankness about his condition. Here there are some parallels with Curtis Mayfield's situation the following decade. Mayfield's post–accident *New World Order,* consisted of newly written songs, collaborations between him and accompanying musicians and producers, reworkings of two previously recorded but unreleased songs, as well as some revisiting of past material, thus displaying a continuity with his pre-accident career. But Mayfield, as the album title suggests, also addresses the major shift in his life on that recording: in part, *New World Order* references the "changes that Mayfield and others with traumatic spinal cord injury and paralysis experience" (Pence 2008, 11). However, if the Pendergrass repertoire—a feel-good blend of soul and desire—was the same, is it possible that the lack of direct address in the music also functioned in some way as a concealment or denial? (I am uncertain whether that is a fair question; or perhaps I think it fair but feel uncomfortable posing it.) Not every singer only sings, and not every singer only sings about their own life. Pendergrass's public negotiation of his disability was culturally complex. In 1998, he published *Truly Blessed,* a detailed autobiography which, while not exactly the warts and all harrowing narrative of some of the most compelling American jazz autobiographies, say, nonetheless spoke with a degree of frankness of his transformative experience, and its struggles and achievements. That is, he went *outside* music (to literature) for his cultural expression of autopathography, but sought in music a continuity with his own past, which was perhaps a combination of solace, memory, the effort to understand and take control of his life, and the pragmatic of trying to maintain his market share. Others, too, have turned from their life in the collaborative art of music to the solitary act of writing as a response to disability. Grace Maxwell, partner and manager of the 1980s Scottish pop star Edwyn Collins, wrote an account of what she called his "restoration" following his two brain hemorrhages in 2005, when he was forty-five. Entitled *Falling & Laughing,* Maxwell's book took its name taken from the very first single Collins had released in 1980. One of the most striking aspects of Maxwell's book is the detail of the support she, family members, and close friends give to Collins to aid his recuperation—an account that stands as a compelling case study of the extent to which disability is precisely not an individual experience or event. In one of their occasional repeated arguments he would say "I've had a stroke you know!" and she would reply "Yep, and I had it right alongside you, dear" (Maxwell 2009, 210). Also, as the manager of a public pop figure, Maxwell understood that she could harness the media if required, and would threaten periodically in order to push her point for Collins's care: "I was precisely that person that hospital trust executives fear the most; a righteous, angry relative with a potential hotline to the media" (2009, 140).[4]

In looking at such instances of other cultural expression, this is not quite to say that Teddy Pendergrass's music avoided addressing his changed experience. What he did in his songs and videos was a subtle but important revisioning of the perception of the sexual allure of the disabled man,[5] the disabled black man: by continuing his late-night love routines with new hits, Pendergrass maintained his reputation as a performer of sexual love songs at the center of his identity, *even while that identity had shifted massively.* He wrote with great clarity and honesty about this in his autobiography.

> With disability, sex goes from being one of the easiest, most natural, most pleasurable parts of your life to becoming a huge question mark for both of you. . . . I like to think that when people hear me sing about romance and sexuality, what they hear in my voice is true. I'm still singing from my experiences now, not just from memories. . . . [T]he videos for "Joy" and "2 A.M." broke new ground by showing a physically challenged person—yours truly—as the object of romantic, erotic interest. (1998, 228, 290)

In the case of adventitiously disabled men, Manderson and Peake have found that "masculine sexuality and masculinity are defined conservatively and phallocentrically. Being visibly disabled (e.g., in a wheelchair) encourages men to be extroverted: 'You can't be a shrinking violet in a wheelchair'" (2005, 237). Pendergrass on stage in a wheelchair embodies *both* these points: a heteronormative phallocentricity combined with the compelling extrovert gesture of being center stage in front of an audience. In his view though, the male singer who is both "physically challenged" and "the object of romantic, erotic interest," the crip uttering *Love Language*, is not conserving a gender and sexual boundary, but breaking one. Nor would Pendergrass be alone in releasing the kind of material that confirmed a sexualized black masculinity for the disabled. Mayfield's "I Believe in You," from *New World Order*, the album recorded vocal line by line while Mayfield was in a quadriplegic state, "is a necessary reminder that people with disabilities are sexual agents regardless of the severity of their impairments" (Pence 2008, 20). Mayfield duetted with Mavis Staples on another track on that album, and Pence observes that Staples "may have been the only person who envisioned Mayfield returning to the concert circuit. If Prince could bring a bed onstage for his act, she reasoned, why couldn't Mayfield?" (2008, 19).

Also, Pendergrass combined his pop profile and his corporeal shock by reinventing himself as an articulate advocate for the disabled, recognized as an authority because of his own experiences, and able and willing to use his pop-given media visibility for social change. Having a special interest in spinal-cord injury put him as a public figure in the United States alongside the *Superman* film actor Christopher Reeves—but Pendergrass also carefully distanced himself from the Reeves campaigning position: "I don't want to foster [an expectation of] cure, I don't think that's a real thing to foster, for me I'd rather foster, emphasise *quality of life*, I think that's more important" (Pendergrass 2007; emphasis in original). An event organized in 2007 gives some sense of the timescale involved in this series of public transformations, successes, and setbacks, by Pendergrass, as well as an indication of the sheer importance of the accident and its implications for the public and private man. A showbiz concert called Teddy 25 took place in Philadelphia, marking the twenty-fifth anniversary of the accident, and the twenty-five years of musical and later campaigning work Pendergrass had been involved in since becoming a disabled man in 1982. One might expect a musician who had been performing since the 1960s, and had tremendous success both as a band member and as a solo artist, to, say, have an event called Teddy 40, celebrating forty years at the top. But Teddy 25, why don't you all join me and remember the day my body got fucked? It is a marvelously pragmatic and unself-pitying exploitation of an opportunity, I think—the kind of event only a singer who decided that his first public gig in a wheelchair would be live in front of a global audience of 1.5 billion people could make. In a way, those wounding words of journalist Dennis Hunt were in the end for Teddy Pendergrass almost correct: when (not if) he sang from a wheelchair, it wasn't the same. It was just the same and different.

A decade or so before Pendergrass, the English singer and drummer Robert Wyatt's own mediated public reappearance as a star with paraplegia took place, accompanied in Wyatt's case with a level of controversy. Following his accident in 1973, when he fell from a fourth-floor window while at a party, resulting in a spinal-cord injury, Wyatt quite quickly returned to recording and performing. One music press report of the accident, headlined "Wyatt Breaks Back," informed readers the week after it had happened that "He will definitely be in hospital for six months. . . . Rehearsals [for the new album] will go ahead with another drummer, as yet unchosen, and on his recovery Robert will return, probably playing keyboards and percussion" (quoted in King 1994, n.p.). As we see in this chapter, such certainty contrasts with other musicians' reactions to a potentially life-changing disability. Wyatt's subsequent album, *Rock Bottom* (1974), contained songs he had been working on before his accident, and which were revised in light of his hospitalization, wheelchair use, and his intriguing subsequent shift from the back (drumming) to the front (singing) of the stage. He talked about this cultural and pragmatic choices of this shift.

> Being in a wheelchair means you have to deliberate what you do. You can't be so impulsive. Not being a drummer any more I then decided to concentrate on what had previously only been a sideline, which was singing. That was all I had left, so that's what I did. Instead of just being somebody's drummer banging away . . . , when I'm my own singer I just stop when I want to. . . . I think I became a better, more concentrated musician. (quoted in King 1994, n.p.)

As we saw in chapter 2, he also sang, if characteristically tangentially, of the impact of his life-changing impairment on his partner, Alfreda Benge, and Benge's voice appears on *Rock Bottom*. Curiously, apparently at his record label's suggestion, Wyatt then recorded and released as a single a cover of the

Fig. 18. Robert Wyatt performing "I'm a Believer" on BBC's *Top of the Pops,* 1974. © BBC Television.

1960s Monkees' hit, written by Neil Diamond, "I'm a Believer." In the run-up to the single's release, Wyatt and band appeared on the front cover of *New Musical Express,* ostensibly trying to descend steps, each of them sitting in a wheelchair of his own. A September 1974 appearance on the television programme *Top of the Pops* to promote the single was arranged, and this was then root of the controversy—a relatively minor event, but one which is still discussed today, on fans' websites and disability networks, as well as on several Wyatt television documentaries and interviews, for instance.[6]

*Top of the Pops* was the BBC's longest-running pop music series, beginning in the mid-1960s and lasting over four decades. At its peak in the mid-1970s (the period when Wyatt appeared) the program had over 15 million viewers. It broadcast weekly the charts for an early-evening audience, ostensibly youth-oriented but frequently attracting the wider family, with a formula that included a chart rundown, restricting appearances to artists whose chart position was rising that week, a regular dance routine to a hit single, and the culminating drama of revealing the new number one. Writing in 1985, Sean Cubitt elaborated on what he considers the show's "deodorised realm":

> Hampered by the early evening slot, the BBC has to censor groups and videos, most notoriously the Sex Pistols and Frankie Goes to Hollywood. Add to this the poor quality of the speakers on most television sets and the result is a sanitising of pop music's sexuality and rebellion, a miniaturisation of its torments, thrills and excesses. (Cubitt 1985, 44)[7]

Wyatt's appearance was initially notable for two facts: his band was drawn from members of the progressive rock scene—including Pink Floyd and Henry Cow, not the normal *Top of the Pops* roster, by any means—and the singer was in a wheelchair. But Wyatt's three minutes on the show have since taken on an enduring other life, as a key popular cultural moment when the official media in Britain effectively sought to censor the work of a disabled artist. Violinist and guitarist Fred Frith recalled that "Richard Branson [of Virgin Records] had bought a beautiful antique wheelchair for Robert to sit on, but the BBC refused to allow it, and in fact wanted to cover the wheelchair completely because they thought it was in bad taste or might upset the viewers" (quoted in King 1994, n.p.). Wyatt's memory zoned in on an argument with the producer: "there was this . . . producer . . . saying 'Could you sit on something else, *wheelchairs don't look well on a family entertainment show*.' I just exploded, the whole atmosphere frightened me, I just thought I was losing control of my life" (quoted in King 1994, n.p.; emphasis added). In the *Top of the Pops* broadcast Wyatt is dressed in a long pale blue outfit that looks rather like a hospital gown, his legs hidden beneath blue material, perhaps a blanket. His wheelchair is static throughout; not pushed nor rolling, its wheels are unused; it is more chair than wheelchair. There are several shots of Wyatt's performance when the crowd is placed in front of the camera to obscure his lower body and the wheelchair, and others are only head shots. Yet the broadcast footage also in fact shows Wyatt clearly in a wheelchair, a standard issue one, as he and the band (the others able-bodied, despite the *New Musical Express* cover image of the previous month) lip-synch and mime the song, which was standard practice at the time. One of the musicians, Frith, even mimics his violin solo, sans violin—a display of artifice containing a certain anti-pop disdain not unexpected perhaps from many in the progressive rock scene. It is intriguing that much is made of Wyatt's sincerity and body truth in the context of a mediated performance—singing a cover version of a song called "I'm a *Believer*", which had, of course, previously been a hit for a manufactured band—which everyone in the television audience would know was mimed—an act the band themselves drew attention to. According to Michael King, a second appearance on the show three weeks later was cancelled "when the BBC's brass learn of Robert's intention for all musicians to appear sitting in wheelchairs" (King 1994), just as they had done on the front cover of *New Musical Express* a few weeks earlier, of course. Wyatt later claimed that the producer concluded their argument with: "You will never work on this programme again!" (Wyatt 2007). As also with the BBC's half-heartedly censorious treatment of Ian Dury's "Spasticus (Autisticus)" the following decade—a single not exactly banned; more subject to a daytime media curfew—the BBC was displaying its policy uncertainty around disability and entertainment, especially in the context of its feel-good, family-oriented popular music scheduling. The rationale may have differed—Wyatt in a wheelchair thought to be upsetting to a family audience, Dury singing "Spasticus" thought to be upsetting to the disabled themselves—but the effect seemed the same: an acceptable pop product being made by a *public service* media organization for the tastefully able-bodied.

## "I've Lost Control Again": Performances of Neurological Impairment

> In a while will the smile on my face turn to plaster?
> Stick around while the clown who is sick does the trick of disaster.
> For the race of my head and my face is moving much faster.
> Is it strange I should change? I don't know. . . .
>
> —Buffalo Springfield, "Mr Soul" (1967)

> Confusion in her eyes that says it all. She's lost control.
> And she's clinging to the nearest passer-by. She's lost control. . . .
> And she screamed out kicking on her side and said "I've lost
> control again."
> And seized up on the floor. I thought she'd die. She said "I've lost
> control."
>
> —Joy Division, "She's Lost Control" (1979b)

How might neurological and cognitive impairments be not only voiced but corporeally performed in music? According to Manderson and Peake, "the injured or diseased body is a body out of control, often at both the cellular and the systemic level, in terms of stability, mobility, and bodily functions" (2005, 232). We will look at a specific pathology in the world of the neuro-diverse, the neurological disorder of epilepsy, which is the most common of the serious neurological conditions—around half a million people in Britain have it, for example. It is an umbrella term for a complex set of conditions—there are over forty types of epilepsy—with the mutual feature being "the tendency to have repeated seizures that start in the brain," caused by the interruption of electrical signals between nerve cells (National Society for Epilepsy website). As we will see, epilepsy is of such interest to us due to its extreme potential within a popular-music context as a physical performance of being out of control, what Oliver Sacks (2007, 255) calls the "kinetic stutter" as a form of involuntary dance. For, when fitting, the body may indeed rock and roll.

The link of neurology and music is not a new one, of course: the pathological category of *chorea*, after all, has its etymology from ancient Greek—dance—and links also therefore with choreography, chorus, choir. Dance, song, disease. In Greek, Latin, and English, neurological disorder is inscribed in the activity of making music and the activity of moving to it alike. Perhaps we should be considering Neil "Shakey" Young and Ian Curtis, our epileptic stage singers, not as the exceptionals, the curiosities, displaying their control issues nightly before the crowd while they sang of them also, but as the very center, the nerve center, of popular music.[8] After all, they are the ones who are shakin' all over, who are all shook up, who show us that there's a whole lotta shaking going on; they epitomize it and they embody it.

At the time of the onset of his epilepsy, Neil Young was a man barely in his twenties in his first successful touring and recording band in the 1960s in America—Buffalo Springfield, part of the folk-rock scene of the West Coast "hippie" counterculture. At the time of his onset, Ian Curtis was a man barely into his twenties in his first successful rock band in England in the 1970s—Joy Division, part of the northern urban punk and post–punk scene. As we have seen, Young already had direct personal experience of disability, and an awareness of the unreliability and fragility of the human body system, as a result of his childhood polio in Canada. It's possible that the potential negative memories of this illness, this family crisis, were tempered by the simple knowledge that he had survived. Curtis had some expe-

Fig. 19. Naming neurology, music, subculture: picture sleeve of English punk rock band The Epileptics's *Last Bus to Debden* EP (1981). Author's collection.

rience of disability, since he worked as an assistant disablement resettlement officer, advising those with disabilities on available government benefits and employment schemes (Middles and Reade, 2009, 49). This involved regular visits to a center for those with serious neurological conditions, including severe epilepsy, and during the early, semiprofessional, Joy Division period, he maintained the day and night jobs together. In a series of letters to his girlfriend in 1980, Curtis textualized rather than sang his "dangerous gift" (see Straus 2011, 40), producing an extraordinary, powerful autopathographic expression of anxiety.

I USED TO WORK WITH PEOPLE WHO HAD EPILEPSY. . . . IT LEFT TER-
RIBLE PICTURES IN MY MIND—YOUNG BOYS AND GIRLS WEARING
SPECIAL HELMETS AND PADS ON THEIR ELBOWS AND KNEES TO
STOP THEM HURTING THEMSELVES WHEN THEY FELL. SUCH LOVELY
PEOPLE IN SUCH A DESPERATE SITUATION. (quoted in Middles and
Reade 2009, 201; typography in original)

Of course, Young usually stands connected to an alternate youthful figure
in the later post–punk or grunge arena of the 1990s—Kurt Cobain—but
here we will explore some different resonances, some other forms of con-
duction, through Young's shared experience with Curtis of epilepsy, of writing and singing songs about epilepsy, and of the physical performance of
that condition onstage, which seems even to have included by each the trig-
gering of epileptic seizures.

Neil Young would regularly have epileptic seizures, including grand mal
convulsions, from about 1966 to, with decreasing frequency, 1974. In Buffalo
Springfield, Young's primary responsibility was as lead guitarist, though he
also wrote and sang some of the songs. At one early gig he was carried offstage on a stretcher; later, other band members suspected him of manipulating seizures "for dramatic effect and attention" (McDonough 2002, 174–
77).[9] For Buffalo Springfield manager Richard Davis, "the seizures were sort
of an event," and seemed to develop into a part of the stage show. Davis was
able to predict when Young was likely to be affected.

> We'd have a system. If Neil was gonna go down, I could always tell—we'd slap
> the lights on and somebody would grab him. . . . There were quite a few seizures
> during the end, and it was "Mr Soul" that would do it. . . . It was a pretty violent
> end to the set. I used to literally see him startin' to fall, and somebody would get
> him offstage. The audience would think it was some sort of strange finale.
> (quoted in McDonough 2002, 175, 226)

The 1967 album *Buffalo Springfield Again* contained at least two songs written and sung by Neil Young that seem to touch on disability, that draw on
and draw his experience of epilepsy: "Expecting to Fly" and "Mr Soul" (see
also Stein 2008, 4–5). (Even the third Young composition on the album,
"Broken Arrow," opens with the band sampling themselves with a brief re-
prise of "Mr Soul," and ends with a human heartbeat, sounding a corporeal
perspective.) At his best, Young is an elliptical songwriter, whose lyrics are

indirect, tangential, partial and contradictory fragments. And, like Bob Dylan, the songs have a legion of sensitive sometimes righteous defenders. My interest in them is centered only on the question of disability, and whether those experiences in Young's life can help us more fully to understand a few of his many songs. When asked once what was the subject of "Expecting to Fly," the song's producer, Jack Nitzche, did actually manage to condense its complexities into a one-word reply: "Epilepsy" (quoted in McDonough 2002, 218). Although the lyric's narrative is set within the convention of a love song, in which emotional turmoil originates in romantic departure, occasional lines jump out that can justify Nitzche's reading. The striking opening image of (presumably a lover) standing "on the edge of your feather" sets the tone for a fragile and precipitate event, which Young's high voice and the higher falsetto vocal and string harmonies compound. (In Ian Curtis's "She's Lost Control" the epileptic girl walks "upon the edge of no escape.") But the opening of the second verse lays bare the actuality of experience in a way that profoundly resonates with anyone having a grand mal seizure: "I tried so hard to stand as I stumbled and fell to the ground" (Buffalo Springfield 1967). As for "Mr Soul," McDonough suggests tentatively that its lyrics are "perhaps a reference to epileptic attacks and hospital stays" (2002, 194), while as we have seen it was during that song when played live that Young would have a seizure onstage during the Buffalo Springfield years. The final verse quoted earlier, the last of three in a song with no chorus, is surely a representation of a body and mind in crisis—its surfeit of rhymes a sign of excess or overdrive. But "Mr Soul" has more to give: the representation (let us say it: of seizure) is set in an anticipatory— feared—frame. The face turning to plaster, the head race and faster face, the strange change: he knows that these will happen to him soon, are unavoidable and inevitable, and he lists them in a prolepsis of pain, the symptoms coming. Finally, the extraordinary line "Stick around while the clown who is sick does the trick of disaster" shows his (Mr Soul's and / or Mr Young's) deep and troublesome and critical awareness of the place of the freak in the entertainment industry, the disabled singer on the rock stage. And let us remember: when playing this song at the end of a Buffalo Springfield set, Young fitted. It was his description of the experience, and it was his trigger for the next one, resulting in a display that would confirm the accuracy of the description, or fulfill it for any fascinated audience member. "Mr Soul" was the soundtrack and the show of the full cultural cycle of the epileptic. It's notable too that Young returns to "Mr Soul" with a new electronic version on the 1982 album *Trans*—the album met with puzzlement and some anger by the public and the record company because it didn't sound like Neil Young, and which was in fact Young's effort to produce music for his multiply disabled son, Ben. Here Young roots around in his own archive for a creative reworking of a song of disability in an album about disability (see also Stein 2008, 6–8, for a discussion of *Trans*).

Young's retrospective view of the Buffalo Springfield years are in large part framed by the onset and regular experience of his epilepsy: "the way I felt and acted was mostly because of nerves, the seizures. It got so I didn't care. I didn't *want* to make it with [that band]. I didn't want to be a slave to the medication I was taking for epilepsy. *I couldn't stand the way I was feeling*" (quoted in McDonough 2002, 231; second emphasis added). The ambivalence of his phrasing is striking—both *I hated the way I felt,* and *Because of the way I felt I could not stand*—and indicates the intensely close relationship between the physical symptoms of his condition and his mental well-being. The other close relationship Young has acknowledged is of the possibilities of creative estrangement from epilepsy—that is, the way in which the transcendent potential of this neurological disorder could contribute to the music-making process.

> Did I get songs from the seizures? Probably. To go somewhere else and you're there and you're talkin' to people and you're part of the thing and you *are* somebody else. Then you realize, "Hey, wait a minute, I'm not—" You don't know who you are because you know you're not the person you seem to be. (quoted in McDonough 2002, 176; emphasis in original)

We can suggest that the temporary psychological identity shift, in the form of subjective and emotional lability—a depersonalization—that Young describes here as a feature of his cognitive experience of epilepsy, gave him something to draw on both for his lyrics and for some of the early time signature-shifting musical accompaniment in his songs. Even without the great studio experimentation unleashed by the Beatles' *Sergeant Pepper* and the Beach Boys' *Pet Sounds* albums, songs like "Nowadays Clancy Can't Even Sing" and "Expecting to Fly" each featured a disrupted chordal and rhythmic progression: the shifts from 4/4 to 3/4 rhythm in both these songs disturbs the linear flow expected of the acoustic part of the instrumentation. Can we understand such musical changes in time as small sonic signifiers of the sorts of disturbance and uncertainty Young was experiencing in his life and exploring in his lyrics? At the very least, these minor rhythmic jolts—types of "formal deviation" and "deformation" in the music of disability (Straus 2011, 113)—contribute the musical strangeness of these songs of disability. McDonough writes of "Clancy" that "the odd time changes threw people" (2002, 179)—which may be one of the reasons the song flopped as a single—but we might think that the arrhythmic musical "oddness" is rather apt in such a neurologically oriented song about music, and about multiple sclerosis, written by a polio survivor and later epileptic.

The sudden, extreme and public experience of epileptic seizure sung of by Ian Curtis in "She's Lost Control" in the late 1970s was also often understood by Joy Division audiences as being displayed by him in his dancing style during instrumental sections of live performances, especially of that song. The stigma of epilepsy is captured by one of Curtis's friends from the time, himself an epileptic: with epilepsy, "you were a mutant. You were handicapped. . . . Ian . . . felt like an alien" (quoted in Middles and Reade 2009, 108). Curtis drew on his experiences working with the neurologically impaired in the lyrics for "She's Lost Control"—"apparently it was inspired by an epileptic girl that Ian knew and was trying to help in his job" (Middles and Reade 2009, 134). Jon Savage has written since of the way in which "his mesmeric stage style—the flailing arms, glossy stare and frantic, spasmodic dancing—mirrored the epileptic fits that he had. . . . Did people admire Ian Curtis for the very things that were destroying him?" (1995, xiii). These factors—song, biography, dance—constitute three external manifestations of a neurocognitive impairment (others include, debatably, his depression-linked suicide in 1980 and retrospective biographies, including the 2007 film *Control*). In neither the small world of British punk and post–punk music nor the bigger world of North American rock did there seem to be any connection made between the epileptic performativity of someone like Curtis back to the stage experiences of Young in the previous decade—even though Neil Young was one of the artists Curtis listened to obsessively in the final weeks of his life (Middles and Reade 2009, 231), and even though in fact these two artists were at the same time in the late 1970s struggling with and producing songs about pop and damage, and the relation between the two. As we will discuss further, Curtis—and the inescapable, sad, and brutal fact of his suicide at twenty-three—stands as an ambivalent figure within disability discourse and culture: "though his gloomy lyrics reflect an internalization of harmful stereotypes about the 'tragedy' of disability, they also portray real and understandable emotions within the disability experi-

Fig. 20. "The 'tragedy' of disability" in rock music: Ian Curtis memorial stone, Maccles-field Cemetery, 2008. Photographer Bernt Rostad ⓒ Wikimedia.

ence. . . . Curtis illuminates problematic ways that disability is consumed within a culture that stereotypically views disability as tragic, and yet romanticizes the naturalizing drive toward (especially self-destructive) death culturally implied by that stereotype" (Church 2006, n.p.).

Joy Division were formed in the punk rock scene in Manchester in the late 1970s, but took a different trajectory to the other punk and post–punk bands, toward a European-style detached aesthetic sensibility. Not much more than 100 live concerts, mostly at small-scale venues, a handful of singles (one a hit) and two albums (one released after Curtis's death) constitute the band's musical output. But their influence and legacy have been tremendous—through the post–Joy Division band New Order, Factory Records and the Hacienda club, and the enduring afterlife of Curtis and his songs. Ian Curtis was diagnosed with epilepsy while his career with Joy Division was taking off. For instance, in January 1979 he appeared on the front cover of *New Musical Express,* and ten days later was seeing a neurologist who recommended the tests that would confirm his epilepsy, and in the interim prescribed anticonvulsant drugs. His own doctor's advice at the time "to get early nights and not work too hard" might have been reasonable but it was also already hugely unrealistic: Curtis was the lead singer in an increasingly emotionally centered rock band that was starting to make waves, which inevitably involved two things for him: late nights, and working himself (up) as hard as possible for every show (Curtis 1995, 71, 82). As for his anti-epilepsy drugs, the trial-and-error prescriptions for which would change as certain drugs were found to be ineffective for his body, mixing them with alcohol and recreational narcotics presented other anxieties. David Church suggests that "Overexertion, dehydration, exhaustion, lack of sleep, extreme concentration or repetition, and moderate consumption of alcohol and marijuana (against his better judgment) could have all helped lower Curtis's seizure threshold" (2006, n.p.). It is not difficult to add other factors: the stress and pressure felt by the lead singer as the band's front person, as he managed audience and industry expectations of their burgeoning success, the return of depression—itself perhaps epilepsy related, perhaps around his failing marriage—the haunting memory of other epileptics he had worked with, and not least the claustrophobically intense internality that was becoming the Joy Division topos.

One concrete act Curtis, the band, and their stage crew did undertake to reduce the likelihood of seizures and the related disruption was to avoid the use of strobe effect lighting in their live shows—a well-known trigger for photosensitive epilepsy (Middles and Reade 2009, 107). For his watching wife, Deborah (when she was permitted to attend concerts), his characteristic dancing would become "a distressing parody of his offstage seizures . . . an accurate impression of the involuntary movements he would make" (Curtis 1995, 74). His physical performances in concert began to be the focus of music press attention; indeed, "the reviews in the music press [were] disturbing . . . they were like psychiatric reports, even using the appropriate terminology and references" (Curtis 1995, 73). And, although Waltz and James state that "epilepsy was never mentioned in any of the band's live reviews at the time" (2009, 371), a July 1979 gig was reviewed by Mick Middles, later coauthor of a Curtis biography, in the weekly British music magazine *Sounds* thus:

> During the set's many "peaks" Ian Curtis often loses control. He'll suddenly jerk sideways and, head in hands, he'll transform into a twitching, epileptic-type mass of flesh and bone. Suddenly he'll recover. The guitars will fade away. . . . Then, with no introduction, the whole feeling will begin again. Another song, another climax. (quoted in Curtis 1995, 83)

While he would sing of losing control, the audience would watch him seemingly doing it, and the journalist would record it for those not there yet so they would know what to expect when they saw Joy Division. Curtis was by now sometimes experiencing successive grand mal seizures, without necessarily recovering consciousness between each one—the medical emergency situation termed *status epilepticus* (Curtis 1995, 82; National Society for Epilepsy website). *Suddenly he'll recover. . . . Then, with no introduction, the whole feeling will begin again.* There was a widening gap between his extraordinary stage and everyday domestic existence—not in itself a remarkable situation in popular music, and in fact commonly enough a motivating factor for those wanting to, as they say nowadays, live the dream. But in Curtis's case the bond between them seemed to be his disability, which was to be managed and medicated against at home during the day, but apparently to be summoned onstage during the evening. While Deborah Curtis "was hardly likely to be impressed by his manic jerking on stage when I spent my life concentrating on eradicating the possibility of any seizures at home" (1995, 85, 86), he was adding a new final verse to "She's Lost Control," which speaks in the first-person singular about "the *urge. . .* to lose control" (Joy Division 1980b; emphasis added).

Drawing on what we have seen in chapter 2 of the rhythmic appropriateness of the vocal stutter—by which I mean the capacity of much speech disfluency in popular music to *follow* the song structure (the stutter features only in the chorus, or it stops on cue at the end of a verse), it is possible to see that the Curtis dance itself has conformist features. That is, the physical loss of control displayed in the dance (and in one song, of course, lyrically sung of by Curtis), is usually controlled. Buzzcocks singer Pete Shelley noted: "it was almost like he was having a fit on stage, *but in one place though*" (quoted in Middles and Reade 2009, 169; emphasis added). Curtis dances during the time onstage when the band is playing and he is not singing, for instance, and stops or reduces the extremity of the dancing on cue, when he is due to sing the next verse or chorus. Also, necessarily, the arms and body move more conventionally altogether when he is playing rhythm guitar—when the instrument and body are strapped together. Not only that, but the flailing arms, which were often accompanied by the "mesmeric" or even "mediumistic" (Jon Savage's words: 1995, xiii, xi) facial expression and eyes, could be a visual response to, representation of, the sonicity of the music—specifically, the drumming. His arms moved to the featured sounds of Steve Morris's kit drums. On the groundbreaking "manic performance" (Savage 1995, xi) of "She's Lost Control," for example, recorded live for a new youth program on BBC television in September 1979, there is a sort of dialogue between Curtis's physical moves and Steve Morris's drum breaks—Curtis is visualizing the music with his limbs. What is perhaps unnerving, though, are his face and eyes in frequent and perfect close-up: eyeballs rolled upwards, eyelids flickering, on an otherwise passive face, which somehow seems to magnify the intensity. These are the kinds of visible facial symptoms often associated with petit mal seizures (National Society for Epilepsy website). The point here is both straightforward and more complex. Obviously, Curtis was the front man and he had a show to perform, which would involve his own special little moves of the unique kind all rock singers want to discover and build up. Signature corporeality is a trick of the trade, and stagecraft a skill to develop, especially for the lead singer. Curtis became an outstandingly distinctive and intense front man, and it is the case that, as Middles and Reade point out, "when Ian danced, Joy Division were instantly a better band" (2009, 145). But his physical dynamic with being in and out of control onstage, with seeming to lose it as he transforms nightly into the "twitching epileptic" of Middles's contemporary review, is a controlled performance he is moving into and out of, in time to the music, on beat and on cue. It is for all intents and purposes a consummate act, which only later in his career becomes a dangerous, self-destructive action. He was, after all, the teenager who had overdosed, and then the inexperienced singer who could self-harm before going onstage; it may not be surprising that the (only slightly) older Curtis's effort to channel the power and fright of the epileptic seizure should come to characterize and then to dominate his stage presence, and then to trigger the very thing he was dancing around. For David Church:

> rock music's countercultural mythos conflates freakery, impairment, and deviance, intentionally exploiting images of disability (for wider sales) by locating them within the person of the rock star (who is rarely ever truly disabled). In Ian Curtis, however, there is a difficult tension between actual impairment (whether intentionally performed as abnormal or not) and the countercultural role of rock star as "freak" (intentionally performed as a punk rock singer). (2006, n.p.)

In Church's view, the Joy Division song "Atrocity Exhibition" is also important to Curtis's cultural exploration of his disability experience, for "it seem-

ingly divulges his feelings of being in a freak show, applauded for performing his apparent abnormality . . . the song becomes a sort of oppositional
reaction to the countercultural conflation of rock shows with freak shows"
(2006, n.p.). It's Curtis's "trick of disaster" routine. Indeed, by 1980, Curtis
began to have seizures onstage, during the middle or latter stages of the
band's shows. These happened in London, Bristol, London again, and he
would be helped from the stage. The Factory impresario, Tony Wilson, remembered that "it was always two-thirds of the way through a set. And it
came to a point where in the last year, you'd watch the group and suddenly
you'd feel Ian may be dancing great and suddenly he's dancing really
great . . . something was happening within a set, doing what he did, that
actually took him to that point," where a seizure would triggered (quoted in
Curtis 1995, 114). Deborah Curtis has described his live performances as "a
public display of his illness. *It was allowed to become an expected part of Joy
Division's act* and the more sick he became, the more the band's popularity
grew" (Curtis 1995, 114; emphasis added). The dancing was understood—
and is retrospectively remediated even more so, for instance, in the 2007
biopic, *Control*—as the clinical exteriorization of his condition(s).[10] As
Curtis sings in "Atrocity Exhibition": "For entertainment they watch his
body twist" (Joy Division 1980a). Curtis wrote privately in 1980 of his epilepsy "attacks" and his music.

> I GET MORE NERVOUS WHEN WE PLAY NOW FOR FEAR OF IT HAP-
> PENING, IT SEEMS MORE FREQUENT. I DON'T THINK I COULD EVER
> SET FOOT ON STAGE AGAIN IF I HAD A FULL STAGE ATTACK WHILE
> PLAYING. . . . I KEEP THINKING THAT SOMEDAY THINGS WILL BE SO
> INTENSE THAT I'LL NO LONGER BE ABLE TO CARRY ON. . . . I HAVE A
> FEELING THE EPILEPTIC CONDITION WILL WORSEN. IT FRIGHTENS
> ME. *IT IS A LIE TO SAY "I'M NOT AFRAID ANYMORE."* (quoted in Middles
> and Reade 2009, 200; typography in original; emphasis added)[11]

There is an uncommon form of epilepsy, the seizures of which are triggered by musical sounds: musicogenic epilepsy, also known as *musicolepsia*.
In it, music is the provocative element. The nineteenth-century music critic
Nikonov unfortunately developed this condition, and wrote a pamphlet
about it entitled *Fear of Music* (Sacks 2007, 24)—and at this moment I am
hearing (admit it, listening to) the twitchy funk and light paranoia of the

1979 Talking Heads album *Fear of Music,* with lyrics which include someone's instruction to "Never listen to electric guitar" (Talking Heads 1979).
There's quite a lot of electricity on that album, and it's just made me think
about the link between the electricity of rock, of the electric guitar—Neil
Young distorting on one, or Peter Hook's bass playing melody unexpectedly
high, out of register, or Curtis occasionally awkwardly strapped to one—the
essential electricity of the rock form, which powers the gig and sparks the
culture, and the electrical disturbance of the neurocognitive condition of
epilepsy itself. (Joy Division's first released recording was, after all, on an album entitled *Short Circuit.* It marked the last nights of the Manchester punk
venue the Electric Circus. My copy, which I have had for over thirty years
(it's not even that good) is the "limited edition on electric blue vinyl": Joy
Division 1978.) In *Musicophilia*—not fear, but love—Oliver Sacks writes of
the musicoleptic experiences of one of his patients, when, as the patient describes it, popular music "touched a chord in me" (quoted in Sacks 2007, 26).

> His seizures start with or are preceded by a special state of intense, involuntary,
> almost forced attention or listening. In this already altered state, the music
> seems to grow more intense, to swell, to take possession of him, and at this
> point he cannot stop the process, cannot turn off the music or walk away from
> it. . . . [M]usic does not just provoke a seizure; it seems to constitute an essential
> part of the seizure. . . . *It is as if, at such times, the provocative music is itself
> transformed, becoming first an overwhelming psychic experience and then a sei-
> zure.* (Sacks 2007, 27; second emphasis added)

Sacks seems to invite us to glimpse the possibility of an epileptic music. I
think we have, with Neil Young's songs doing the "trick of disaster" and Ian
Curtis's doing the "body twist," heard fragments of what such electric music
might sound like, in the popular music soundscape anyway, and more specifically how the body dances to it.

Young has talked about how managing epilepsy has informed his wider
living practice: "I think I learned something, dealing with that condition.
It's helped me in other ways. . . . [O]nce you start controlling that, then you
control all kinds of things. Maybe that's why I'm still here" (quoted in Mc-
Donough 2002, 178). As I write and rewrite this book I have moved into my
sixth decade—hey, am still walking, don't knock it—(I am old, I am old, but
I will wear the bottom of my trousers rock 'n' rolled); from my perspective,

old Young is the pivot, not Curtis (nor, for that matter, Kurt Cobain)—the necessary and present elder's counterbalance to the tragic disability and rock self-destruction of youth suicide. Thinking back to the Buffalo Spring-field and epilepsy period, to his own twenties, Young has recalled that "you take things very heavily when you're that age. You don't realize you're gonna live through it." An obvious flipside of youth is its lack of life experience, which can be magnified by the fact that you also know everything. Young asks a wonderful question too, of the kind only an older person could: "Does my music suffer because I survived?" (quoted in McDonough 2002, 196, 701). The absolute fact I know for certain is simply this: music doesn't suffer by being made, *ever,* even if it's crap. Music suffers most of all by the terminal silence of withdrawal, for whatever reason. Of course, I recognize that that produced silence might resonate over the music that was made, rendering it more precious, fragile, or, where its aesthetic revolved around some form of suffering, authentic. In industry terms, Curtis had something to live up to in rock that was not available to the same extent to Young when he was that age: a confirmed template of youthful rock star death and its romantic afterlife—Hendrix, Joplin and, most of all for him, Morrison. (We will return to this in chapter 5.) Rock afterlife occurs variously but for our two there is something in common. Jimmy McDonough's 2002 epic Young biography is entitled *Shakey;* Anton Corbijn's 2007 Curtis biopic is entitled *Control:* in each instance, there is an initial and fundamental biographical gesture to situate the life and work within the neurological, perhaps specifi-cally electro-epileptic, frame. Each biography is (of) a control experiment. Even if it becomes in the course of telling also something else, the drama of the life story opens with and is centered on the singing body's struggle to control itself, a narrative of (self-)restraint and its failure, the corporeal and psychic experience of that narrative dynamic, and its musical expression and performance. That's why we—fans in general, as well as readers of this book—are interested in it too, of course. And that struggle is central to rock and roll's aesthetic practice: after all, to control means to roll in an opposite way (*contra + rotulare*).

In this chapter we have looked at ways in which the disabled body of the pop and rock singer presents and performs his (mostly) own disability. This focused on those singers who have negotiated their transition from able-bodied to disabled primarily as a result of spinal-cord injury in the pop and rock gaze; learning to employ and adjust to assistive technologies, changing—or significantly keeping the same—musical approach, vocal style, repertoire. Then the critical gaze shifted to those whose neurological disabilities have informed or impinged on their stage performance and how they sing about it. Such visibly disabled male rock and pop stars were and are the front men for a revolutionary corporeal sonic culture that has sought and may continue to seek a "knowledge of selfhood and body-truth," as Petra Kuppers has put it (2003, 92).

## CHAPTER 4

# Johnnie-Be-Deaf

## *One* Hearing-Impaired Star, and Popular Music as a Disabling (Deafening) Culture

> They come out to see what the freak is like.
>
> —Johnnie Ray, on his audiences, 1952
> (quoted in Whitefield 1994, 133)

> . . . without your hearing, you have nothing.
>
> —Ray Charles (n.d.)

WE TURN NOW to look at the one key star of deaf pop—a singer, songwriter, and pianist whose hearing impairment was visible, present, and negotiated throughout his extraordinary career, in a "queercrip"-informed (McRuer 2006) analysis of the pre–rock-and-roll figure of Johnnie Ray. We then go on to explore the terribly ironic cripping capacity of pop and rock as a deafening mode through music-induced hearing loss, the other symptom of which is mature regret. Here, a number of rock artists are discussed—in particular, from later life, when the occupational hazards of a career in the reckless and excessive industry of loud music have presented as medical symptoms. We will also discuss the hearing loss of fans in relation to music technology (amplification, personal stereos).

Music is first and foremost an aural cultural experience, and one that remains hugely popular with young people even in, and as part of, an interactive digital multimedia world. One recent survey of research into young people's exposure to loud music found that, "on average, people in the group aged 14 to 20 years listen to over 3 hours of music per day"; further—in a key point to which we will return—"the more they liked the music, the louder they preferred it" (Vogel et al. 2007, 124, 128). For the vast majority of people, central to the corporeal experience of music is the place of the ear—or rather, as Oliver Sacks corrects us in *Musicophilia*, "the huge but often overlooked importance of having *two* ears" (2007, 146; emphasis added). Technological developments in recording and transmission (such as stereo or surround sound), or innovations in consumption such as the Walkman or iPod, infer a normative and fully functioning binaurality in a largely phonocentric globe. The shift from mono to stereo recording and records was popularized in the wake of rock and roll, one might argue effectively in parallel with the rise of popular music itself from the 1950s to the 1970s. Although stereo recordings were easier to transmit on tape, the first stereo records were produced for sale in America in 1957, and what "started as a luxury good for the technically minded elite in the 1960s became a mass-produced consumer good in the 1970s" in the form of the home stereo system (Millard 2005, 215, 222). Stereophonic sound, with its capacity for the listener to aurally discriminate between different instruments or sections in the recording by locating them in different sound-spaces, has become such an industry standard and audience expectation that, during the early digital era, vintage mono recordings were constantly being remastered for stereo consumption. This was not only a marketing innovation: such technological and industry developments dictate that it is not enough simply to hear popular music (which is often pretty loud anyway); one ought best be able to hear it stereophonically, via the two different ears and the two sets of sounds they simultaneously process.

According to Sacks, "our auditory systems, our nervous systems, are . . . exquisitely tuned for music" (Sacks 2007, xi). Indeed, the very terms eardrum or tympanic membrane suggest a fundamental connection between physiology and musicality. For human beings, the "functional utility" of the specialized organ of the ear is not so extraordinary as it is in, say, bats, with their sonar—humans may even have "the most limited range of all mammals"—but the utility does, in the view of A. J. Hood, "find its highest expression in our ability to communicate by means of the spoken word *and in our appreciation of music*", not least because of "the superlative pitch discrimination possessed by the ear" (Hood 1977a, 32, emphasis added; 41). Although hearing is a neurophysical operation of tremendous sensitivity, the hearing mechanism of the ear—the organ of Corti—is, in fact, rather "well protected from accidental injury; it is lodged deep in the head, encased in the petrous bone, the densest in the body, and floats in fluid to absorb accidental vibrations" (Sacks 2007, 132). But it remains the case that there are numerous ways in which our hearing can be affected by popular music: the use of very loud volume, the placing of the music source near or in the ear canal (as by using headphones or earphones), and the lengthy and regular duration of listening, for instance, all present potential hazards.

While deafness is often considered one of the invisible disabilities, this is not necessarily the case. It can combine with other associated symptoms to manifest in a physical manner; as Hood explains, because the ear is an organ of the sense of both hearing and balance, "it is not unusual to find deafness accompanied by disorders of balance, the most classical example being Ménière's disease, in which fluctuating attacks of giddiness and deafness are the rule" (1977a, 36). The ear is the primary organ for consuming music and maintaining a sense of balance alike. Also, as we will see, the technology of hearing aids was quite cumbersome in the early days of popular music—and remained so until the introduction of digital microtechnology in the field—and anyone who used one then would have been easily identifiable as hearing-impaired.

Yet, before going further we do need to consider the extent to which this chapter belongs in this book. Both their mobilizing history and the more recent impetus of identity politics have helped to produce a powerful community of people with hearing disorders, who in recent years have begun to self-identify as "Deaf." To be Deaf rather than deaf is to claim the identity of the Deaf as possessing and living a separate, distinctive, and complete culture, with, vitally, its own (sign) language(s). As Lennard J. Davis puts it in *Enforcing Normalcy,* the Deaf "feel that their culture, language and community constitute them as a totally adequate, self-enclosed, and self-defining subnationality within the larger structure of the audist state" (Davis 1995, xiv). For American Sign Language speakers, the place signed and typographically represented as DEAF-WORLD is the nation they inhabit (Lane 1995, 161–62). Further, many within the Deaf movement have not only questioned but rejected the inclusion of their own social and corporeal experience of hearing impairment within a discourse of disability (and even the term "hearing *impairment*" as a part of that discourse). There is a "political element" within Deaf identity groupings that, because of the self-identifying minority language status of Deaf culture, "distances itself from both phonocentric society and from any suggestion that they are people with impairments or disabled people" (Scott-Hill 2003, 89). Debates about the position of d/Deafness in relation to disability have become more compelling as the theoretical and social ideas of the two have become more sophisticated, and there is transatlantic consensus. One leading British Deaf activist, Paddy Ladd, has put the view from that community: "We wish for the recognition of our right to exist as a linguistic minority group. . . . [L]abelling us as disabled demonstrates a failure to recognise that we are not disabled in any way within our own community." The American Deaf leader M. J. Bienvenu has asked: "how can we fight for official recognition of A[merican] S[ign] L[anguage] and allow ourselves as 'communication disordered' at the same time? . . . Disabled we are not!" (both quoted in Lane 1995, 159). One thorny issue identified in a strong Deaf rejection of disability is that that rejection may replicate a normate view: Deaf people are avowedly not disabled, "[t]hey are NOT that. Not crippled, not blind, not crazy, not sick. Disability is 'othered' to the extreme" (Doe 2004, 35). What Mairian Scott-Hill calls "the tension-ridden relationships between Deaf and disabled people" is "evidenced not only by the marginalisation of Deaf people from disability politics, and *vice versa,* but also by the separate evolution of Deaf studies and disability studies" (2003, 88). In her view, Deaf people "perceive themselves to be excluded from the dominant areas of social and cultural production by the perpetuation of a phonocentric world-view. They may also feel excluded from the disability movement because the movement is seen to reflect this world-view in the way in which it is socially organised around phonocentric language 'norms'" (Scott-Hill 2003, 89). For Harlan Lane, the demands and expectations of each group, disabled and Deaf, are not only different but *mutually exclusive:* where disabled groups campaign for independence, the Deaf desire interdependence; rather than mainstreaming in education, the Deaf want dedicated institutions with their linguistic specialism; the Deaf reject medical intervention (for example, around cochlear-implant surgery for Deaf children) and have little need of important areas for many disabled people such as personal assistance or rehabilitation (1995, 161–62).

Nonetheless, for a book such as this, concerned with a cultural form in which the activity of listening is an—no, *the*—essential corporeal behavior, hearing impairment or absence can be, has been, understood as a reason to be fearful; to be denied admission to the party. For instance, the visually impaired singer Ray Charles has articulated starkly the common sense view from within popular music about the centrality of hearing: "I believe so strongly that without your hearing, you have nothing. Of course, that's especially true when it comes to music" (Charles, n.d.). This is perhaps the very kind of absolutist remark, *from the wider disabled community,* that betrays a lack of understanding and sensitivity about the experience of hearing impairment, and that would legitimate for the Deaf community its urge for separatism from the disability movement. But, in music, hearing helps—there is even a phrase for it: a gifted musician is said to have "a good ear." Practicing a specific form of popular music—jazz—is predicated on the musicians' act of listening to each other as they improvise; the brilliant opening word and instructional sentence of trumpeter Miles Davis's autobiography is, after all, "Listen" (1989, v). This is not to suggest, in disability studies, the return of the traditional deficit approach, but it is to acknowledge the legitimacy in Tom Shakespeare's observation that "impairment is not neutral, because it involves intrinsic disadvantage. . . . [P]eople with impairments will always be disadvantaged by their bodies" (2006, 43, 46). The extreme position of Ray Charles notwithstanding, we may assume a level of disadvantage in making music when one cannot hear it, accurately or without noise interference, or indeed at all. That being so, the nonlinguistic sonic order that is music may become the cultural limit case for the disability of hearing and deafness. Deafness has a special place within music—it being commonly understood by audiences since Beethoven as a symptom of a profound and pathetic lack, the never-ironic absolute limit case for the perception let alone the pleasureful consumption of our unseen free-floating signifier.[1] But that is a very stark position, and we would do well also to keep in mind the argument offered by Joseph N. Straus about the different kinds of "ways in which people with disabilities listen to music, specifically to the ways in which the experience of inhabiting an extraordinary body can inflect the perception and cognition of music" (2011, 158). So Straus discusses autistic hearing, blind hearing, mobility-inflected hearing—and deaf hearing—in a compellingly more nuanced understanding of what it means to hear (music).

## Johnnie Ray: "The Scrawny White Queer with the Gizmo Stuck in His Ear"

He's sincere and shows he's sincere.

—Hank Williams, on Johnnie Ray (quoted in Whitefield 1994, 85)

But where, really, are our deaf stars? Is it so impossible that popular music should permit the hearing impaired on its stage, and I mean central stage, and while at the youthful (usually, for pop) peak of their careers? There is one—only one!—deaf (rather than Deaf) young thing who sang and played piano while wearing his hearing aid on stage and screen and took the pop world by storm for a while, who made the youth quake before the *youth-quake* was even termed so: the American artist Johnnie Ray (1927–1990). Not "poor old Johnnie Ray," as sung of by Dexy's Midnight Runners in their 1982 hit "Come On Eileen," nor the one Van Morrison would sing dismissively of in his own 1997 song "Sometimes We Cry." (When Morrison cries, claims Morrison himself, they are real tears: "I'm not gonna fake it like Johnnie Ray.") Yet in the first half of the 1950s especially, audiences in the United States and internationally were not pitying toward (Dexy's) or dismissive of (Morrison) the new phenomenon. Ray—vocalist, pianist, and songwriter—had four million-selling singles, and other major hits in countries around the world (Hardy and Laing 1990, 658–59). According to Ray's still-active fan-club website, his double-sided hit record "Cry" / "The Little White Cloud that Cried" (released in 1951) would go on to sell over 21 million copies (elsewhere the website claims 35 million global sales), and would win a Grammy Hall of Fame Award in 1998. It is noteworthy, in the racial context of 1950s America, that his early singles, including "Cry," were released on Columbia Records's subsidiary for the black music market, OKeh Records; Ray had started his professional career in the black and tan (cross-racial clientele) clubs of Detroit in the late 1940s, and drew on blues and some jazz for his repertoire—early on, some record fans and radio-industry people thought he was a black singer (Johnnie Ray Fan Club website). He even said in an article in the African-American magazine *Ebony* in 1953, of working at Detroit's Flame Showbar: "I was the only white singer on the bill but sometimes, because of makeup, you'd never know it" (quoted in Whiteside 1994, 64).[2] He appeared singing live regularly on American television, including numerous occasions on the leading national programme Ed Sullivan's original *Toast of the Town,* subsequently renamed *The Ed Sullivan Show.* (It should be acknowledged that his one big break in Hollywood—appearing alongside Marilyn Monroe in the 1954 film musical *There's No Business Like Show Business*—was a career flop that effectively ended his film work.) When he is described, Ray is often cited, with a good deal of legitimacy we should acknowledge, as the (missing) link between Frank

Sinatra and Elvis Presley (see Whiteside 1994, blurb; Johnnie Ray fan-club website). As a bisexual man, he gained a different kind of notoriety with court appearances under charges of "accosting and soliciting" (one conviction in 1951 before fame; one later sensational acquittal in 1959), and featured regularly in the Hollywood scandal rags of the period (Harrison 1957, Linder 2010). In this context he offered a "boundary-crossing presence of queer space . . . at a seemingly queer-hostile time" (Stephens 2005, 307). As Cheryl Herr points out in an area I discuss further later, this "queercrip" combination of identity experiences makes Ray a "poster child" (Herr 2009, 327) for Robert McRuer's theoretical category (though curiously Ray makes absolutely no appearance in *Crip Theory,* McRuer's study of "cultural signs of queerness and disability": 2006).

But it was Ray's vocal and live performances that caused the storm. Ray's biographer Jonny Whiteside describes the innovations in his performance, noting that he was

> the first white pop singer to stand at the piano; the first to send a piano bench flying with a swift backwards kick; the first to wrest a microphone from its stand and carry it about the stage with him, the while vibrating through a kinetic series of convulsive, violent gestures, each wild movement instinctively calculated to emphasize the lyric. He tore at his hair, shot his arms out at the audience, spasmodically clenched and flexed his fingers. He bent over backwards; he went down on his knees; he crouched; he leapt; he rolled on the floor. (1994, 68)

With Ray, the pre–rock-and-roll-era young white singer who rode an extraordinary wave of febrile popularity from American youth while sporting a hearing aid in performances—and was black-sounding, supportive of black musicians, openly disabled with a potentially discreet—even invisible—disability, publicly bisexual, emotionally vulnerable: there are so many richly resonant cultural complexities, and always wonderfully competing subtexts. Notwithstanding the odd name check in a later lyric, he is arguably one of the great lost figures of American pop (and we may wonder about the extent to which that in itself is connected with his—uncool?—disability), though the impact of Ray's out-of-control physical and emotional excesses would be obliterated within less than a decade by the new sounds and corporealities of rock and roll. But in the early 1950s it was Ray, shining on himself, who was making up onstage the supreme new pop musical act, balance trick, of *being authentic and performing authenticity,* as

Fig. 21. Johnnie Ray
1950s publicity post-
card. Author's
collection.

disabled country singer Hank Williams kind of uttered at the time. As for
the subtext(s), the lyric of a late hit song like "Just Walking in the Rain"
from 1956—even though in this instance Ray did not write the words—
signifies multiply for a musician who could not hear properly, and who performed with a highly visible electrical device protruding from a hole in his
head (hearing aid in his ear) with a cable running from it to his body (where
a six-pack of batteries was strapped to a harness round the chest or neck:
see Herr 2009, 336).

> People come to windows
> They always stare at me

Shake their heads in sorrow
Saying who can that fool be. (Ray 1956)

They stare at him because he is a character walking in the rain; he is emotionally low, but we must also think they (we) are staring at him as the
performer wearing a hearing aid, so very unusual in a pop singer. And, being disabled, his intelligence must be doubted: he is a "fool," after all. Joseph
Grigely has mused on the strategy for visiblizing his own impairment: "we
have been conditioned to presume difference to be a visual phenomenon,
the body as the locus of race and gender. Perhaps I need a hearing aid, not
a flesh-colored one but a red one . . . a signifier that ceremoniously an-
nounces itself" (quoted in Siebers 2008, 102). Though Ray's aid was often a
Caucasian flesh-colored one, its protruding presence alone renders a blush-
ing strangeness—and in fact he sometimes wore a mauve-colored one. The
technology available to him was commonly described in the literature of
the hearing-aid industry itself at the time as "cumbersome" and "unsightly."
Herr remembers it appearing "abnormally large" as she watched him on *The
Ed Sullivan Show* as a youngster (Herr 2009, 336, 338). To understand the
significance of Ray wearing the aid in performance and in public generally,
its power or shock value—and the way it could construct a different form of
masculinity—we can compare Ray's actions with the experiences of a later
singer such as Abdul "Duke" Fakir of the Motown vocal group the Four
Tops, who developed sensorineural hearing loss in both ears in older age.

> Who wants to admit that they can't hear? I didn't want to admit it for a long
> time. I stayed away from hearing aids. *I guess it was a macho thing.* I just didn't
> want anything hanging off my ear. . . . [The new miniature devices] are sleek and
> sexy *and completely unlike hearing aids a generation ago.* I love them. . . . Today's
> technology is efficient and *nearly invisible.* (quoted in Better Hearing Institute
> website, n.d.; emphasis added).

Yet the hearing aid was an essential constituent of Ray's performance. He
wore it and he used it; he needed it to be able to hear more clearly what he
was singing and playing, and where he was in relation to the band or orchestra's musical accompaniment. For conductive deafness, a hearing aid
can supply sufficient amplification for even complete restoration of speech
recognition, yet, as A. J. Hood has explained, in the context of technological
and design innovations, "miniaturisation imposes severe restrictions on the

frequency response of hearing aids so that the full spectrum of sounds so necessary for musical appreciation and enjoyment is lacking" (1977b, 325). The aid gifted problems, too: Ray's road manager Tad Mann recalls that both musicians and audiences were "familiar with him turning the volume [on the hearing aid] up so loud in order to hear the music that it would screech with feedback. . . . He could never get the volume the way he wanted it. He often lost his place and the notes . . . were off key" (quoted in Herr 2009, 335–36).

Another Ray song, "It's the Talk of the Town," is also ostensibly about breaking up in a relationship, though Ray's attraction to such songs seems regularly to be on the social embarrassment and awkwardness of rejection rather than the personal pain experienced. Interestingly, the song had been recorded by polio survivor and wheelchair user Connie Boswell two decades before—do its lyrics resonate for singers with disabilities? Ray sings:

> I can't show my face
> I can't go any place
> People stop and stare
> It's so hard to bear (Ray 1953)

The starers in these two songs, who might be *not* emotionally overwrought, rejected and young, or *not* disabled, or *not* bisexual, or just *not* famous, either gaze out through the safe glass of their homes or are frozen still in public by the freakish surprise of what they see before them. This unwanted and unsought audience experience Ray turns into material for his own yearning crowds. Curious how reading lyrics of songs by a disabled singer like Ray half a century later in the context of cultural disability studies might make *us* stop and stare. But how curious should that be? After all, many of pop and rock music's lyrics are expressions of unhappiness—the key trope of being misunderstood, of suffering, exclusion, alienation. And some of Ray's audience members—not the street starers—came to concerts to gaze and listen precisely because he *did* visiblize his disability. For instance, we know that Ian Dury attended one of Ray's astonishing London Palladium concerts as a youth. One of Dury's biographers makes clear what he understands as the link between the two singers—each being disabled, and connecting the body and voice: "Ray performed with a hearing aid and contorted his body as he sang. His unusual singing style probably left its mark on Ian" (Balls 2000, 53). Dury marked by Ray. Polio survivors like

Dury were among the most notable of disabled people during these years, and one of the small band of female admirers and informal helpers who followed Ray loyally on tour in the early 1960s was Bonnie from Connecticut, a polio survivor and wheelchair user (Whiteside 1994, 304).

There are occlusions in the biographical information we have about Ray, which may make the critical discussion more difficult: Cheryl Herr points out that we do not know what brand and kind of hearing aids he used, nor do we have full information about his autopathography, the variations in his aural capacity, for instance. We do know that Ray lost the hearing in one ear in a childhood accident; *or* we do know that he had a congenital hearing defect which resulted in degenerative hearing loss—it depends which biography or memoir one reads, and indeed which story Ray himself offered to interviewers at different times about his impairment (Herr 2009, 330–31). What we actually *do* know is that Ray was not deafened by popular music. The reasons for his hearing impairment were (probably) twofold: a childhood accident at age thirteen in 1940, and failed attempts at surgical correction as an adult in 1958. The most frequent narrative of the accident tells us that, at a Boy Scout Jamboree in Oregon, during a game of "blanket toss" using a canvas tent, Ray was tossed high in the air and on the last occasion fell out. He was concussed, and worse: an upright strand of dry straw penetrated his left ear and "severely traumatized the ear canal and punctured the ear drum membrane. Johnnie . . . immediately lost fifty per cent of his hearing" (Whiteside 1994, 21). Thinking or hoping it would get better or go away, Ray did not even tell his parents what had happened, and it was a year before he was diagnosed and supplied with a hearing aid, during which time he withdrew socially and regressed at school. From extrovert and confident, the now "loneliest boy in the world [was] adjust[ing] to the narrow little world into which I had been shoved," as he put it in a 1953 interview (quoted in Whiteside 1994, 25). Whiteside even speculates that "he was probably unaware of when his voice changed" (1994, 25). But he did plunge into his music, and Whiteside paints this retrospectively as pivotal: "the bleak silent year . . . instilled a powerful ability to express himself in song . . . with a depth of emotion" (Whiteside 1994, 29). In fact it was not a "silent year" at all—Ray had at least one fully functioning ear, after all. Yet this adventitious childhood disability had a profound impact on Ray, which he referenced quite frequently in interviews through his career. For instance, after attempting and failing to get a break in Hollywood in the late 1940s, a triumphant return as a star in 1952 saw him explain his history in an feature in the *Los Angeles Daily News:* "Hollywood plain told me to get lost. They didn't like me because I wore a hearing aid. I was told to forget about a career. . . . I told 'em to go to Hades. I proved the public will accept me" (quoted in Whitefield 1994, 97). (Actually, although his invisible disability was displayed by his use of a hearing aid onstage and in front of the television cameras, when filming for *There's No Business Like Show Business,* he was told that he could use his hearing aid during rehearsals but was required to remove it for shooting (Whiteside 1994, 178). So he never quite defeated what Lennard J. Davis calls, in another context, "the hearing establishment": 1995, 172, n4.)

Ray's condition would also cause balance problems—as Whiteside puts it, "the law of gravity was never very kind to Johnnie" (1994, 37)—a not uncommon related symptom of hearing impairment, since the functions of the inner ear are concerned with both the sense of hearing and of balance, of course. But is it so surprising then that one of Ray's trademark stage moves—embodying being overcome by emotion, but also a physical display of the secondary effect of his disability—was to fall to the floor? Or that his massively excessive consumption of alcohol and some narcotics over decades would lead to him frequently losing physical control? As one later manager, Bill Franklin, recalled, perhaps with some weariness, "There had always been a lot of falling down" (quoted in Whiteside 1994, 385). We begin to glimpse some of the ways in which his performance, onstage *and* in life, was informed or influenced by his daily experience of disability. Herr retrospectively diagnoses bipolar disorder, too (2009, 335). Through 1960, struggling with tuberculosis, Ray would complain, "I'm either on stage or in a hospital." His own publicity, such as copy from an Australian tour program from the time, drew his personal health into the narrative of his performance of emotion and vulnerability.

> There have been times when Johnnie may not have been feeling well, but once he gets onstage, it is the greatest tonic he could have. At every performance, he gives to the utmost of his ability, even though at times, unbeknown to anybody else, he may have been painfully suffering. (both quoted in Whiteside 1994, 275)

By the late 1950s, Ray's hearing had deteriorated further and he decided to undergo surgery to correct or at least improve the situation. Although he claimed he could lip-read "to a certain point," as he put it (quoted in Whiteside 1994, 178), as far as is known he could not sign and never learned to, "despite his intensely gestural rendering of songs," as Herr notes (2009, 339). The surgery was disastrous, although press reports were quickly filled with stories such as "Johnnie Ray ear miracle thrills New York," or the gushing words of the Voice of Broadway columnist (and one of Ray's long-term lovers) Dorothy Kilgallen: "Johnnie Ray passed his Big Test with flying colors—came onstage at Philadelphia's Latin Casino without his hearing aid and performed with all his old vitality and exuberance." The reality appears very different: Whiteside explains that "the surgery completely eradicated what remained of his left ear's hearing and also diminished that in his right ear by almost 60%." Instead of the hoped for no hearing aid, according to his manager Franklin, he now "had to begin wearing his hearing aid in his *right* ear" (see Whiteside 1994, 238–39; emphasis added).

Known as the Nabob of Sob, the Prince of Wails, the Cry Guy, the Cheerful Tearful, the Master of Misery, the Anguished Bard, among others, Ray became internationally famous for his hyperemotional vocal and physical renditions of songs, extraordinarily crystallized in the titles and lyrics of his double-sided first hit single "Cry" / "The Little White Cloud that Cried," the B-side of which he himself wrote. The sheer number of names coined for Ray by the entertainment media (over a dozen: see Whiteside 1994, 120 for others) confirms the greater than "queer-crip" multiple identity which he seemed to embody. According to Herr, "Ray's great talent was less singing than it was emoting. He was skilled at employing vocal markers of emotion, in particular feelings of acute distress and ebullient joy. These emotional states were very much grounded in the words that he sang" in these trademark songs (Herr 2009, 328). There are reports of Ray's speech being intermittently articulated, "almost like that of someone with a hearing problem, very poorly modulated" (Bill Franklin, quoted in Whiteside 1994, 300), and this may help explain his vocal innovation in singing. Once again, we can locate the "weird voices" (Neil Young's phrase, remember: quoted in McDonough 2002, 98) of popular music within disability discourse, we can further understand their meanings. The characteristic delivery and enunciation of lyrics he introduced with "Cry" in 1951 and then developed further consisted of "drawing out each word to impossible lengths, dramatically phrasing each sustained syllable" (Whiteside 1994, 80). It was an inarticulate semi-melisma, though one practiced more on the first syllable of words and especially on single-syllable words—particularly those beginning with hard consonants—so that it could extend into a stutter. "It's the talk of the town," for instance, is Ray's master class in the *mal canto* style, with a sophisticated and understated jazz-blues accompaniment that projects the vocal line even further out. He sings the words a little like this: "You-ou-ou le-e-ft h-hm-me-e-e . . . hm-hm-my-y hea-art . . . we ss-send out invitations . . . h-hwe-e-e-e ca-an't stay apart, Don't let ffffoolish pride . . ." The sense of the words is stretched to near senselessness in a song that starts with the repeated phrase "Baby how they *talk*, baby how they *talk*" and has a middle eight section ending with him singing "What can I *say*?" Speech and its difficulty are at the heart of the lyrics and the vocal performance alike. While this mannered and stylized speech disfluency was presumably intended to capture or present the emotional uncertainty and vulnerability of the singer, it is surely also a voicing of disability. Ray's physical performance spoke of a difference or struggle too, as Herr describes it in the context of "the singer's vulnerability," which managed to combine "an abruptly volcanic physicality—loose-limbed, urgent— . . . [with being] endearingly clumsy. Reinforcing the tortured affect of his facial expressions, he intermittently raised his arms to the ceiling or fell to the floor, skipped to the left and then Charleston-shimmied to the right, banged his torso on stage equipment and clapped his pockets . . . perhaps kicking the piano" (2009, 325). One 1953 reviewer wrote of his vocal and stage routine and its effect on the audience.

> While cry-boy delivers his lachrymose songs, the on-lookers stamp and clap, weep and groan, and by the time Mr Ray completes his whining, stammering performance an indescribably hypnotic spell seems to have been cast over the entire audience . . . and then Mr Ray, his face wet with perspiration, panting from exhaustion, walked off. (quoted in Herr 2009, 326)

"Whining, stammering": just a touch of the queer falsetto break to accompany the fragmenting *mal canto* here. Yet his shows had already been even more incendiary. Ray's American concerts in 1952 became happenings of incitement and unpredictability for the performer and crowd alike—for a time, Ray would descend into the crowd, though fans bringing razors and scissors to try to clip a souvenir off the singer made that dangerous ("they would've taken my ears if they could," he remembered about the more wild of his European fans: quoted in Whiteside 1994, 160). Sometimes even tear-gas bombs were exploded by audience members in the auditorium. In a remarkable interview at the time, Ray explained his understanding—of his audience, his appeal to them, *and* his self-identification.

> They come out to see what the freak is like. . . . They want to know what this cat has got. I know what it is. I make them feel, I reach in and grab one of their controlled emotions, the deeply buried stuff, and yank it to the surface. (1952, quoted in Whiteside 1994, 133)

*They come out to see what the freak is like.. . .* The pentametric rhythm and lyrical feel of the sentence enhance its power, but there is also a claim being made on the part of the disabled: Ray's disability gives him access to secret places and knowledge, "the deeply buried stuff." In this moment, he publicly self-identifies as freak, but also a kind of savant, and violent emotional channeler. He takes them out of control. We must intertwine with this reading that presented by Stephens: "The novelty and emotional release Ray offered audiences coupled with his carefully managed image allowed him to openly access and utilize public space to add queer textures to the music and performance culture of his era" (Stephens 2005, 291). They come out to see what the multi-freak is like . . . armed with razors and bombs.

The singer Tony Bennett was an early admirer of Ray's style, and recognized that there was a connection between the disability, the sound of the voice, and the physical onstage performance: "he smashed all the rules. He did everything. He jumped up and down, he jumped onto a curtain. He hit the audience with that piano, standing up at the piano, no one ever did that. . . . [B]ut he had this tremendous problem of not being able to hear himself, and hoping that he was singing in tune, and not being sure of that—but when he wasn't sure, something would take over . . . and it would become . . . a great visual performance" (quoted in Whiteside 1994, 74). Ray's mode of compensating for the professionally embarrassing and potentially catastrophic situation that was the singer losing his place and his tuning in his own songs gave him the means to innovate and entertain in other dynamic ways, and prefigured the shift that took place in rock and roll from the voice as site of meaning to the body. Another out-of-tune crip singer in pop, or actually the first, the *mal canto* originator? (It is fair to say that surviving footage of Ray in live performance from his peak period in the 1950s—in the form of archive television broadcasts, for instance, accessible on the Internet—does not do full justice to the performative range and sheer physical eccentricity of the live shows as described in many reviews and memoirs, and captured in photographs. Probably this is due to a certain nervous cramping of style in front of the live broadcast television camera, as well as an awareness on his part of the need to accommodate his movement to the relative immobility of cameras at that time. It may also be a further contributory factor to the relative neglect that Ray has experienced from later popular music historians and enthusiasts.) Onstage, the drummer was increasingly Ray's key musician, as Whiteside notes: "Since the failed ear surgery [of 1958] his drummer was more important than ever . . . he was the only one able to get him back in time and tempo should he lose his way mid-song" (1994, 281). Ray acquired the jazz drummer Jimmy Campbell in 1962, and Campbell articulated his practical and musical support for Ray in performance.

> He had a jazz mind. . . . Musically, he was a very adventurous kind of person, and liked to try all kinds of different things, but the hearing was a handicap, as far as venturing away from a melody. He carried it off though. I would put my drums on a platform at the front of the band instead of in back, and if he got confused with his hearing about where he was at, he would come stand on the platform and the vibrations would give him an idea of where the hell he was at. And he didn't get lost too often, either. It became pretty well ingrained. . . .
>
> Once in a while if he did get off, he'd turn around and I could tell he was lookin' at me—he'd put his foot out and I'd hit real hard for him and then he'd be right back on. (quoted in Whiteside 1994, 282–83)

In this preference more for what Joseph N. Straus distinguishes as "sonic vibration [rather] than 'normal hearing,'" Ray here confirms one aspect of "the deaf relationship to music [which] tends to be visual, tactile, and kinaesthetic. Deaf people often prefer to see the sources of the musical sound, to feel the musical vibrations, and to engage music with bodily movement." Indeed, such "deaf hearing may thus also be hearing out of time" (Straus 2011, 32, 29, 170). It is possible as well to ascertain the impact of Ray's impairment on his musical repertoire and stage setup: as Campbell notes, while he would like to play jazz, involving vocal variation and improvisation around a melody, an anxiety about getting musically lost—a lead singer's nightmare, coming in in the wrong place—led to him falling back on "ingrained" song structures and approaches. The focus on pop songs (rather than jazz numbers) was not only a result of industry or managerial pressures to deliver what (they thought) the public wanted, it was also a pragmatic choice by Ray, since such material tended to be more rhythmically secure and melodically straightforward.

What should we make of Ray's emo-ness, and its effect on his audiences, in the context of his disability? As noted, the powerful emoting Ray performed vocally and onstage is captured also in the lyrics. In a survey of what he terms "crying records," "tearful tunes," and "weeping themes" in pop, B. Lee Cooper observes that "vocalists have utilized songs to assess personal grief, to examine romantic cycles, and to plumb the depths of human emotion" (2004, 107), but Ray is so overpowering in his entire package of performativity in this regard, and so complex in what he offers in corporeal and sexual terms—and so successfully foundational to the generic practice—that such a view is insufficient. Herr positions his disability absolutely at the center of the emotional style of his musical performance: "Ray's delivery is seen to be caused by his deafness. Expressing his hearing loss, acting out his aural abandonment as if his ears were lovers who had abandoned him. . . . [I]n 'Cry' *Ray basically performed the emotional impact of his disability*" (Herr 2009, 327; emphasis added). Is there not something reductive though with this kind of reading? One limitation of identity politics is that the lens of identification becomes a malfunctioning monoglass, distorting through limitation, through Nancy Fraser's process of the "reification of identity." As Iain Ferguson puts it, "an emphasis on a shared identity [of disability] can discourage attempts to explore other intragroup divisions such as gender, sexuality and class" (2003, 82), and we have seen how Ray the multi-freak is more complex. During his early years, Ray's disability would combine with his burgeoning recognition of his bisexuality, and, trying for his first break in the black and tan joints of the cross-racial music scene of Detroit, he started to receive attention as, in biographer Whiteside's phrase, "the scrawny white queer with the gizmo stuck in his ear" (1994, 55). Race, sexuality, disability: a potentially explosive and dizzying combination (razors and bombs again?). We cannot isolate the emo-ness of his disability from its other potential causes, and need to acknowledge that, in Vincent Lamar Stephens's words, "his tendency to perform 'as though his life depended on it' and willingness to express pain 'queered' male singing by breaking with musical conventions of rhythm, phrasing and tone and fully integrating a gender subversive visual intensity to his performance" (Stephens 2005, 301).

Ray's targeting by the authorities and some media was a sign of his discomforting strangeness (which *was* partly due to his disability), and the targeting contributed to the complexity and contradictoriness of the public profile of an outsider figure who had at the time an extraordinary emotional and visceral power over young people. He was a makeup wearing crip crier, and such factors "marked him as a gender outsider compared to [the] John Wayne-style grit, Sinatra-style swagger" of popular culture masculinities during that time (Stephens 2005, 292). Not only did the hypermasculine heteronormative Detroit police notice him, and react negatively—twice—some in the male-dominated music industry did too.

> male reviewers and critics chiefly described Ray's extroverted performing style by surveying how his body and its movement signify emotiveness and vulnerability. Ray's voice, gestures and stage movement provided a map of his unusual style which reviewers often contrasted with other male singers. Ray's voice, gestures and audience were an index of what appears unusual or queer to male observers many of whom found him disturbing. (Stephens 2005, 295)

Ray was, during those turbulent pop star years of the 1950s, a rather stark challenger to the master narratives of what McRuer links together as "compulsory able-bodiedness and heterosexuality" (2006, 151). (That the non-deaf English singer Morrissey's curious and controversial wearing of an old-fashioned hearing aid with the Smiths in the early 1980s was explained away as Morrissey's homage to Ray signals at least the recognition by one of pop's sexually ambivalent stars of an important precursor. Queer vulnerability and, more problematically, crip chic, are embraced in Morrissey's camp package.) His queer masculinity—bisexual, emotionally open in performance, vulnerable, and uncertain—also makes sense in the context of how disability *feminises* masculinity. Mixing codes, Whitefield argues that Ray became "America's first culture-shocking misfit," with his "unorthodox blend of male power and female sensitivity" (1994, 115), and his black-inflected sounds and repertoire. If we combine these with Ray's open bisexuality (even if open as a result of various exposés of his criminal record in the American scandal sheets), *and* his disability, we have a portrait of a remarkable pre–rock-and-roll star queer-cripping his way through the new landscape of popular music—or, more accurately, forming that new landscape and mapping its contours at the same time, ensuring that those contours included, at pop music's sonic start, *pre*-rock and roll—a bit of a queer-crip space for "weird voices."

## *A Deafening Mode*—Popular Music as a Disabling Culture—Music-Induced Hearing Loss

> I have unwittingly helped to invent and refine a type of music that makes its principal proponents deaf.
>
> —Pete Townshend of The Who (2006)

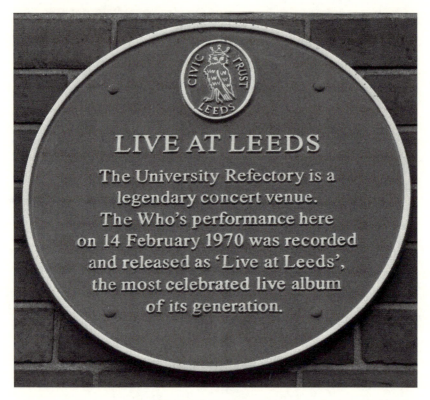

Fig. 22. The Who *Live At Leeds* wall plaque, Leeds University, commemorating a legendarily loud concert recording from 1970. ⓒ Wikimedia.

Much of this book is concerned with ways in which the relation between popular music and disability is a positive, enhancing, or empowering one, regardless of how complicated that might sometimes appear. So, for example, the repertoire of popular music lyrics includes the representation of the experiences of being disabled, its singing voices mark a connection with the extraordinary body, its bodies themselves find affirming and expressive space in the culture and performance of freakdom or deviance that some pops and subcultures have innovated, and sometimes its musical forms are capable of denoting a physical difference. In ways like these, even while we may be surprised by the generous fact, the culture can include the marginalised disabled. But we need also to consider situations in which popular music can function as a *disabling* culture. What should strike us is the extent to which some consumption and production practices in pop and rock have begun consistently to contribute to an experience of disability. Varieties and degrees of hearing impairment—tinnitus, difficulty with the auditory discrimination of simultaneous sounds, deafness—figure prominently here. *Pop crips. It really can.* While, "typically, people with NIHL [noise-induced hearing loss] complain of loss of perceived clarity of speech and greater difficulty than normal following speech in a background of noise" (Scientific Committee on Emerging and Newly-Identified Health Risks 2008, 34), musicians with music-induced hearing loss experience these *and* the anxiety of professional instability. This is confirmed in the plaintive tone adopted above by Pete Townshend, guitarist and songwriter for The Who, who in 1976 claimed the record as "officially The Loudest Band in the World," playing live at levels consistently of 126 decibels (dB) (Barnes 2009, 3). A seemingly perverse situation is an increasingly common one, due primarily to the popularity of extremely loud amplified music at live concerts and nightclubs on the one hand—an issue or danger for musicians and fans alike—and technological innovations in personal music consumption, from Walkman to iPod, on the other—an issue for fans. How unique or unusual is this situation? (I return to the disabling nature of pop in consideration of the psychological effects of the pressures and temptations of the industry on its new young stars in chapter 5.) In the consumption of cultural forms, how many are potentially dangerously and irreversibly disabling? Watching a film, reading a novel, looking at a painting—none of these is usually strongly connected with visually impairing the spectator. By and large, more or less, generally speaking, most culture does not crip—its consumption or production is not disabling. But pop—and more specifically, rock—seems to have developed a self-negating potential. The irony is indeed profound; it's heavy. The very discriminating organs that make most possible profession and pleasure *in* popular music are those under threat of dysfunction *by* popular music. Lennard J. Davis has written of the way in which the activity and phenomenon of critical "writing [is] a deafened mode"—dependent on silence and thought in both production (reading and writing) and consumption (reading, thinking) (1995, 181, n64); my approach, in the critical context of popular music, is to explore the extent to which *music is a deafening mode*—with the echo (we need not hear it to understand it) of mode as a musical scale. The average loudness discomfort level, as otologists term it—the level of sound intensity which one would find unpleasantly (though not painfully) loud—is around 100 dB (Hood

1977b, 329), though prolonged exposure to 80 or 90 dB and above is generally accepted as having the potential to cause hearing damage. Indeed,

> industrial regulations require employers to take action whenever their workers
> are exposed to noise over 85 dB for 8 hours a day. . . . Listeners using portable
> music players can expose themselves to the same level of loudness in 15 minutes
> of music at 100 dB that an industrial worker gets in an 8-hour day at 85 dB. . . .
> A recent study found that, in a typical nightclub, the sound intensity ranged
> from 104 to 112 dB. (Daniel 2007, 226–27)

It should be acknowledged that music, along with everyday sound and
noise more generally, has become louder in recent decades: a Hear Education and Awareness for Rockers campaign organisation (H.E.A.R.) leaflet
from 2004 points out that "Americans are increasingly exposed to noisier
lifestyles." So, while the pain threshold for hearing is at 125 dB, a rock concert nowadays, with enhanced amplification technologies, may be up to 130
dB—mundanely above the exceptional loudness of rock concerts such as
The Who's record-breaking event of 1976 (H.E.A.R. 2004, 7).[3]

As noted, the experience of music-induced hearing loss in the context of
popular music belongs in the main to two groups: practitioners and enthusiasts of very loud popular music forms (typically, though as we will see not
exclusively, hyper-amplified rock music and some experimental genres),
and listeners to personal stereos. The cultural and technological innovations that have made these possible date from the 1960s and 1970s (the early
popularity of rock and then heavy metal music), the 1980s (the populariza-
tion of the Sony Walkman personal stereo cassette and then CD player), the
1990s (introduction of MP3 personal stereos) and the 2000s (the introduction of the Apple iPod). We can postulate from this both that there are now
generations of middle-aged and older people affected by music-induced
hearing loss, and that there is a significant health concern for younger music fans about their levels of consumption and volume via digital personal
music devices. Surveys of recent studies have shown that, as Ineke Vogel et
al. report, some "musicians consider playing louder than any other group to
be prestigious" (2007, 128). From a quick scan among my old albums and
singles (actually it took me an entire morning, for I was diverted and ended
up re-listening to my youth), I was reminded that the back cover of David
Bowie's 1972 album *The Rise and Fall of Ziggy Stardust and the Spiders from*

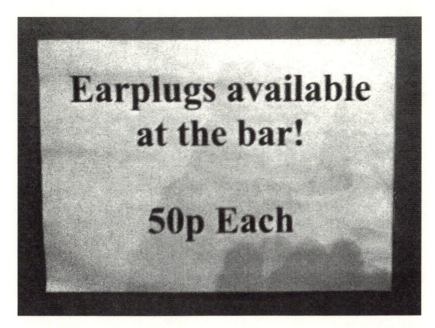

Fig. 23. Club sign for ear protection from loud music (Two, please). Author's collection.

*Mars* contains the instruction TO BE PLAYED AT MAXIMUM VOLUME, for example. The contemporary English experimental rock band My Bloody Valentine were notorious for employing loud volumes in live performances; their reunion concerts in 2008 and 2009 were noteworthy for the controversy around the extreme loudness, with earplugs on offer at the doors and some audience members leaving because they felt "physically distressed" by the noise (Barnes 2009, 3). Band leader Kevin Shields (who, perhaps unsurprisingly, has tinnitus) has defended the band's sonic aesthetic—which include trying to induce a state of physical unbalance or disorientation via the volume and frequency of the sounds produced—but also acknowledged the difficulty.

> We play with low frequencies that are nothing like anyone has ever heard before—it's a chaos that sets off a kind of inbuilt alarm system. . . . We'd like to say that it is cool to wear earplugs; it's not cool to get your hearing damaged. And anyway, feeling the music is a great experience. (quoted in Barnes 2009, 3)

Elsewhere, I recently saw for sale some personal stereo earphones called Monster Jamz; the associated advertising copy tempts buyers with the promise of "eardrum beating bass punch. . . . You'll be shocked how big your music can sound." (The company's website contains "safety tips," which include "avoid listening at high volume levels for prolonged periods. This may cause permanent hearing damage or loss." You may one day be shocked how little your music can sound: Monster website, n.d.) Is it then so surprising that "many young people believe music is enhanced when played very loudly," and have done so for decades (Daniel 2007, 229)? Even the playing of some (non-amplified) folk forms can lead to hearing loss: studies of the percussive/melodic combination of music practiced by steel-band orchestras ("pannists"), for example, "demonstrate the potential for the intensity of noise generated in a steelband to cause sensorineural hearing loss. . . . The noise level at the core of the band is consistently above 100 dB(A). This is comparable to the level 2 to 4 meters from center stage of a rock and roll band . . . [S]teelband players are at a high risk of developing hearing losses, which is directly dependent on the length of time of exposure" (Juman et al. 2004, 464).

According to research on hearing disorders—that is, not simply hearing loss, but *other* disorders too—among musicians by Kim Kähäri et al., "a large number of rock/jazz musicians suffered from different hearing disorders (74%). Hearing loss, tinnitus and hyperacusis were the most common disorders and were significantly more frequent in comparison with different reference populations" (2004, 627). Rock and jazz musicians experienced greater hearing disorders than the other musicians looked at, classical players. In terms of gender, male musicians had worse hearing than female ones, not infeasibly because "more men than women played the loudest instruments such as woodwinds, brass winds and percussions" (Kähäri et al. 2004, 629). The gendering of potential music-induced hearing loss is confirmed in Vogel et al.'s survey of young people, in which

> males were found to have more social noise exposure, and were more interested in noisy sports, home tools, and shooting, and in playing in a band. They also used and preferred higher music levels, used their portable music players for a longer average time, expressed less worry about the presence of hearing-related symptoms, had more positive attitudes toward noise, showed lower levels of desired behavior change, and were less likely to use hearing protection. (2007, 127)

Social class, smoking, and diet are all factors in the onset of hearing loss—so much so that, in a campaign article, one of *Rolling Stone* magazine's recommended "five ways to save your ears" is "quit smoking: it doubles the risk of noise-induced hearing loss" (Ringen 2005, n.p.). Yet in very recent years the place of the personal stereo as source of both diversion and motivation in contemporary exercise or gym culture has led to the ironic situation that, "whereas participating in physical activity is generally seen as part of a healthy lifestyle, doing this in combination with high-intensity music could constitute a risk for hearing loss" (Vogel et al. 2007, 129).

Let us consider each of these cases of popular music-induced hearing loss in a little more detail, looking at, in turn, the rock aesthetic of loud volume, and the impact of the use of personal stereos. (The technically improved sound systems of nightclubs in recent years are a further source of intense levels of music: Scientific Committee on Emerging and Newly-Identified Health Risks 2008, 27.) Over the past few years there has been a slew of journalistic and academic articles about, as one put it, "music making fans deaf," and musicians. These writings have been prompted by the hearing loss experiences of the ageing rock generation combined with new concerns about young people's encounters with loudness via personal stereos. Writing in *Rolling Stone* in 2005, Jonathan Ringen maps out the affected male generation: "in 1989, Pete Townshend admitted that he had sustained 'very severe hearing damage.' Since then, Neil Young, Beatles producer George Martin, Sting, Ted Nugent, [Fleetwood Mac drummer Mick Fleetwood] and Jeff Beck have all discussed their hearing problems" (2005, n.p). An advice booklet produced by Hearing Education and Awareness for Rockers quotes the following statistic: "60% of inductees into the Rock and Roll Hall of Fame are hearing impaired" (H.E.A.R. 2004, 5). (The sheer loudness of much amplified popular music, particularly in the enclosed space of the indoors venue, has made hearing disorders an occupational hazard for musicians and fans alike—could one go "deaf forever," (Mötorhead 1986), as the English heavy rock band Mötorhead sang on a 1986 single of the same name?) In rock music, it is woven into the excessive aesthetic, alongside other perhaps potentially precarious practices of music performance and consumption, like "the worldwide phenomenon of head banging": a dance form soberly (or drily) defined in the *British Medical Journal* as "a violent activity associated with hard rock and various subgenres of heavy metal . . . [the] violent and rhythmic movement of the head synchronous with music" (though originating, apparently at a Led Zeppelin concert

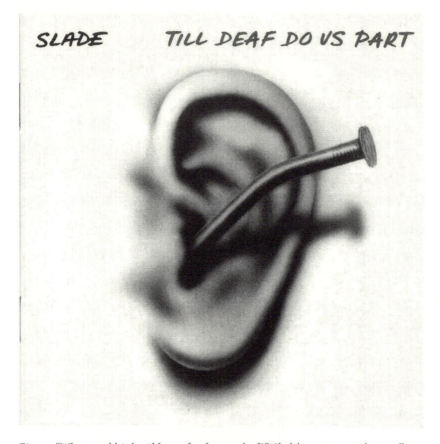

Fig. 24 "What would it be if [your fans] went deaf?" Slade's controversial 1981 album cover. © Union Square Music Ltd., London. Used with permission.

in the late 1960s, in the indisputably dangerous practice of fans banging their heads on the stage in time to the band: Patton and McIntosh 2008, n.p.).[4] To be a headbanger is to be a member of a subculture centered on rock music, the movement of the body, and the at least potential for physical damage. Other rock fans would position themselves by or with their heads actually in the speaker boxes at gigs. As well as being a display of extreme fandom via excessive consumption to less committed adherents of the music in the crowd, this is also obviously a potentially disabling action.

In rock, then, loudness is part of the package: this is seen clearly in album titles like Nazareth's *Loud 'N' Proud* (2010) and Ozzy Osbourne's *Live*

*& Loud* (1993), or song titles such as Kiss' "I Love it Loud" and "Shout it Out Loud" (available on the album *Sonic Boom*). The career of British glam rocker chart-toppers Slade exemplifies the aesthetic: their 1970 album, their first with the name Slade, is called *Play It Loud;* their final album in 1987 *You Boyz Make Big Noize*. The first of their three singles to enter the British charts at number one was "Cum on Feel the Noize" (1973), later covered by Quiet Riot and by Oasis; intriguingly, the effect of the group's characteristic misspelling of song titles works only in, in Lennard J. Davis's term, deafened mode. But it is Slade's 1981 album *Till Deaf Do Us Part,* their most heavy rock- rather than pop-oriented record, which is particularly notable. Guitarist Dave Hill claimed responsibility for the album title, explaining the curious thought behind the "twist on words": "What would separate you from your fans, what would it be if they went deaf?" (quoted in Ingham 2007, 5). The original album front cover featured an image of an ear with a large nail penetrating the ear canal. The delicate pencil-style drawing and shading contrasts with, and accentuates, the violence of the image. The nail is bent—force has been applied—and its point protrudes from the *back* cover. The ear can only be profoundly damaged; the head well and truly banged. The lyrics of the title song connect heavy rock, live performance, masculinity, extreme volume, and the infliction of pain and death on the audience via the loudness of the music: "Coming over to slaughter you . . . / Do you want us to torture you?" (Slade 1981). (The employment in recent years of rock music as instrument of torture or military intimidation provides a graphic illustration of the extent to which loudness in certain forms of music can be damaging, and is even a form of violence. See Johnson and Cloonan 2009.) Although there is an element of self-caricature within Slade's culture, of course—singer Noddy Holder opens the album with a mock "rock and roll preach" promising an "earholy catastrophe" to follow—at the time of its release some record stores refused to stock the album because of the "offensive" cover (Heslam 1992, 364). The American heavy rock guitarist Ted Nugent was notorious for his use of extreme volume in live performances—an apocryphal but still much-repeated story from his 1970s heyday told of one outdoors gig where a pigeon was killed in midair by one of his power chords. Like Slade, Nugent used volume as part of his marketing strategy, and it inspired his repertoire too. His most famous slogan was "If it's too loud you're too old"—which challenged as well as defined his (non-avian) audience, by their youth. That is, generational difference in popular music is also articulated through the possibility of

impairment, with its implication that hearing loss is for older people, not cool youth.[5] Because it is commonly associated with ageing (presbyacusis, age-related hearing loss), the state or onset of impaired hearing bears further anxious traces within the youth-oriented cultural zone of pop—this may help explain American rapper Foxy Brown's bewilderment with and initial denial of the public discovery of her own sudden and severe sensorineural hearing loss in 2005. Indeed, studies have shown that young people still reject protection from the potential damage to hearing of loud music because of "cultural pressures to conform to stylistic norms and *youthful* images of attractiveness and healthy bodies" (Vogel et al. 2007, 129; emphasis added). Nugent's 1976 song "Turn it Up" encapsulates the aesthetic practice of heavy rock, with lyrics such as:

> Turn it up, turn it up, make it louder than hell
> Turn it up, turn it up, make it ring like a bell . . .
> Turn it up, turn it up, turn it up, louder, louder, yeah! (Nugent, 1976)

The song title, repeated lyrics, the bulk of the chorus, and even the fade-out coda (when the volume of the recorded music is actually, of course, decreasing) all instruct us to "turn it up"—and it is essential to make the effect endure: the ear must "ring like a bell," making the experience of tinnitus a central experience as well as a reminder of the gig. In fact, Nugent himself began to wear earplugs onstage, and has experienced hearing loss since his thirties (Gosch 1984). In rock, then, loudness is part of the pleasure, and its effects on hearing accepted, even celebrated, by fans and musicians alike, as Mike Barnes has explained.

> that ringing in your ears could be likened to a bonding experience, recounted with the same sort of jocularity-in-adversity with which you might discuss a hangover with fellow sufferers. But if the inner ear is damaged, the next-day ringing—temporary threshold shift—may become tinnitus, a hissing or whistling sound in the ear which can be permanent. One guitarist and DJ who has tinnitus reckoned that it was as much "a badge of rock'n'roll honour as my Chelsea boot-squished toes or impaired liver functions." (Barnes 2009, 3)

The proudly damaged male body of the rock-and-roll wreck, half-fucked from head to toe, self-presents as an authentic figure who has so far survived the culture's excess, as well as presumably the passing deaths of the less fortunate or the more appetitive. Sporting his "badge of . . . honour," he has attempted to cheat the ageing process and its natural infirmities (though remember Tobin Siebers: "there are no survivors": 2008, 7) by enthusiastically embracing the disabling opportunities his culture has tempted him with before life did it anyway. Very rock and roll.[6]

How does what Michael Bull (2005, 344) has called the "privatised auditory bubble" public listeners create for themselves by their use of personal stereos in urban environments function less as a secure, closed experience, and more as a disabling potentiality? There is at least one link with the consumption of rock music, since, among users of portable headphones, research has shown that, of different music genres, "rock and heavy metal was played the loudest by both males and females" (Daniel 2007, 227). Otologists and medical academics confirm each other's findings about the dangers to hearing of popular music consumption in the new loud, mobile era—in particular, around the impact of Walkman and iPod technologies on young people. Writing in a survey of recent research in the field in the *Journal of School Health* in 2007, Eileen Daniel found that, "while age and hearing loss is linked, there appears to be a rise in hearing impairment among children and teenagers, usually related to recreational noise exposure. Unlike industrial contact, many young people voluntarily expose themselves to loud noise via headphones, car sound systems, loud concerts, and nightclubs" (2007, 229). The microtechnology of personal music consumption—in this instance, the earphone or headphone—is important: "the actual sound level at the eardrum is . . . influenced by the insertion depth of the ear-bud in the ear canal. It is possible to obtain sound level of about 120 dB(A) in the worst case scenario. . . . Furthermore, using software available on the internet enables to exceed these levels and reach values of 130 dB(A)." Also, the development in personal stereos of "high-performance digital players"—as opposed to the older cassette Walkman, for example—"with an increased dynamic range, has facilitated the listening to music at high levels due to reduced distortion at these levels" (Scientific Committee on Emerging and Newly-Identified Health Risks 2008, 9, 11 n7, 42). Another survey of recent research on "Young people's exposure to loud music," covering over thirty articles in the field, published the same year, open with the observation that

> with the massive growth in popularity of portable MP3 players, exposure to high noise levels has increased dramatically, and millions of young people are

> potentially putting themselves at risk for permanent hearing loss every time
> they listen to their favorite music. Music-induced hearing loss may evolve into
> a significant social and public health problem. (Vogel et al. 2007, 124)

While Vogel et al. qualify their understanding, projecting music-induced
hearing loss into a future scenario, Oliver Sacks seems in less doubt. His
present is replete with dangers for those musicophiliacs who are

> plugged into iPods, immersed in daylong concerts of our own choosing, virtu-
> ally oblivious to the environment. . . . This barrage of music puts a certain strain
> on our exquisitely sensitive auditory systems, which cannot be overloaded
> without dire consequences. One such consequence is the ever-increasing prev-
> alence of serious hearing loss, even among young people, and particularly
> among musicians. (Sacks 2007, 48)

Sacks's future is more bleak, while the present is deafening enough: "problems can be expected to increase exponentially for people who play iPods or
other music at too-loud levels. It is said that more than fifteen percent of
young people now have significant hearing impairments" (Sacks 2007, 132,
n1).

Yet it is possible that innovations of personal stereos are the pleasureful
prosthetic for auditory culturalists like music fans. Walkman earphones,
and, even more, iPod buds, as well as the wires connecting them to their
players, have arguably removed the stigma of unsightliness associated with
hearing aids that, say, Johnnie Ray's generation felt so powerfully, and which
Ray directly confronted, not least with his colored devices. Personal-stereo
earphones are now constructed as an icon of coolness. For instance, the
advertising copy for one product line, Heartbeats earphones, reads: "The
incredibly unique style of Heartbeats came straight from Lady Gaga herself.
Who needs earrings when you've got head-turners like Heartbeats?" Wearing pop celebrity-designed earphones "make[s] on-lookers do a double
take"—which is a quite different reaction from the "double-take" regularly
experienced by Ray's generation of ear-device users (Heartbeats website).
The cultural cachet of Apple products, the technology of choice of the
world's creatives, touches the ears. In the past, hearing aids have been at-
tached and therefore disguised on the ear frames of spectacles, for instance—
the discussion now is of them as an integrated technology with the personal
stereo itself. The development of, for instance, Apple personal device ap-

plications (apps) into medical and disability fields has seen assistive technology apps produced for the iPhone and similar Apple products that mean it has the potential to function as a hearing aid. One hearing-impaired blogger, responding to the discussion thread about a new hearing-aid app called soundAMP, writes of how "the irony of the iPod, with the hearing damage caused by its loud, long playing ability, and nearly universal use, now coming to the aid (pun intended) of the hearing impaired, is music to my ears!" (quoted in Berke 2009). Others have criticized Apple for not ensuring that the iPhone is hearing-aid compatible (see comments thread to Kincaid 2009). Among other available medical apps for hearing is one called Hearing Check, developed by the leading British charity, the Royal National Institute for Deaf People, which is "designed to be the best method of checking for sensorineural hearing loss (due to age or noise exposure[,] for instance) without seeing a medical professional" (RNID website, n.d.). Developments like these may be employed to enable personal music device producers—elsewhere, as we have seen, the target of criticism from academics, journalists, and health professionals for the disabling possibilities of their modes of consumption by some, especially younger, users—to counteract the deafening negativity lined up against them.

This chapter has explored the fundamental and seemingly dichotomous relationship between popular music as a sonic art and the incapacity on the part of musicians and fans to hear it by focusing on one of the very few key artists to have made a career as an international star while being deaf and becoming deafer, and by looking at the causative place of popular music in hearing impairment—the terrible irony of music-induced hearing loss for rock musicians and pop fans. In the final chapter, we will look further at the disabling nature of some aspects of the popular music industry, as well as at its campaigning responses around the social issue of disability.

# CHAPTER 5

# Crippin' the Light Fandango

## An Industry That Kills and Maddens, *and* Campaigns

> My greatest achievement is that I've stayed alive in the music
> industry for this long.
>
> —Slash, Guns 'N' Roses guitarist, 2010

> Now put your hard-earned peanuts in my tin.
>
> —Ian Dury, "Spasticus Autisticus" (1981)

THROUGH THIS BOOK we have uncovered and interrogated some capacities of both pop and rock to function as themselves *dis*abling cultures, with the profoundly ironic place of loud rock and dance musics as contributors to musicians' and fans' hearing loss at the heart of the discussion. Others we have touched on in music more widely are the historic figure of the castrato, and the (often minor for many but major for musicians) industry-related injuries caused by stress or repetitive strain through instrumental practice. Are there further disabling capacities in popular music, which we might reasonably characterise as a voracious, careless and indulgent industry? We have also explored the greater number of significant instances in which, arguably despite its remorselessly presentist focus on healthy, normatively sexually attractive, youthful bodies, popular music in fact often functions as an *enabling* cultural zone for those of its workers and enthusiasts with disabilities. As the industry has matured over (roughly) the past sixty years or so, and its people—the survivors, anyway—have grown older and less able-bodied, it may well make greater sense that pop and rock begin to inhabit or become an inclusive, supportive space. We should note Joseph N. Straus's argument about the "late style" of music-making here, that "what we have been calling late style may be better understood as a disability style" (2011, 102). We would also do well to recall the view of singer Marianne Faithfull, spoken in song in her best (that is, worst, post–*Broken English*) voice, that, "After a certain age, every artist works with injury" (Faithfull 1995). The industry's enabling capacity is probably one of its more surprising features, but is certainly one that requires careful qualification and delineation.

Nonetheless, I hope one of the surprises of this book (for its popular music specialist readers at least—disability studies scholars may know this score a little better) will have been the cultural and performative variety and the experiential and emotional depth of crippery on record, onstage and on video. I have been struck by these features anyway; my hope is that I have been able to capture and transmit enough of the artists' energy to keep you interested and in turn invigorated. Are you like me, going back and listening again, anew, or for the first time even, now cripped?

In this final chapter we look at two important extramusical aspects of the subject, which may seem in turn critical and praiseworthy. That is, together they offer the opportunity for a dialogic consideration of the positions of pop and rock regarding our question of disability. As suggested, they are focused less on the music, voices, and bodies of the stars and fans than on the contributory role of the industry itself, and its relation with disability. As constituents of a cultural industry, pop and then rock music—and then, as it emerged, the music-media end of *celebrity* culture—have developed certain practices of behavior and lifestyle, of business engagement and (let us be in no doubt that we are uncertain—a rhetoric of) social advocacy, for instance. These have become so embedded in the industry that they now function as a behavioral expectation or norm. And these industry practices and pressures matter particularly when we introduce disability to the discussion, when we crip 'em.

First, we will consider the relationship between the pressures and temptations of the industry as themselves disabling and the tropes and practices of rock suicide and "madness"—cultural cognitive impairment. It is apparent that there are industry-specific conditions, which tend to target certain kinds of pop workers: singers—front men, and women—appear most vulnerable. Why the singers? Perhaps because there is arguably a closer relation between their instrument, which is the voice, and the body; perhaps because they are the focus in the band of fans' attention, and feel the adulation and pressure more; perhaps because the singer is often also the lyricist, who writes the band's subjective and expressive text. In Laurie Stras's view, "the jazz or pop singer has a privileged and vital role . . . as an agent through whom identification becomes easier, less intellectual or abstract, more corporeal" (2009, 317). Pop stardom is an illness that can seriously, even fatally, threaten health and undermine ability; to do well in this career is frequently to be or to get a bit or a lot fucked up. Its workers employ medical terminology to express the condition. His then manager described the unattractive transformation of Ian Dury, following the chart-topping success of the single "Hit Me With Your Rhythm Stick" in 1979, as the result of him suffering "a very bad attack of number one-itis" (quoted in Balls 2000, 205). Shortly afterwards, Dury himself wrote a song called "Delusions of Grandeur," in which he sang of the egotistical pleasures and symptoms of the career—"I'm a dedicated follower of my own success . . . I've got megalomania"—as well as of the insecurities—"Oh, look at me, just another pathetic pop star" (Dury 1980). When a band member congratulated him on the astute self-confessional lyric, Dury, extraordinarily, vehemently denied the song was about him, arguing that it drew on what he had observed in others (Drury 2003, 112). He did, though, himself say, of the industry's traditional trajectory to success and beyond (usually back), "after people make it, a malaise sets in" (quoted in Balls 2000, 205). Deborah Curtis notes that, round the same time (the punk scene had inscribed within it a self-referential narrative about its own relationship with the industry, a symptom of its political unease with its own commercial imperatives), as Joy Division became more successful in late 1970s Britain, her husband and that band's front man "Ian [Curtis] contracted what was known as LSS (Lead Singer Syndrome)" (1995, 93). *Number one-itis* and *LSS* are the medical metaphors that describe the industry's sheer damagability, which may be focused most on, but is not restricted to, those who make it. The pop and rock industry has a notable capacity to facilitate the ruination of its workers; it's a high-risk, hi-vis workplace culture where one is never quite safe. And, extraordinarily, it seems where there is never quite enough trust to go round. This feature is a neglected area of research in popular music studies. Consider the kings of the scene, the King of Rock 'n' Roll, Elvis Presley (died 1977), and the King of Pop, Michael Jackson (died 2009), whose own controversial physicians prescribed the fragile men in their care huge amounts of drugs in the periods leading up to their deaths. Dr Feelbad. Pop's unsettling medicine is a repeat prescription—a systemic regicide for the subjects to follow.

Second, remembering that in this chapter we are focused on the industry itself, we will look at the roles of disability advocacy and activism as cultural intervention within the realm of popular music. The main argument is that disability campaigning in the mid-twentieth century set a template for much of the recent and current pop activism, although the contribution of disability campaigning has been historically neglected in popular music studies. While the familiar story of Anglo-American pop activism would stretch from Live 8 (2005) back to Live Aid (1985) to, at a push, the Concert for Bangladesh (1971), we will go back to the 1930s and 1940s to examine the role of American popular music in polio campaigns initiated by President Franklin D. Roosevelt. This leads to a discussion of more contemporary critiques of charity from the disability-rights movement, focused on the expression of those critiques in grassroots music production from disability arts. The sweep is from a Presidential Ball to a village hall, each with its music and cripolitics. To contextualize this historical revisioning, we will consider pop activism in the field of disability, and its limits, which would frequently include those organizations that are individualized—that is, structured through the artist's own self-promotion (from the Johnnie Ray Foundation to, say, the Amy Winehouse Foundation). This is the final section of the book's readings; I want the book to end on a high note (which may or not be voiced in some kind of cripping falsetto). By doing so I seek to confirm, even if problematically, the enduring capacity and indeed defining desire of disability culture to function as advocacy, the active space of cultural disability studies as a politically engaged one, the significance for popular music studies of crip awareness. Effectively, then, this final chapter asks questions of the ways in which industry practices, alongside the rock 'n' roll lifestyle as it developed to embrace extreme hedonism and campaigning advocacy alike, disable and enable their own stars. There is a destructive economy within this creative economy.

## Popular Music as Destructive Economy

> No-one's got the emotional tools to deal with being looked at by a
> million people. Live the dream? Live the nightmare.
>
> —Robbie Williams, Take That (quoted in Leigh 2011)

> What kind of fuckery is this?
>
> —Amy Winehouse, "Me and Mrs Jones" (2006a)

English jazz-pop singer Winehouse's sung question, the opening verse line from a song on the hit album *Back to Black,* contains a startling tabu neologism for a pop lyric—one of the signs of Winehouse's freshness, her creative innovation, of course—which resonates in the context of her lyrics' self-dramatising commentary on her life and her love life, yes, but also I suggest on her position in relation to the industry. *Back to Black* is, after all, the album that famously (perhaps now we must say notoriously) opens with a song and a hit single called "Rehab," in which the young woman, barely into her twenties, recounts, to a fabulous retro 1960s-soul-style dance track, the twin pop lifestyle pressures of health and hedonism. "Rehab" is in fact a refusal of treatment, a rejection of advice, with listeners singing along to its refusing chorus—no, no, no; we are complicit. The control / rock 'n' roll dialectic discussed in chapter 3 when looking at the out-of-control performing pop body is relevant here too, in the context of the industry's treatment and behavioural expectations of its own lead workers. If we speak the cultural policy language of creative industries or creative economy, we should acknowledge too that there is and has long been a destructive economy at work in popular music.

Winehouse died in 2011 at the age of twenty-seven, and there was following her death recirculated popular talk about "The 27 Club": a grouping referring to those rock and pop musicians who have died, accidentally or deliberately, aged twenty-seven years. As well as Winehouse, this lamentable club's most famous members include Brian Jones of the Rolling Stones (died 1969), Jimi Hendrix and Janis Joplin (each died in 1970), Jim Morrison (1971), Kurt Cobain (1994). It has been reported that Cobain even spoke as a youngster of joining the 27 Club. Facts appear malleable regarding qualifying membership: bassist Richey Edwards of the Manic Street Preachers (who disappeared in 1995) is often included, though the circumstances of his disappearance and timing of his presumed death by suicide have remained unclear; blues singer and guitarist Robert Johnson (died 1938) is sometimes cited as the founding member, though, as Elijah Wald points out, "we have documentation for [Johnson's] birth years of 1907, 1909, 1910, and 1912" and, besides, Johnson's death certificate gave his age as twenty-six (Wald 2004, 299, n1). Nonetheless, the mythic narrative and its periodic repetition and consolidation tells us something about the health and lifestyle model of the industry and/or about the public perception and expectation of that model, which is condensed in one of the great phrases of pop about itself—famously from an Ian Dury song—the un/holy trinity of "sex

Fig. 25. "They wanted me to go to rehab": Amy Winehouse, live at Virgin Festival, 2007. Photographer Napalm Filled Tyres ⓒ Wiki-media.

& drugs & rock & roll." A recent *British Medical Journal* study has explored the place of youthful death in popular music, searching in particular for evidence of "a peak in risk at age 27" among number-one pop musicians in the British album charts 1956–2007. According to its authors:

> Our final sample contained 1046 musicians, with 71 deaths (7%). The sample included crooners, death metal stars, rock 'n' rollers, and even Muppets (the actors, not the puppets). The sample consisted mostly of men (899, 86%). The median age at first number one was 26 years. . . . Our analysis found no peak in the risk of death for musicians at age 27. . . . The study indicates that the 27 club

has been created by a combination of chance and cherry picking. We found some evidence of a cluster of deaths in those aged 20 to 40 in the 1970s and early 1980s. This pattern was particularly striking because there were no deaths in this age group in the late 1980s, despite the great number of musicians at risk. This difference may be due to better treatments for heroin overdose, or the change in the music scene from the hard rock 1970s to the pop dominated 1980s. (Wolkewitz et al. 2011)

The overall conclusion of even a relatively modest, and nationally centered, statistical study such as this is indeed that "famous musicians . . . *do* have a generally increased risk of death during their 20s and 30s" (Wolkewitz et al. 2011; emphasis added). The popular music industry is a dangerous and damaging place to work, for younger performers, and, even more so, fans in particular. Guitarist Pete Townshend has explained his decision effectively to disband The Who for most of the 1980s as a direct result of the industry's recklessness: "I blamed the rock industry for the death of Keith [Moon, Who drummer, in 1978], of Brian Jones, of Jimi [Hendrix], for the death of 11 kids at Cincinnati at one of our shows. I felt that we hadn't looked after our own, and *there was something wrong with our business*"(quoted in Garfield 2006, 27; emphasis added). The indulgence and excess offered by the business to its youthful talent, the possible fragility of creativity, the destructive cycle of public pressure and rehab withdrawal, the narcotic temptation of self-medication, the demands of authenticity or of the touring lifestyle, and the construction and mediation of celebrity, are all potentially destabilizing aspects of the pop music industry itself—in the cognitive context, the question is the extent to which pop *disables* its own artists, and how far its fans ("short for fanatics," as I like to point out that Adorno points out: quoted in McKay 2005, 31) confirm that disabling narrative both in their desires and their own actions.[1]

Yet does this cultural industry madden (or just let down) its workers, or does it particularly attract, say, proportionally more of those who manage to combine that unstable combination of being sufficiently introspective to want to articulate emotions and struggles with being sufficiently extrovert that they are willing to do so in public performance? Does it attract more of those people who are culturally or socially eccentric? Add to this the relatively youth of most new pop and rock people—enthusiasm, energy, arrogance, inexperience, vulnerability as key factors—and there is a potent mix made. But it is not just pop and rock that are dangerous to one's health. Indeed, according to Alex Lubet:

> performing any kind of music seriously is potentially far more hazardous to our health than we care to admit. For certain kinds of trauma, evidence points to Western classical music, perhaps surprisingly, as most dangerous of all. Large studies of professional orchestral players . . . agree that a majority have upper limb injuries. (2011, 22–23)

While Lubet's suggestion that classical music is the "most dangerous of all" music practices attenuates in the context of pop's litany of youthful fatalities, even if classical musicians' entrainment injuries can be functionally career-threatening for them—nonetheless, it is worth reminding ourselves of the wider potentiality between creativity and damage. In the discourse of popular music, and perhaps especially of rock (via jazz), a romantic eschatology has developed and endures, which can in some genres become an extreme and urgent ending, though in others it is melodramatic or pathetic. This is confirmed by the favored perspective of the media industries on young musical death, in which, for example, "popular movies were made about Mozart, Charlie Parker [,Ian Curtis] and Kurt Cobain, not about Aaron Copland (died age 90) or Eubie Blake (died age 96)" (Sartin 2010, 112). Live fast, die young. Bird lives. And now he's gone. I hope I die before I grow old. Time takes a cigarette. Goodbye my friend, it's hard to die. No future. Death disco. Is there life after birth? Do it, do it. I hate myself and I want to die. It's better to burn out than to fade away. When we're dead they'll know just who we are. I'm just gonna close my eyes. Teenagers scare the living shits out of me. No, no, no.

The industry has developed a special self-destructive capacity—a culture of negation. There is a kind of fatal medical model in pop. And, as we have noted, how they die, some of them perhaps old now for pop stars but still far too young. They have died on and of medication, seeking tranquility through tranquilizers: the King of Rock 'n' Roll, Elvis Presley, in 1977, aged forty-two; the King of Pop, Michael Jackson in 2009, aged fifty. Sacrifice is the ultimate reward for pop royalty. Presley's personal doctor, "Dr Nick" (George Nichopoulos), had written almost 200 prescriptions in Presley's name for *10,000 doses* of narcotics in the eight months of 1977 before Presley's death alone, and many years later had his license removed. He claims he also gave Presley elaborate placebos, and said he even arranged for "the manufacturers of Dilaudid, Elvis's favourite painkiller, to press a special batch of a thousand pills without any active ingredients. It took a year of letter-writing and legal wrangling. But they looked just like the real thing" (Higginbotham 2002). Die loaded? In Dr. Nick's view—and I accept that this is not breaking news about the industry—the narcotic requirements were a part of the lifestyle and culture of popular music: "My job was taking care of the whole entourage. There were about 150 people I took care of. You had a couple of bands. You had the songbirds. You had the people that set up the stage . . . And all these people were night people [like Elvis], too" (quoted in Higginbotham 2002). Presley would take uppers before a show and downers after it—and sometimes there were two shows a night (Higginotham 2002). Jackson's own doctor, Conrad Murray, was convicted in 2011 of causing the singer's death—criminally negligent involuntary manslaughter. Murray ordered "gallons" of the surgical anesthetic propofol, to aid Jackson in combatting his insomnia (Gumbel 2011). Real or contrived aspects of Jackson's own medical situation are well-known and widely circulated—wearing surgical masks in public, sleeping in an oxygen tent; we may wonder how far he thought of his fans as pathogens. The range and amount of drugs given to Jackson while under his doctor's care was described in court as a "pharmaceutical experiment" (quoted in Anon 2011), while the polypharmacy that was Presley's pre-death experience was evident in the autopsy that found fourteen drugs in his system (Higginbotham 2002). The slurring inarticulate voices and shambolic performances of singers from Billie Holiday to Hank Williams to Elvis Presley to Jim Morrison to Michael Jackson to Amy Winehouse to Whitney Houston would be a feature of their later years (or still, younger years, but final ones)—surely a sad state for once extraordinary, and in Presley's case even revolutionary, pop performers. The sadness is located in the individual's situation, but in the context of the industry, the persistence and longevity of the downward performative trajectory is striking: singing the fall has become an essential part of the pop story. A recording of Jackson's voice, which requires a transcription in order for a listener to make sense of it, was played for the Los Angeles jury and the global media audience at his doctor's trial. It was recorded by Murray on his mobile phone in 2009, a few weeks before Jackson's death. On it, Jackson is slow speaking, sounds semi-comatose, and completely slurred in vocal delivery, while the impact of the recording is enhanced by the fact that he is talking about how great the comeback shows in London are going to be. On this recording, which is the length of a pop song, the quality of the singer's voice and the lyrics he speaks are largely disconnected, until Jackson's final words. The recording ends with periods of silence from Jackson and then the extraordinary words "I am asleep" (*Today News* 2011).

And what about the extreme damage of suicide, where self-destruction cancels life? We should pause to consider how far rock suicides belong here, not least because of the place of suicide in rock mythologizing and its more extreme discourse of authenticity. Think of English singer-songwriter Nick Drake, whose songs included "Poor Boy" from 1970, with its lyrical refrain "Oh poor boy, so sorry for himself / Oh poor boy, so worried for his health." Drake (probably) killed himself in 1974—just perhaps it could have been an overdose—at the age of twenty-six, following repeated bouts of severe depression, leaving a modest musical legacy of three albums that have been subsequently cherished and fetishized by fans. What Plathian pall is cast over that music now? Or we can think of the more recent suicide (probably) of Richey Edwards, lyricist and guitarist with Welsh rock band the Manic Street Preachers—who notoriously displayed both authenticity and the performance of authenticity (that is, in a certain way, *in*authenticity) by using a razorblade to carve "4 REAL" on his forearm in 1991 while doing a post-gig interview with a music journalist and a photographer (the key, now iconic, photograph was reproduced in the *New Musical Express* the following week, and subsequently used as a poster image promoting an American tour by the band: Lamacq 2000). Edwards was still in his stage gear, wearing a Situ-punk stenciled shirt with the words, drawn from one of the band's early song titles, SPECTATORS OF SUICIDE. In 1994, in Thailand, Edwards self-harmed at a concert, using a knife given to him by a fan to cut his chest, and the following year he disappeared—suicide?—being finally officially presumed dead in 2008. The Manic Street Preachers used Edwards's surviving writings as the lyrics of their 2009 album *Journal for Plague Lovers*. And of course, the dominant figure in this narrative is Kurt Cobain. Such artists matter in particular for us because of the effects of their deaths on their fans and other musicians (Neil Young, in Cobain's case), and the debates raised at the time about ways in which music might, if not facilitate mental illness, be accused of glorifying or at least making more acceptable self-harm. Edwards, Cobain, and indeed Ian Curtis, referenced the death cult or death culture of the industry in discourses prior to their self-inflicted deaths. That is, by the times of their pop moments, in the 1980s and 1990s, there was a strong and accepted—*expected*—tradition in the culture of mas-culine self-destruction.[2] Debbie Curtis remembers how, even when a teen-aged schoolboy, Ian

> would choose certain songs and lyrics such as "Speed child, don't want to stay alive when you're twenty-five," or David Bowie's "Rock 'n' roll suicide," and be carried away by the romantic magic of an early death. . . . Anyone who had been involved in the young, arty medium of any form of showbusiness and found an early grave was of interest to him. (Curtis 1995, 7, 15)

In his suicide note, Cobain describes himself as the "self-destructive death rocker that I've become." Although the figures on the blogosphere report a mass cluster of up to sixty-five copycat suicides following Cobain's death (see, for example, Monacelli 2010), one authoritative study focused on Se-attle is more considered and informed: "the expected 'Werther effect' [named after Goethe's romantic suicide and the copycat following events] apparently did not occur" (Jobes et al. 1996). According to David A. Jobes et al., in their article "The Kurt Cobain Suicide Crisis":

> What can we conclude from the immediate aftermath of Cobain's suicide? First, it seems much was done right by the media. . . . The general message was, "great artist, great music . . . stupid act, don't do it; here's where to call for help." Sec-ond, Cobain's use of a shotgun countered any romanticized visual image of a lonely, misunderstood star (e.g., Marilyn Monroe) drifting off into a sleepy, overdose death. . . . Third, it would seem that various efforts within the Seattle community to perform outreach and provide support and education may have been effective. . . . The net result . . . was that the Seattle Crisis Clinic's services were remarkably well used. (Jobes et al. 1996)

While Jobes et al. point out that one fan did go home from the Cobain vigil and commit suicide by self-inflicted shotgun wound, overall, in fact, there was no spike in youth suicides following Cobain's own; locally there was a spike in telephone calls to the crisis helpline.

Some popular music is occasionally but persistently perceived to play a negative role in the construction of its fans' mental health and life choices. In the splintering taste and style subcultures characteristic of rock it can possess a label, like emo. The death by hanging of a young teenaged girl in Britain in 2008 sparked a press controversy about her music fandom: she had recently been self-harming, and listening to a new band for her, My Chemical Romance, which was described in the right-wing, family-oriented British newspaper the *Daily Mail* as an "Emo 'suicide cult rock band'" (Levy 2008). Earlier youthful suicides were also connected to the music being listened to: in a 1990 American court case brought by their parents, an album by the British heavy metal band Judas Priest was found not to have incited two young men to shoot themselves. Curiously—or satanically, if that is your bag—the case rested on claims of the record containing subliminal messages and of reverse soundings—that is, words heard when the record was played backwards. The self-shootings had taken place in 1985, when LPs rather than CDs were the norm—a technology easy to play backwards. Apparently the words included "Do it, do it" (Moore 1996; Moore acted as an expert witness for the defence). Heavy-metal music had other controversial fan deaths—most notably, a series of suicides associated with the 1980 Ozzy Osbourne song, "Suicide Solution." While Osbourne claimed that the song is a lament about the alcohol-related death of AC/DC singer Bon Scott earlier that year, and guitarist Rhoads claimed he wrote the lyrics about Osbourne's alcohol abuse at the time—in each case, the *solution* of the title is not an *answer* but an alcoholic *liquid*—several young American fans would hear in it an imperative, and attempt suicide by self-inflicted shotgun wound. The lyrics mostly do deal with alcoholic danger and damage—living "inside the bottle"—and there is also a surprisingly great existential question, one that arguably resonates in disability studies: "is there life after birth?" But there is too in mid-song the striking couplet "suicide is the only way out, don't you know what it's really about?" Could a listener (not) think that suicide is what it, the song, is really about? The verses are followed not yet by a guitar solo but by a middle eight section in which fragments of a word which may be "suicide"—"sui, sui, sui . . ."—or which may be "shoot, shoot, shoot"—are heard, a fragmented vocal line that echoes disturbingly through and out-of-time across the medium tempo rock guitar, and that switches swiftly, perhaps unnervingly, across the two stereo channels (Osbourne 1980). The several unsuccessful court cases brought against these heavy-metal artists following attempted and achieved youth suicides may speak not only about the fear of music—though bear in mind Robert Walser's assertion that "none of these critics is able to connect heavy metal directly with suicide" (1993, 143)—but also about (in)comprehension and the desire to blame, the right-wing cultural policy articulated and mobilized by the Parents' Music

Resource Centre during these years, and even the national culture of litigation itself (see Walser 1993; Kahn-Harris 2007). Intriguingly, here it is not only the fans but the enemies of metal music—more so its enemies—who seek to confirm its disabling capacity.[3]

With the later subgenre of death metal a more extreme sonic and discursive transgression would take place. "The names of the bands themselves are an indicator of this: Cannibal Corpse, Death, Dismember, Obituary, etc. Album titles speak for themselves—*Butchered at Birth, Scream Bloody Gore, Cause of Death,* etc. . . . Some death metal and grindcore bands use the destruction of the body as their major lyrical resource" (Kahn-Harris 2007, 35). Such fascination has arguably been taken further in pop performance: in 2003, American industrial rock band Hell On Earth advertised a live concert that would feature onstage, as a part of the show, an actual suicide. I think this was a hoax, a tasteless publicity stunt, but the stage act was being justified in the context of a terminally ill person campaigning for the right to die. As the band's publicity explained: "A Euthanasia Society member will carry out the suicide to raise awareness for dying with dignity. The Euthanasia member, who suffers from a terminal illness, is using the event as a platform to help make back-street suicides a thing of the past" (Hell On Earth 2003). The key point for us though, in the context of disability studies, is the place of metal music as an extreme articulator of cognitive impairment, and its repeated performative discourse of self-harm or self-destruction.

Of course, the excessive lifestyles of pop and rock, and their associated risk behaviors, do not inevitably lead to the final drama of death, but do have other health implications as well. The "damage done" (Neil Young) works other ways too. According to medical doctor Jeffrey S. Sartin, in his study entitled "Contagious Rhythm: Infectious Diseases of 20th Century Musicians":

> more contemporary rock musicians have experienced an epidemic of hepatitis C infection and HIV/AIDS related to intravenous drug use and promiscuity. *Musical innovation is thus often accompanied by diseases of neglect and overindulgence, particularly infectious illnesses,* although risky behavior and associated infectious illnesses tend to decrease as the style matures. . . . Again and again, as new musical forms have surfaced, innovative artists have pursued unorthodox lifestyles that put them at risk for lethal pathogens. (Sartin 2010, 106; emphasis added)

Such a creative/destructive musical template is not new, and was arguably established during the romantic period, as Sartin notes: "many prominent composers of the 18th and 19th centuries led disordered lives punctuated by financial instability, romantic turmoil, and alcohol overuse, often leading to health crises" (2010, 107). Similarly, for early jazz musicians in the twentieth century, common causes of death were pneumonia and tuberculosis, often related to alcohol and substance misuse, while "other infection[s] of note related to dissolute behaviour [that] plagued jazz musicians" included syphilis and chronic viral hepatitis (Sartin 2010, 109). The expressive culture of jazz and the lifestyle choice of narcotic became intertwined in both popular consciousness, and, to a fairly disastrous extent, in the musical community itself.

> Many jazz musicians lived and died by Charlie Parker's dictum that "If you don't live it, it won't come out of your horn." Early jazz musicians imbibed alcohol and marijuana freely, but the introduction of heroin into the music scene in the 1940s was devastating and the major factor in spreading viral hepatitis. (Sartin 2010, 110)

We can view these forms of substance abuse in a music scene as a less-than-careful practice of self-medication, and this is especially attractive and easy reading in the context of the use of street drugs in the existential and cultural struggle of the expressive musician in the margins of jazz. After all, there is a certain "persistence of the myth of the mad genius" in music (Lerner and Straus 2006a, 2), and it is prominent in the history of jazz from the founding figure of New Orleanian cornetist Buddy Bolden onwards. It is said that Bolden's prodigious tone and his introduction of improvisation contributed significantly to the pioneering sound of African-America in the early twentieth century—I write "it is said" in acknowledgement of the fact that, as jazz historians like to point out, "if Bolden had not existed, someone would have had to invent him" (Shipton 2001, 84). There are no recordings of him playing, perhaps only one photograph of him in existence, and Bolden was incarcerated in the Louisiana State Asylum for the Insane in 1907, while still in his twenties, until his death in 1931 (Shipton 2001, 82). Shall we say, after Bolden, that jazz music is predicated on disability?[4] In jazz, the fascination would go on to center on the intuitive expressiveness of the solo, as Miles Davis exemplifies in his analysis of bop innovator pianist Bud Powell's experience: "Before Bud went to Bellevue [psychiatric ward in 1946], everything he played had a wrinkle in it; there was always something different about the way the music came off. Man, after they bashed his head in and gave him shock treatments, they would have done better cutting off his hands" (Davis 1989, 102).

We are beginning to shift our critical gaze from the health dangers of a reckless narcotic-centered lifestyle and music practice to the romantic fetishization within many music forms of a cognitive impairment. If we seek to replicate a dismal jazz romance across pop and rock, what is changed in the process? As we have seen, there is a lyrical topos of emotional suffering that is a preferred one in pop and rock, but this can extend to forms of mental disability. Mental illness has frequently been referenced in the romantic trope of (often masculine) suffering, as evidenced in the persistent strain of anti-psychiatry in countercultural music like King Crimson's "21$^{st}$ Century Schizoid Man" (1969) or David Bowie's "The Bewlay Brothers" (1971) and *Aladdin Sane* (1973) (see Spelman 2009), and indeed in the "crazy diamond" syndrome of Pink Floyd's 1970s efforts to come to terms with the reclusive figure of original 1960s member Syd Barrett. While, as Giles Perring notes, "the commodification of 'madness' and 'deviancy,' through 'wild men of rock' like Jim Morrison, Keith Moon, and Jimi Hendrix, is an essential marketing tool in a countercultural package" (Perring 2005, 180), it is also the case that some countercultural musicians found other ways of exploring their fascination with the mad or deviant. Arguably this may be the situation when rock music depicts a sort of "critical madness," in which the subject is "less about literal madness than about madness as a trope for unconventional thought" (Walser 1993, 155). We are dancing around crude versions, even misrepresentations, of experiences of cognitive impairment with some of these examples—nonetheless, they do illustrate the culture's enduring enthrallment with certain figures of disability and are probably eminently crippable.

Frank Zappa's lifting from the street and recording of Larry "Wild Man" Fischer in 1968 is a case in point: the sleeve notes for the 1969 double album *An Evening with Wild Man Fischer,* released on one of Zappa's boutique labels, Bizarre, tell us that passersby "thought he was crazy" and that Fischer's mother "had him committed to a mental institution several times" (quoted in Perring 2005). "Bizarre indeed," writes David Sanjek, "these were the works of a paranoid, schizophrenic, manic depressive street performer" (Sanjek 2013, 151). But Fischer fed Zappa's "fascination with the transgressive" and confirmed Zappa's privileging of "intuitive performance and non-conventional technique and sonorities" (Perring 2005, 180–81): in Zappa's eyes and terminology, Fischer was a *real* "freak" (though this is undercut by the problematic cover portrait, which shows a wild-looking Fischer performing his cognitive impairment by holding a knife to his "mother"'s throat). Zappa himself included in the sleeve notes a plea to the listener: Wild Man Fischer "has something to say to you, even though you might not want to hear it" (quoted in Sanjek 2013, 156). What Sanjek calls "the sonic irreducibility" of Fischer's painful (to listen to) autopathography here signals a certain approach to music as a practice of the outsider artist (Sanjek 2013, 154), playing a mad parade outside societal and musical norms alike, and we may think of an emblematic contemporary version of this naïf, impaired, outsider music in, say, the career of singer-songwriter Daniel Johnston. From the DIY aesthetic of Johnston's early bedroom recordings—tinny, lo-fi, with vocal and musical accompaniment distorted, released on cassette and sold at gigs in the 1980s—to contemporary appearances and occasional tours of his performances of awkwardness with an acoustic guitar, there is a place in popular music, a small (male) place, for such expressive anti-musics as Fischer's and Johnston's. This is notably so when the music is located in a countercultural context, which favors the authentic(ity of the) freak or deviant.

To conclude this discussion of the destructive musical economy, we revisit the point articulated above by Pete Townshend, that "there is something wrong with our business." How do songs sing of pop's own industry experience? I have in mind not self-regard or postmodern playfulness here, nor is our focus on self-reflexive lyrics that might deal with the sharp business practices of rip-off record companies, or groupies, or the toils and temptations of touring, or bands' personality clashes and musical differences, or the bloated boasts of star rivalries.[5] No: what I seek is the song where the industry's damaging capacity is critically explored in its own product. There is a pair of such pop songs by female singers in the early twenty-first century, that draw on the experiences of the singers' pop and celebrity lives, that lay bare in the lyric some of the pressures for women artists. Both were international hit singles—crisis narrative sells, not least when it has an authentic story, memorable melodies and choruses, great production, and a top promo video. That each performer is a solo singer confirms the added pressure of being in the front line, possibly more so even when there is not a band (often formed of old friends) behind you. The high-profile gendered narratives of the late Amy Winehouse and Britney

Fig. 26. Daniel Johnston (2008): "naïf, impaired, outsider music." Photographer Dick Johnston at www.hihowareyou.com

Spears may be performances and confirmations of what, as we have seen, Winehouse called in one song the sheer "fuckery" of the transatlantic pop process, particularly as in recent years it has been more aligned with celebrity culture. Winehouse and Spears are medical models—their young, female, sexualized, centrally presented bodies signifying either cool, attractive, threatening tabu (Winehouse with extensive tattoos, piercings, flamboyant beehive hair and heavy Egyptian makeup, imperfect jazz vocalities, young death) or healthy, fresh, accessible (school)girl next door (Spears with athletic body, blonde hair, a famous winning smile, physical dance routines, though intriguingly an increasingly technologized voice). Winehouse's "Rehab" (2006) describes one of the tempting life cycles of pop—in and out of rehabilitation as the fame increases and pressure rises— though the song was issued on what was Winehouse's breakthrough major international album, *Back to Black*, itself only her second album release. Winehouse's work on *Back to Black* is a quite stark exploration of self-image and self-worth in her love life and professional life—she often stated that one of her favorite songs was the Crystals's extraordinary and controversial 1962 single "He Hit Me (It Felt Like a Kiss)," which illustrates her understanding of female performance and complex emotional terrain, as well as of her awareness of pop music history and style. But for us it is not the female confessional or tragic chanteuse (Billie Holiday, Janis Joplin) tradition that is of primary interest here, beyond the observation that that gendered tradition offers a template for the retro-style, jazz- and blues-influenced Winehouse to conform to and further confirm in due course—she did "tread a troubled track," as the title song, "Back to Black," puts it, and she wrote and performed songs about that.[6] Rather, we listen because the hit single "Rehab" is in part *about* the industry—its expectations, problems, and medical options. From the title and repeated chorus on these are the song's subject. It sings of pop's disabling propensity. The lyric includes a short dialogue with a male medical figure or psychiatrist:

> The man said, "Why do you think you here?"
> I said, "I have no idea" . . .
> He said, "I just think you're depressed"
> This me: "Yeah baby, and the rest." (Winehouse 2006b)

But it is her defiant and restated refusal to commit to "seventy days . . . ten weeks" in rehabilitation, to address what is in the song identified three times as issues with alcohol, that is the core. "*They* wanted me to go to re-hab" she opens with . . . but who are "they"? Her management team, par-ents, band members, concerned friends, early fans? (Now fans leave You-Tube comments to the "Rehab" video, saying things like "OMG shd ve gone to rehab Amy why didn't you.") This is a song about some of the industry norms of medical treatment. While Winehouse refuses (though later she did "go to rehab"), we can see that the song presents and affirms the *normal-ity* of the kinds of health options available to those who succeed in this work sector. We already knew that, of course, from our voracious consumption of celebrity media reports about the papped foibles of our film and pop stars, but to make a song, a hit single, out of the drama, which is a portrayal of both personal crisis and standard industry practice, is a critical and gen-dered reflexive act. Rehab is what happens when one is losing control; pop is what happens when one is losing control.

That "Rehab" was Winehouse's very first transatlantic top-ten single success arguably undercuts the extraordinary world-weariness of the lyric. I make this observation in comparison with Britney Spears's hit single "Piece of Me" (2007), which reflects on her veteran rather than near-novice status in the media and music industries. From her preteen childhood years on television on the 1990s revival of Disney's *The Mickey Mouse Club* to her leading of "the new Lolitocracy" (Merskin 2004, 99) in pop in the late 1990s, Spears has grown up in the media and popular music celebrity worlds, with an increasingly intensely sexualized image. Writing in 2004, Debra Merksin identified a group of female pop artists in "Britney Spears, Christina Agu-ilera, Destiny's Child, and Beyoncé [who] are 'just adult enough to be avail-able, just young enough to be nonthreatening'" (Merskin 2004, 99). Soon though—by the following year—Spears is pregnant, and displaying "a body that is expanding and leaky," which in turn leads to her being mocked in media and celebrity circles for being overweight, and unhealthy. Spears's was by then a "'messy' lifestyle *and* body" (Meredith Nash 2005; emphasis added). Hounded and trapped by a ruthless paparazzi culture—the situa-tion admittedly clouded by her own complicity in media celebrity—there is a great interest in Spears's music still, but even more so in her fragmenting life: two marriages in 2004, the first, in Las Vegas, lasting only fifty-five hours; stories about and photographs of her dysfunctional parenting skills; in and out of rehab; and, in February 2007, a very public display of break-down, as reported breathlessly in, for example, Hollyscoop celebrity web-site.

Wow this girl has lost her marbles. According to reports, Britney Spears walked into a salon in Tarzana, CA and she demanded the stylist shave her head, when she refused, Britney grabbed the clippers and shaved it herself. She then went to a tattoo parlor in Sherman Oaks. Britney got a black-white-and-pink cross tattooed on her lower hip and red-and-pink lips on her wrist. The price: $80. . . . What does Britney's manager . . . have to say about all this? . . . "Britney knows that she needs help, and is already going through counseling, she knows what needs to be done and is slowly rebuilding herself step-by-step." (Hollyscoop 2007).

Losing it in that part of the public sphere that is not the specifically delineated one of the stage is the celebrity displaying and performing her own cognitive instability in an everyday situation. But Spears will essay a musical reclamation of such public moments of celebrity pop madness. By the time of "Piece of Me," toward the end of that same year, 2007, Spears's music has developed to a sophisticated electro-pop, exploiting the potential of technological manipulation, especially around the digital voice, as Stan Hawkins and John Richardson write.

Enhanced and animated through the prominence of voice filters, vocoder audio plug-ins, and stat-of-the-art software, the voice occupies center stage. The recording consists of a wash of vocal strands that titillate at the same time as they impress. . . . Spears' vocals are digitalized to evoke a multiplicity of the self through the body. (2007, 616)

In their reading of Spears's 2004 single "Toxic," the extended voice manipulation creates an alternate persona for Spears of "cyborg diva"; her "performance is toxic because of an overdose of technical virtuosity that sculptures her as an aural and visual spectacle depleted of human characteristics" (Hawkins and Richardson 2007, 616, 617). But "Piece of Me" also employs remarkable technological manipulations of the voice over an electro-pop dance track, yet its representation is not of an extra-human cyborgean diva. The voice technology and the lyric the voice sings on "Piece of Me" present an altogether less comfortable "multiplicity of the self," all-too-human in its fragile but knowing self-knowledge. There are eight distinct first-person identities in the song—Spears singing of eight different versions of herself, as constructed by the media and pop industries, available as product. She presents herself as each of them in turn, effectively formally introducing herself (herselves) to the listener. Plural Britneys speak of dysmorphia—"I'm Mrs She's too big now she's too thin"—and of fantasy—"I'm Miss American Dream since I was 17," or "I'm Mrs Lifestyles of the rich and famous." But what is important for us is that plural Britneys are media and pop Britneys as well—"I'm Miss Bad media karma . . . I'm Mrs Extra! Extra! This just in." Most interesting for us is when plural Britney combines media and music in her critical gaze.

> I'm Mrs Most likely to get on the TV for stripping on the streets
> When getting the groceries.
> No, for real. Are you kidding me?
> No wonder there's panic in this industry—I mean, please. (Spears
>     2007)

In that brilliant spoken aside, "I mean, please," we hear dismissal and exasperation about the febrile state of the pop industry, that will allow or expect its stars to get in these situations and then panic when it happens.[7]

From *Back to Black* by a twenty-three-year-old to the following year's *Blackout* by a twenty-six-year-old, there seems not so much an echo as a correspondence from major female artists about gender, celebrity, and breakdown in pop. Winehouse and Spears each endured ongoing comments from the media and the public about their bodies, the unsuitability of their partners, critical comment and a regular pursuit by the paparazzi especially for the unflattering snap, vilification for poor live performances, and much more: such a living, making it, is an out-of-control living in pop. As British singer Robbie Williams—no stranger to the celebrity pages—puts it above: "Live the dream? Live the nightmare" (quoted in Leigh 2011). What they further share in the industry is the experience of its pressures and temptations, and the double standards applied to its female stars, which are duly explored in songs that are reflexive commentaries on those very experiences. We should note though, in the spirit of evaluating authenticity claims, that Winehouse wrote her own song herself; Spears's was written for her by a songwriting team, who apparently ignored express orders from her not to produce material about her personal life. Nonetheless, to self-dramatize in voice and performance in ways which also comment on the industry with these powerful songs is impressive; but there is a sobering reality too for these talented young pop women in their run-ins with the destructive economy of pop. Spears has had custody rights for her children removed and been placed on involuntary psychiatric hold in a Los Angeles hospital, and Winehouse is dead, memorialized by a rush-released final album padded with demo tracks and studio out-takes. Lionesses? I mean, please.

There is one further song of industry I wish to discuss, moving us from global superstardom at the top of the pop tree to—let us be kind—the lowly first branches of cult status. In "Having a Party," from 1978, the lyrics of which are accompanied by a medium slow and very sparse guitar and bass drum motif—precisely not party music, then—the great lost English singer-songwriter Kevin Coyne (1944–2004) offers his critical judgment on his years as an artist on Richard Branson's Virgin Records. The title of the album on which this song appears, *Millionaires and Teddy Bears,* is taken from its lyric—which signals that the singer must have considered "Having a party," the album's keynote song. The party is an industry gathering at a millionaire's house, with "squealing" girls on the patio, and Coyne is a misfit because, as the drinking executives point out, he has never had a golden disc (though he has had a "nightmare boogie" in which he "dreamed I was trapped in a whole full of" them). Coyne's modest sales career may well have been in part due to the focus through his entire thirty-five-year oeuvre on people at the margins of society, the northern working class, dysfunctional families, women in trouble, maudlin lovers, the "mad"—and specifically, the institutionalized. It was a social-work approach to pop: his first solo album in 1972, after all, was called *Case History,* and featured a song entitled "Mad Boy." *Case History*'s sleeve note informed his fans that he had "worked at Whittingham (psychiatric) Hospital near Preston, Lancs., till 1969 as a social therapist [and] at present works for the Camden accommodation scheme (Soho Project) as a social worker" (Coyne 1972). Curiously— shall we not say distastefully?—the front cover of his 1976 album *Heartburn* even shows a representation of suicide—a human figure leaping off a building as a backdrop to a head-and-shoulders portrait of Coyne. Coyne appears to be looking over his shoulder, as though he can sense the anguish of the unseen-by-him event: Coyne's marketing via an apparent hypersensitivity to suffering was part of the appeal for his fans.

Coyne was never really popular—in fact, he never even had a *silver* disc. At Virgin Records, the press office referred to him, attempted to market him, as their "anti-star" (Clayson 2004). Probably, too, his musical practice restricted the shifting of units: his anti-technique approach to the acoustic guitar (open-tuned bar chords played with only his thumb from the upper

Fig. 27. Kevin Coyne's *Heartburn*, 1976 album cover, with its representation of a suicidal act. © Virgin Records, London.

side of the fingerboard), his use of prerecorded tapes and other avant-garde performance techniques to disrupt the flow during gigs. Not being able, or electing not, to play the instrument "properly," and hearing other voices while singing: there is something culturally disabling about each of these artistic choices, quite apart from the lyrical terrain. Some years, or decades, lost mid-career to alcohol and depression didn't help. The best he could hope for was that uncommercial role a few can reach: an acquired taste who could only be a cult figure. Yet on "Having a Party," his gaze at the marginal and disenfranchised of society extends to the workers in his own industry, to those who have been successful, as he offers critical comment in music on what he viewed as the careless destructiveness of pop:

> Smoke up the chimney
> Bones of pop stars
> They say you've got to be tough and rough
> And tough and rough and tough and rough
> If you wanna be a . . . pop star.
> [*Sotto voce:*] Bollocks. (Coyne 1978; ellipses in original)

If over the years the characters in Coyne's songs were familiar with the experiences of mental illness and of institutionalization, how surprising should it have been that he could find these very characters and experiences in the creative industry of pop? Working in pop after mental health and social care, his attuned gaze identifies institutional pressures not all would be able to bear ("you've got to be tough and rough"), particularly the sensitive ones who might be most necessary for emotional insight and articulation. Coyne also makes a startling accusation: what is required is a stream of victims, of *successful victims*, to keep the house warm, the business—the party—going ("Smoke up the chimney / bones of pop stars"). Pop will eat itself becomes, in his Molochian view here, a kind of culture of cannibalistic consumption.[8] "Having a party / Oh what fun," Coyne sings, unfunnily.

## Disability Activism and Advocacy in Popular Music

> . . . dancing that others may walk.
>
> —President Franklin D. Roosevelt, birthday ball radio
> broadcast, January 30, 1940

I feel we may have moved, in our critical fascination with the (self-)destructive capacities of the music industry, a little far in this chapter from the cultural and experiential core of disability. Let us get back, to look in this final section of the book at the role of disability activism and advocacy in the development of popular music's public social agenda. The primary argument is distressingly familiar: disability has been overlooked; more precisely, disability has been overlooked in historical narratives of the music's articulation and display of a social conscience. We will address that, to illustrate one further way in which disability has fundamentally shaped popular music. But there is a *double-crip* to be done. Not only will we crip this part of pop history by illuminating the contribution of people with disabilities to its social campaigning—and social campaigning in pop is often enough viewed as an all-round and unquestionably good thing—we will then also consider the complex and nuanced attitudes of people with disabilities active in the disability rights and grassroots disability arts movements to charity and advocacy work—that is, we are also cripping those.

Fund- and consciousness-raising for and about social issues have been a central activity of popular music for many decades—from playing a local benefit gig to organizing a global media "mega-event," pop and rock musicians have been consistent and high-profile contributors to this industry practice. Rebee Garofalo explains that, broadly speaking, "mega-events and socially conscious mass music have been the beneficiaries of a left-leaning orientation which has characterized popular music since the rock era" of the 1960s (1992b, 32). Much work has looked at the place of the pop festival or one-day open-air concert as pivotal phenomena, because of their visibility and impact, of course—not one star attraction but many, on the same bill—but also because of their mediated other versions: the live benefit album or film of the event, or the live telecasting of it for a global audience, say. Here, key events regularly referenced include George Harrison's Concert for Bangladesh in New York in 1971 (actually two concerts—a matinee and an evening performance), and the Live Aid simultaneous concerts in Philadelphia, London, and Sydney in 1985 (see Garofalo 1992a; McKay 2000; Garofalo 2005; Street 2012). A second central activity would be the recording and release of the benefit single, particularly where it features a raft of artists, which is aimed to raise funds in response to a specific crisis. The single, of a song sometimes specially written, is released to be bought by a sympathetic and concerned public; generally, artists give up their time and their royalties for the cause. After Harrison's innovative 1971 single "Bangla Desh," "Do They Know It's Christmas?" (1984, UK) and "We Are the World" (1985, U.S.), each produced in response to news reports of a terrible famine in Ethiopia, are probably the best-known examples. In self-congratulatory mode, the industry also celebrates its own charitable work: in 1996, for instance, the BRIT Awards introduced a new prize in its annual ceremony, the Freddie Mercury Award, in recognition of outstanding charitable work by popular musicians. There are too directly politically engaged artists and movements—from Rock Against Racism to Rock the Vote—as

Fig. 28. 1950s deaf singer Johnnie Ray (far right) features on a 1973 Better Hearing Institute campaign leaflet cover. © Better Hearing Institute. Used with permission.

well as more radical ones: Fela Kuti challenging the corruption of the Nigerian state with his heroic belief that "music is a weapon" (see Veal 2000), or musical subgenres or scenes such as, in Britain, the second folk revival of the 1950s (communism) or anarcho-punk of the 1980s (anarchism). Sometimes the radical sub-pop offers a comment on the pop mega-event; music activism critiquing the act and motivation of industry charity. I am thinking here of the British anarchist popsters Chumbawumba, whose first album in 1986 was called *Pictures of Starving Children Sell Records*—the band's comment on Live Aid.

But where is disability advocacy and activism in these stories of rock-and-roll charity and campaigning? With one or two exceptions—Neil and Pegi Young's annual Bridge School benefit concerts of leading rock and country musicians, first held in 1986 to raise money for a new school they cofounded in California for children with "severe physical and speech impairments," including the Youngs' own son Ben (Bridge School website, 2012); Ian Dury's controversial 1981 single "Spasticus Autisticus"—they are largely absent from popular music history. Yet there is quite a powerful and persistent tradition of, at the very least, the establishment of eponymous advocacy organizations within popular music. I have in mind, for instance, the Johnnie Ray Foundation for Hard of Hearing Children, the Stevie Wonder Home for Blind and Retarded Children, the Teddy Pendergrass Education/Occupation Alliance for the Disabled, the Elton John AIDS Foundation (though this one does not draw on John's personal experience), perhaps the posthumously established Amy Winehouse Foundation. Clearly, there is a showbiz imperative here, alongside a commercial pragmatic recognition of brand awareness. Frequently, the campaign organization is intimately related to the autopathography: a deaf or a blind musician campaigning in some way about hearing or visual impairment. Others are less self-oriented in their advocacy or campaigning, and are more likely to include references to the social experience of disability in their musical work, too. As we have seen, the prime examples here are the portfolios of songs and live performances by disabled singers like Dury, and Young, for whom "disability . . . [has indeed] been a powerful artistic muse" (Stein 2008, 4). The one figure we have so far only touched on, Stevie Wonder, arguably has employed both advocacy and activism approaches.

We should reflect here on what is debatably the highest-profile popular music fund-raising and campaigning event specifically around disability today. Neil Young's sustained involvement in the Bridge School benefit concerts, with his wife, Pegi, as school and concert organizer, has extended significantly beyond one of his own disabled sons' attendance as a youth at that school. That both of his sons are disabled helps explain the parent's commitment, of course, via the simple fact that disability is "still part of Young's everyday existence" as a father (see Stein 2008, 6–7).[9] We have seen how in the 1960s and early 1970s he produced music, lyrics, and performances drawing on his own experience as a disabled man, and in the early 1980s made other music recorded specifically for his more severely disabled son, but since then the Bridge School concert series show Young working as an erstwhile curator of music acts, fund-raiser, and quiet campaigner around disability (though he puts it more modestly: "It's all Pegi. I'm just the public relations man": quoted in McDonough 2002, 608). Annually, he has exploited his own pulling power and industry contacts alike to ensure that Bob Dylan, David Bowie, The Who, Patti Smith, REM, Elvis Costello, Emmylou Harris, Brian Wilson, Jerry Lee Lewis, Metallica, Paul McCartney, CSNY, Bruce Springsteen, Simon and Garfunkel, among others of his work "friends" (see fig. 29), turn up to play at charity concerts in California, to raise funds for the specialist school. This is Young's local parallel activity to the annual Farm Aid open-air concerts, which he cofounded and has also played regularly at, a series of post-Live Aid "mega-events" first held in 1985 to raise money for struggling American farmers. That both Farm Aid and the Bridge School concerts have endured over many years is significant, as

Holly George-Warren has pointed out about the former: "what began as an act of compassion regarding the Farm crisis in the 1980s turned into ongoing political action—a 'process' that has more of a chance of making changes politically than a one-time 'band aid' that raises a bunch of money during one event" (quoted in Garofalo 2005, 335). The musical "process" of the Bridge School concerts over quarter of a century has been to support the development of innovative practices in disability education and assistive technology with children, and to help disseminate those by activities such as professional training for teachers and parents, lecture series, and international visiting fellowships. The concerts happen over one or two days each October—a major event in the school year to which all the children are invited. At each concert the schoolchildren themselves form the backdrop to the stage shows—the stage is therefore partly in the round; the youngsters a permanent visual presence for the rest of the audience as they become, just possibly, starees and mini-stars alike (I am reluctant to write that they are almost but not quite on the stage), while some artists turn their back on the ticket-paying audience and sing to the kids in chairs and their caregivers— and short talks by teachers or parents, sometimes children when they can, are interspersed with the musical acts. The music itself is to be played on acoustic instruments, an unplugged aesthetic even for the rock bands, who "are forced to re-interpret their most popular compositions and present them within this unfamiliar, stripped-down framework. . . . Just like the children enrolled in the school, musicians performing at the benefit are discovering alternative modes of communication they might previously have assumed to be ineffective" (Stein 2008, 8).

We might observe that, the Bridge School aside, many of the star-led disability campaigns and organizations previously cited are rather modest, or precariously short-lived—being predicated on unreliable funding from almost inevitably temporary pop success and profile. It is a moot point whether such organizational activity is anyway the most useful strategy for exploiting in a social context pop's profile and visibility. Perhaps singing or musicking "about" disability is actually still one of the best things for musicians and popsters to do, if cripoliticking is what they want to engage in. John Street sort of makes this point, more widely, in the context of discussing bands playing at political pop events: "although some musicians make speeches and some sign petitions . . . [m]uch more significant are the performances they give" (2012, 73). When the performance is by a musician or band with disabilities, that very fact can itself have effect. So singer Teddy

# WHO'S FRIENDS WITH NEIL?

**DAVID BOWIE**
**SIMON & GARFUNKEL**
**TRACY CHAPMAN**
**DON HENLEY**
**PRETENDERS**
**PEARL JAM**
Elvis Costello
**TOM PETTY**
**PATTI SMITH**
**MINISTRY**
**BONNIE RAITT**
**BECK**
**NILS LOFGREN**
**LOVEMONGERS**

For over a decade, Neil Young has been the driving force behind an annual series of Northern Californian concerts designed to help sustain and enhance The Bridge School, an innovative educational program designed to help provide children with severe speech and physical disabilities the greatest opportunities for communication. Despite being a worthy cause however, The Bridge School Concerts have become legendary in themselves as a result of their line-ups which have seen some of the worlds most talented performers stripped down to mostly acoustic sets and playing with all the passion they can muster. The Bridge School Concerts Vol. I is the first ever collection of these renowned performances from Neil and friends.

Fig 29. Bridge School concerts live recordings advertisement: Neil Young and some of his 'friends', making music for disability. Author's collection.

Pendergrass has written of the effectiveness of his role as a disabled public figure as a pop advocate: "I've met, spoken with, and received mail from thousands of people with disabilities, and I know that simply by being a public figure and continuing to achieve and succeed in the public arena, I've helped others" (1998, 263). It's more complicated than that, of course, as we have seen: Pendergrass's impact was a result of his being a public figure *who became disabled*, his focus within campaigning on everyday living with disability rather than possible future spinal-injury cure, as well as his choice not to change his love-song repertoire, but to be onstage a sexual man—just one who happened to use a wheelchair. Overall, though, we must ask if the invisibility of disability in the advocacy and activist field of the popular music ecology warranted? The answer, both in terms of a brief survey of star-led organizations, and more historically, is clear: no. We turn now to earlier popular music and mass media in the twentieth century, as they uncovered and began to exploit the potential for engaging with social agendas, to explore the extent to which disability in fact functions as an important popular music charity and campaigning precursor.

The embodied experience of popular music through the rhythmically coordinated physical act of dance has played an important role in the drive against, as well as in the articulation of the experience of, polio at different times (see Shell 2005a, 109–17). The most important acts of dance were organized in the United States—a series of activities known under the collective title of "Paralysis Dance" (Shell 2005a, 117). Franklin D. Roosevelt was president of the United States from 1933 until his death in 1945, and a polio survivor, having contracted it at the relatively late age of thirty-nine. One of Roosevelt's health-campaign tactics informed by his own experience as a significantly mobility-impaired man, a direct result of his polio, was the president's birthday balls—a series of fund- and consciousness-raising events held across the country in his name, each January 30 from 1934 until 1945. The birthday balls consisted of prestigious headlining events at which the leading dance bands and singers of the day appeared, as well as many smaller dances and parties featuring local town bands, which would develop to involve, in Roosevelt's rosy words from 1939, "every state and county, every city and town, every hamlet and crossroads community" (Roosevelt birthday ball radio broadcasts). Monies raised from the birthday balls would be split between Roosevelt's therapeutic center for polios, the Warm Springs Rehabilitation Institute in Georgia, and local groups and organizations. (In 1938 a second, newly formulated popular music and film star-endorsed fund-raising campaign was launched, informally named the March of Dimes, focused more on funding the new National Foundation for Infantile Paralysis's research into polio prevention, rather than rehabilitation. Named after the coin, it sought in the form of mass donation, we can see the March of Dimes as a historical instance of the situation where "capitalism and cripples . . . [are] sometimes inexorably linked" (Snyder and Mitchell 2006, 15).) It is worth emphasizing that the birthday ball was, from the first, not simply a glittering dinner and dance event attended by Roosevelt family members at the Hotel Astor in New York; it had a more ambitious cross-media design and scope, aided by the mediated nature of Roosevelt using an annual birthday radio broadcast to the nation to introduce and champion the idea, and exploiting the film industry too for support (Gomery 1995). As Roosevelt put it to radio listeners across the nation in 1934, drawing on the language of sentimentality and disability made possible by the fact that polio was primarily a children's disease: "I would like each one of you who hears me to remember that what you are doing means the enriching of the life of some crippled child. I know and you know that there could be no finer purpose than our will to aid these helpless little ones" (Roosevelt birthday balls radio addresses). In fact, that first January saw 600 individual events organized across the United States, including "a dance for those in wheelchairs at Warm Springs" (Gomery 1995, 128); within a few years Roosevelt was talking in terms of 25,000 events being held nationwide, so that, even during wartime, "laughter and music [would] still ring out from coast to coast" (Roosevelt birthday balls radio addresses). In the perhaps unsurprising view of Roosevelt's own Presidential Library:

> the funds raised by the Birthday Balls and March of Dimes financially supported the creation of a polio vaccine by Jonas Salk in 1955, eradicating the disease throughout most of the world by the 1960s. Franklin Roosevelt's dedication to finding a cure for polio benefited millions of children worldwide, but it was the participation of Americans across the nation in Birthday Balls that made the campaign a success. (FDR library website)

Let us pause to acknowledge the driven scientific invention that has indeed—yes!—very nearly eradicated poliomyelitis as a major disabling disease around the world today. (The Western model of private philanthropy established by Roosevelt for polio retains its pivotal role, in polio eradication and education drives funded by the Rotary International or the

Bill Gates Foundation. See fig. 31.) Problematically, though, the Presidential Library's hagiologic history grandly sweeps controversy and criticism away—actually, at least some experimental vaccines and theories directly funded by the president's birthday ball commission were, at the very least, "inadequate . . . [and] made costly and dangerous mistakes" (Gould 1995, 70). Also, while some African-Americans were active in the birthday balls, Roosevelt's rehabilitation center at Warm Springs was a whites-only facility (Gould 1995, 78–81; Rogers 2007, 787); one 1937 African-American newspaper headline captured the outrage: "We Donated, But They Left Us Out" (quoted in Rogers 2007, 790). The National Association for the Advancement of Colored People declined to support the Birthday Balls, until "polio became a civil rights issue" later in the 1930s, in the drive toward what Naomi Rogers calls an "integrationist epidemiology" (Rogers 2007, 793, 785). Indeed, the complex growing relations between disability awareness and campaigning, civil rights, and the cultural politics of popular music would be actively revisited in following years. A political sensibility and activism informed by even such tentative links in identity politics from race and disability perspectives is present, articulated by or through popular music. For example:

> during a 1957 March of Dimes campaign, gospel singer Mahalia Jackson refused to perform in a segregated hall and reminded local organizers of the March of Dimes' national policy, "which is dedicated to all people, regardless of race." She was not, she explained, "urging my people to turn their backs on the drive against polio. I know what sickness is. I think race hatred is a sickness too." (Rogers 2007, 793)

Nonetheless, the point remains that, in the phenomenon of the birthday ball, popular music, in both live and radio broadcast form, was early on employed as a mass activity for the purpose of social change. Indeed, popular music interventions in politics seemed at a high point during Roosevelt's presidency: "he probably inspired more commercial song writing than any other president, before or since," wrote Patrick J. Maney in 2000. "Published or recorded works dedicated to FDR came in all forms—orchestral pieces, polkas, fox trots, and gospel, blues, and hillbilly songs" (Maney 2000, 85). Notably, for us, bringing together star songwriter and star musician, in 1942 Irving Berlin wrote a song then recorded by bandleader Glen Miller entitled "The President's Birthday Ball." It was a special gesture by

Figure 30. Polio disability campaigning: President's Birthday Ball poster (dated on rear, 1939). Library of Congress. Posters: WPA Posters. POS-WPA-NY .01 .P75, no. 1 (B size) [P&P].

Berlin, marking Roosevelt's sixtieth birthday. Perhaps it is unnecessary, or unfair, to point out that the song's uninspired lyrics did not sing of cavalier scientists whose experiments might be killing or infecting children, or of poverty and racial segregation in accessing health care: "Check our sorrow 'til tomorrow / For the heavens will soon be bright / And we're gonna have fun tonight" (Miller 1942). Both Berlin and Miller were heavily involved at this date in a patriotic cultural propagandizing in support of the U.S. war effort, of course, while Marc Shell notes that "polios understood at once the *political and financial rhythms*" of Berlin's song (2005a, 117; emphasis added). Other popular songs, including from stage musicals, were co-opted into the American campaign against polio, notably "Brother, Can You Spare a Dime?" (originally from 1932), for its lyric's relevance to the March of Dimes, and, because of its resonance around mobility impairment, a common result of polio infection, "You'll Never Walk Alone" (1945). This last may seem a curious choice of song, or one that laid bare the differences in perception between campaigners and the people with disabilities being campaigned about. Shell informs us that "You'll Never Walk Alone" was used widely "by many charitable polio organizations in order to publicize 'walkathons,'" yet his own youthful reception of it seems altogether more ambivalent.

> To us polio-children, the words of this love song meant both that we would never be able to walk without braces and that we would always be dependent on someone to lean on. When young polios performed the song before [telethon] audiences . . . the adults' tears would flow along with their money. (Shell 2005a, 141)

Notwithstanding such ambivalence, the history of an individual song can illustrate for us its place in disability culture, the song shifting resonance according to public health and impairment contexts. But also the song's crippled history evidences the contribution of popular music to disability advocacy, points to our important prehistory for fund- and consciousness-raising within pop. This is the conclusion we can draw from Shell's tracing of the other disability uses of "You'll Never Walk Alone," which function after and as a result of its use in polio campaigning through the 1940s and 1950s.

> "You'll never walk alone," long associated with Jerry Lewis's Labor Day muscular dystrophy telethons, has also been adopted by such causes as . . . the annual

> AIDS Walk campaigns. Marilyn Horne, Joan Baez, and others have sung "You'll
> never walk alone" at AIDS Walk rallies . . . and in 1992 Patti Labelle made a new
> recording of the song for a national AIDS Walk public service announcement.
> (Shell 2005a, 271 n7)

The disabled lives or multiple sonicities of "You'll Never Walk Alone"—
polio, muscular dystrophy, AIDS, identified by Shell from the 1940s to the
1990s—both precede and extend beyond civil-rights activism and countercultural music, confirming our reading of popular music's longstanding
and enduring engagement with disability activism, and at the same time
confirming the importance of reinserting disability activism into our reading of the social movement politics of popular music.

As noted, the American popular film industry, too, was increasingly involved alongside music and musicals, and radio: film stars as celebrity sup-
porters, film plots telling polio stories, cinemas themselves as collection
points for the March of Dimes (Gomery 1995; Shell 2005a, chapters 4 and 5).
Many American music, film, and radio stars would endorse the wider fund-
raising activities of the March of Dimes campaign, to the extent that Gomery can describe the organisation in 1945 as "the most beloved (and richest)
charity in the USA with coffers brimming over with totals measured in the
millions of dollars" (1995, 132), while Shell notes its agenda-setting significance: "entertainment cult celebrities and private foundations proved both
successful in its time and influential through the rest of the century" (Shell
2005a, 142). The March of Dimes even seemed to have transcendent potential on everyday folk: saxophonist and polio survivor Dave Liebman's
mother was famously active as a fund-raiser in New York, because of her
son's disability: "She collected $20,000 in dimes ringing door-to-door in
Brooklyn. . . . Mom was [treated] like a movie star because she did this"
(Liebman 2012, 12). Arguably, the multimedia, multi-million-dollar charity
or campaigning extravaganza known today as the popular music "mega-
event" (Garofalo 1992b)—Live Aid or Live 8—has, with its combination of
radio, live and recorded music, dance and party events, film-industry engagement, a hugely successful precursor in a national annual "mega-event"
of the birthday ball and the March for Dimes. For us, this is especially important because it illustrates not the marginality of disability within popular music history, practice, and understanding, but its *centrality*. Of course,
in this rewrite of pop (campaigning) history we should acknowledge the
differences as well as continuities. The birthday balls were established from

the heart of government and then certain popular musicians of the day invited to become involved: the organization was instituted and the agenda controlled centrally, even if there quickly developed a nationwide localized structure of happenings. The Concert for Bangladesh, Live Aid, and Live 8 were initiated by musicians themselves, and a critical challenge implicitly or explicitly thrown down to political leaders. Even at such contradictory grassroots mega-events, though, the political waters are muddied, as John Street charts the organizational necessities in a British context.

> Live 8, for instance, involved political negotiations between the Band Aid Charitable Trust and the Prime Minister's Office, the Treasury, the Department of Culture, Media and Sport, and the London Parks Authority. It also required global negotiations between political and bureaucratic actors in seven other major cities. These were supplemented by further negotiations with broadcasters. (2012, 75)

The birthday balls of the 1930s and 1940s had other curious minor musical resonances. The domestic intimacy Roosevelt achieved with the mass of Americans, in large part achieved via his fireside radio broadcasts, had another intriguing result in the context of popular music. Thousands of ordinary Americans wrote to the Roosevelts during his presidency, including with their correspondence copies of songs they had composed in the president's honor. Maney (2004) estimates that 14,000 songs were written and sent, by primarily nonprofessional musicians, in an extraordinary musical-political dialogue, that must have been at least in part inspired by the events of the birthday balls. One of these songs, marking Roosevelt's first election victory, by a Mary Davidson, of Cumberland, Maryland, is entitled "The Spirit of 1933," and its lyrics include the following clumsy but direct verse:

> Hail to our new Chief
> I'll tell you folks he's grand.
> Although he is a cripple,
> He knows just when to stand. (quoted in Maney 2004, 86)

(Elsewhere, too, people were "dancing [so] that others may walk." In Britain, during the vaccination drive against polio in the later 1950s, one tactic employed was the "jabs while you jive" campaign, targeting young people at Mecca Dance Halls and youth clubs [Gould 1995, 174]. There is something

Figure 31. Rotary International polio eradication drive publicity poster for 2011 "This close" campaign, featuring Congolese band of street musician polio survivors Staff Benda Bilili. Used with permission.

to be said here about the attractive and pleasureful physical activity of dance through popular music by young people being employed to counter a potentially physically devastating virus that mostly targeted youth: rock and roll is pinpointed reflexively as the very kind of activity that would be under threat from polio.)

But how has the work of disability charities been viewed and revised in the decades since, especially with the rise of the disability-rights movement? Marc Shell argues that such political-cultural responses to polio in the United States as the birthday balls and the March of Dimes were responsible for "a remarkable institution of 'handi-capitalism' supported by celebrity culture and the entertainment business" (2005a, 10). He later goes further, in terms of both critical commentary on the development of *handi-capitalism* and beginning to trace the links between early disability cultural advocacy and later popular music activism we have been exploring in greater detail.

"Crippledom" was a good thing for the March of Dimes. It furthered money collection and a cure. It allowed telethon masters to use polios as distinctly dehumanized and deformed money collection props. . . . Polios were likewise definitively *commodified;* thousands of children became naked patient demonstrators in surgical theatres and orthopedists' advertisements. This exploitative practice was the origin of Live Aid: the studios, and later the celebrity community, raising funds in the private sector, seemed to make the public sector both weak and unnecessary. (Shell 2005a, 145; emphasis in original)

From a rhetoric of help, support, and charity we move toward one of dehumanization, commodification, and exploitation. As the disabled-rights movement developed post–civil rights, many disabled people began to express a profound "unhappiness with charitable discourse: some had even experienced being thrown coins in the street" (Shakespeare 2006, 155; see also Watson 2003, 44). Charities were now viewed with suspicion, as reinforcing the notion of disabled people as dependent rather than independent or interdependent; they produced "a dependency born of powerlessness, poverty, degradation, and institutionalization"; a dependency "saturated with paternalism" (Charlton 2000, 3). Also, there was distrust that disability charities were, in Michael Oliver's distinction, "organisations *for*" as opposed to disability groups being "organisations *of*" (quoted in Shakespeare 2006, 157; emphasis added). This new critical positionality would be encapsulated in a key slogan of the disability-rights movement—a slogan with the purpose of refusing dependency: "Nothing about us without us" (see Charlton 2000). The American independent-living campaigner Ed Roberts would spell out the trajectory of his activist education: "if we have learned one thing from the civil rights movement in the US, it's that when other people speak for you, you lose" (quoted in Charlton 2000, 3).

Nick Watson has written of ways in which some disabled people today understand what they experience as their continued "oppression as the *product* of charity" (2003, 44; emphasis added). That is, the charitable activity is viewed as the problem which maintains the subaltern social position of the disabled, rather than part of the liberatory social-change agenda (even as it might speak a language of liberation or advocacy). Like Shell's handi-capitalism, an altogether more critical reading of fund-raising for, as the language of Roosevelt's time put it, the "helpless little ones," is articulated, in which the state of helplessness is—a little like the repeated one-word title, lead chorus, and backing voice support of Neil Young's 1970 song of polio, "Helpless," which is, well, in the end, unhelpful—replicated, confirmed, inescapable as the crip life experience par excellence. British disability-rights activists began to target disability charities, in actions that may have seemed bewildering to charity bureaucrats, as Tom Shakespeare recounts.

> One of the consistent themes in the British disability rights movement has been a vehement opposition to charities which claim to represent and support disabled people. . . . Throughout the 1980s and 1990s, demonstrations against charity fundraising . . . were important political events in the development of a disability rights consciousness, bringing together disability activists, and challenging traditional responses to disability. Key slogans of this period, seen on banners, placards, t-shirts and in the protest songs of Johnny Crescendo and Ian Stanton were "Rights not charity" and "Piss on pity." (Shakespeare 2006, 153)

That Shakespeare mentions protest songs illustrates the important place of popular music in grassroots disability activism during these years, where it functioned as soundtrack, as entertainment—channeler of truth-telling, comedy, or anger—as fund-raiser, and was by virtue of these multiple roles also a core part of the movement. Folk singer Stanton's 1992 song "Tragic but Brave" was made available on his self-released cassette entitled *Freewheelin'*, which neatly references both the musical tradition of Bob Dylan and the everyday fact for Stanton that he was a wheelchair user. The song draws a picture of a disabled person moving from self-denial to the beginning of a politicized identity; the process taking place against a backdrop of a news report about a disability direct action protest:

> And she looks at the crowd on the TV news
> With their wheelchairs, their sticks, and their guides
> They are brandishing banners, they are pissing on pity
> And they celebrate difference with pride
> Something stirs inside. (quoted in Cameron 2009, 393)

Direct action, identity politics, mass media, popular music, disability rights: Stanton's lyric covers all of these. The places in which songs like "Tragic but Brave" were sung live matters too, as Colin Cameron explains: "the power of the music . . . is also entwined with the community and grassroots locations in which it has been performed. Access is at the heart of disability arts, and in practical terms this has meant that gigs have usually taken place in small venues . . . where disabled people have been able to get to" (2009, 382).

Within disability arts, certain forms of popular music have been privileged, argues Cameron, for their traditions, their aesthetics, and, we might conjecture, their relative ease of playing.

> Blues is music born of oppression and which gives voice to the oppressed. Folk emerges from a rootedness and groundedness that is certain of its own values. Punk is the noise of the alienated, the disregarded and disrespected. Each of these forms is used to articulate anger at the established order. Furthermore, each has traditionally been associated with a rough and readiness. Polish is not the main thing. It is authenticity that counts, the spirit of what is being sung rather than how perfectly manufactured it sounds. This is about the oppressed making their own use of available cultural resources to make their voices heard. (2009, 382)

Such participatory forms as these, which privilege DIY aesthetic and access, are clearly important popular musical practices that speak to some or many within disability activism. But there are also other participatory approaches, as noted by Melissa C. Nash, in the context of performance and music workshops: "much of the lives of people with profound and multiple disabilities is passive. *Involvement in the avant-garde may be a way out of such passivity*" (Melissa C. Nash 2005, 199; emphasis added). It is possible that community music, for example, particularly that school of community music that draws on an instrumental jazz tradition, offers other participatory routes to creative music-making in the community (see Everitt 1998; Moser and McKay 2004; McKay and Higham 2011). While usually in jazz instrumental technique is central, community musicians have used that music, working with people with disabilities, to produce "alternatives to the hegemony of technique in virtuosic and conservatory traditions" (Perring 2005, 185). Arguably, free improvisation, for example,

> has opened some practitioners up to musicality within people with learning difficulties that virtuosic traditions might overlook. Some musicians, such as [English free jazz drummer and founder of Community Music] John Stevens . . . have explored what is possible at the *edge* of technique and what occurs with what might be described as *non-* or *anti*technique. (Perring 2005, 181; emphasis in original)

In this discussion we have moved quite quickly a long way from the charitable Presidential Birthday Ball, but also maybe not so very, very far: I wonder if any of the thousands of small, local events that happened across the United States each January in the 1930s and 1940s—now I am imagining a giddy wheelchair dance, or someone singing a raucous folk song with bad (we know it's good) guitar accompaniment about their experience of being disabled—could have had a touch of the spirit of anger or wit or sheer attitudinality we hear in the grassroots music and protest gigs of the disability-rights movement. Failing that, if this fantasy is just too flighty, too unrigorous, let's settle for this conjecture, quite unsubstantiated: notwithstanding the rhetorical and political shift from "helpless little ones" to "piss on pity," the first produced the second.

## Shakin's All Over

> One of the primary tasks of disability studies is to cultivate media and textual critics . . . who can intervene in the cultural images of disability that influence our responses and ways of imagining human differences.
> —Sharon Snyder and David Mitchell,
>  *Cultural Locations of Disability* (2006, 202)

Well, I have volunteered myself to disability studies to contribute to this important task, from my existing research field in cultural and popular music studies. The fresh dialogue here and elsewhere between disability studies and popular music can only enrich both. In *A History of Disability*, Henri-Jacques Stiker writes in passing of the idea of "social contagion," that the love of difference (let us not even stretch love, but talk more modestly of simply the tolerance by the currently nondisabled of those with disabilities) could be socially contagious. What about *cultural* contagion? Stiker continues: "there is only one recourse beyond the ethical imperative, and that is to make it part of our culture" (1997, 11, 12). Sheila Riddell and Nick Watson put it more straightforwardly: "the struggle for social justice, then, involves *a quest for cultural recognition* as well as economic redistribution" (2003a, 15; emphasis added). One of the aims of *Shakin' All Over* has been to map the sonic history and tracks of that quest for cultural recognition—to discover that cultural expressions and explorations of disability have been the already heard of pop since its foundations were both established and shaken on day and night one, whenever they were.

Terry Rowden shows us a cultural challenge for the disabled in pop and rock, for their musicians "are performers in popular forms, and thus the possibility for them to see their music-making as a form of self-expression has always been tempered by their realization of the economic necessity of attracting and entertaining" normates (2009, 10). Failing the balance trick—I know that feeling—they become *un*popular. Neil Young recalled in 1986 that his advisers used to urge him to "keep all this weird polio/epilepsy shit quiet" (quoted in Stein 2008, 5). Among all the pop and rock in this book, there is a good deal of unpopular music.[10] After all, in this chapter alone we have seen the "anti-star," a musical "rough and readiness," and "anti-technique," all employed within a disability context. But then we would do well to bear in mind the observation of Greil Marcus that "to make true political music, you have to say what decent people don't want to hear" (quoted in Street 2012, 155). *Shakin' All Over* argues for a pop that maintains a persistent and publicly profiled performativity, in which the disabled body onstage demands rather than deflects the stare, in which pop's apparent ephemerality and consensus is compellingly destabilized by lyrics of the experiences of the disabled, and in which fans strategically employ pop discourse and its modes of behavior to represent their impairment and to negotiate others' responses to it. Here I am thinking again of Ed Roberts, who, on returning to school after years of home education and bed rest following polio, saw his new schoolmates watching him being lifted from the car, suddenly thought of and felt like Elvis Presley and so "I decided to be a star, not a helpless cripple" (quoted in Sandahl and Auslander 2005, 3). Roberts reached for popular music, not as a compensation, not only as a cultural prosthetic, but as an attitude, a way of performing, of presenting the body, and claiming the scene—and "making the choice to perform his disability was the starting point of his life as an activist" (Sandahl and Auslander 2005, 3). We can go further here than individual performance, and think about the very act of people forming a band. From a disability perspective, the motivation for the formation and membership of a band may speak more of the desire for interdependence and community, whereby the band functions as support, network, and facilitation device, as well as being a collective space for cultural work.

In the course of researching and writing the book I have had the great pleasure (usually) of going to see artists and shows I thought relevant—a crip popper or rocker onstage? I'd be there in the audience, the one with the notebook. The evening that really stands out was a concert I'd never nor-

Figure 32. Stevie Wonder, opening the 2nd International Conference of African and Diasporean Intellectuals, Salvador, 2006. Photographer: Antonio Cruz / ABr ⓒ Wiki-media.

mally have gone to, since I am a lover of mostly small interior music. It was a very expensive concert in a very large hall by a global superstar, the kind of gig where (if you have some sight) you screw up your eyes to see the key figure moving not onstage but on the large screens either side of the stage. At least the sound (if you have some hearing) at such gigs is usually pretty good nowadays. But you know what? I was totally blown away. I was moved. I was inspired. I was energized to get back to the book, to do the songs justice as far as I could, as well as to ensure that the critical politics and disability theory would not be lost in the close pop readings. And, looking back, I think I was reassured that my own experience of disability—Charcot-Marie-Tooth disease, progressive muscular dystrophy—which to be honest had been doing my head in a bit, making me feel like Dury's "one-legged Peter / who knows bloody well / he's got worse ever since he came in" (Dury 1980)—was, straightforwardly put, livable with. Yes, I got all that from one pop gig. It still seems a lot to me, and on the way home I felt lucky. And this was from a pop star whose songs I had *quite* liked, rather than ever loved, who was there in my big sister's record collection when I was a 1970s teenager listening to prog and glam rock, then Kevin Coyne, then Ian Dury and the Pistols. It was when the superstar—I am not supercripping here, believe me, though I fear you will think I am. I don't think I am, anyway. Maybe I am. I am. Reclaim the supercrip from abjection or overcriticality—it was when the superstar moved from singing his extraordinary back catalogue and talking about the history and legacy of the civil-rights movement to one simple direct statement spoken between songs (hmm. So: not sung) about the personal experience of disability, the rights of the disabled, and a demand for greater access and social mobility through urban design for all people with disabilities, and 16,000 audience members cheered massively. I wasn't in that moment thinking about Stevie Wonder as freak or wonder, nor even as "a prosthetically enhanced and up-to-date cyborgean soulman" (Rowden 2009, 119). I wasn't thinking about the Braille lettering on some of the album covers, or the classic albums' resonant names for a blind man—*Talking Book, Innervisions*—that seemed to confirm the cliché of blindness in music as offering "an enhanced interiority" (Straus 2011, 6). Nor did I have in mind the sonic urban painting that was "Living for the City" (at the press launch in 1973, Wonder had all the journalists blindfolded on a tour round New York: Werner 2004, 193), though I had danced joyously to that song already that evening. Nor the later experimental film soundtracks (the *blind* guy doing the *film* music?), pushing the boundaries of cross-media collaboration. No, it was not these critical items in my mind then, at my pop concert, where I was being a fan. It was really the quite specific spoken demand for disability awareness and access, delivered onstage by the disabled musician at his pop concert, and the way that that utterance had been so cheered by everyone, that powerfully struck me. The shakin's not all over, is it? The world still needs shaking up. Stevie told me that one night in Manchester and I agree with him.

# NOTES

## Introduction

1. According to Laurie Stras, "in the 1920s and 1930s, jazz was indeed 'disabled music,' considered by many to be aesthetically and functionally impaired to the point that it . . . was an active agent of medical and social disorder. Most commonly, jazz and its consumption were seen as both the origin and the product of mental or 'nervous' disorder" (2009, 300). Arguably, as we will discuss further, some sort of template was being set: such "contagious rhythms" (Sartin 2010) would also be strikingly evident three or four decades later via the "risky behavior" of rock and roll and then rock lifestyles. Medical doctor Jeffrey S. Sartin points out: "Bill Haley was a lifelong alcoholic, and Elvis died of a heart attack after years of drug abuse. The rock lifestyle carried many insidious dangers, among them the twin scourges of hepatitis and HIV" (Sartin 2010, 110).

2. The boy stared at Johnny. While *The Boy Looked at Johnny* is a well-known British punk rock book from the late 1970s by then-young music journalists Julie Burchill and Tony Parsons—the title drawn from quoting a Patti Smith lyric—I am thinking of myself round the same time, as a seventeen-year-old watching the Sex Pistols live, and wondering now, as a fifty-something, about the attraction. The man looking at the boy staring at Johnny. What was his body saying to mine?

3. I give credit: this book, above all others, opened up for me the space and I feel gave me the legitimacy to explore disability and culture. I read *Extraordinary Bodies* first during a period when my mind needed opening up (it wanted to close down, as I was realizing that that's what my body was doing) and it worked. I was in a private panic, and it allowed me to transform or channel my febrility into intellectual production and textual energy.

4. In *Music, Disability, and Society,* Lubet calls the research field "music DS" (2011, 5).

5. Though Cheryl Herr has pointed out the methodological difficulty inherent in a project which seeks to explore "an individual's putative inability to do certain things typical of the majority of human beings (for instance, walking, talking, seeing, hearing,

maintaining socially acceptable mental function and emotional balance). . . . For a scholar of popular music to bring such questions to bear on a particular performer ideally requires access to an unusual depth of information about the individual, the kind of biographical data that is rarely available even for the most cherished and widely written about musicians of our own era" (2009, 323).

6. Richard Bruno has written of such "pretenders and wannabes" that they suffer from a form of "factitious disability disorder" (quoted in Shell 2005a, 279, n76). Another relevant term might be "disability paraphilia" (Shell 2005a, 279, n82), though Tobin Siebers offers something which sounds less medically authoritative for the impersonating performance of disability, as when a nondisabled actor plays a disabled part—usually in "bombastic" style—: "'disability drag' . . . [which] represses disability and affirms the ideology of ability" (2008, 115, 114).

7. For those interested, my reviews of some of them are available: Rowden (McKay 2010a), Lubet (McKay 2011).

8. Kirk addressed it himself at the time, by inviting the critic, Steve Race, who had recently described Kirk as like the famous white-faced (insult to injury) clown Charlie Cairoli, part of whose act involved playing instruments poorly, up to the piano to join in for a number at Ronnie Scott's jazz club in London, where Kirk was appearing. According to the account of audience member Ron Malings, Race stumbled through the piece, embarrassed, out of his depth (Malings 2009).

## Chapter 1

1. In respiratory centers in 1950s United States, groups of young ventilator-dependent polio survivors often produced mimeographed news sheets. Referencing the "rocking" technique of physical movement recommended to aid artificial breathing for some, newssheet titles reflected youth and pop music tastes of the time: *The Rocking Reporter, The Rock 'n' Roll* (Gould 1995, 194). This is cited as small evidence of the generational correspondence of (late) polio and (early) pop.

2. Compare figures for the scale of the disease elsewhere: in the 1980s in the USA there were over 600,000 polio survivors, and in India an estimated 12 million (Gould 1995, 223).

3. I keep qualifying in this way because polio nowadays is primarily framed within medical history in the developed world, as a problem that was resolved half a century ago by successful mass vaccination programs (though Shell 2005a, chapter 9, challenges such easy historicizing, asking "What can we (still) learn about polio?" [204]). An international eradication effort in the decades since has led to the virus being active in probably only three or four countries today—and a sustained effort from 2010–11, championed by Bill and Melinda Gates, with funding also from some Western governments, seeks its absolute eradication across the globe. See discussion of the Staff Benda Bilili song "Polio" later in chapter 1.

4. Though not all jazz instrumentalists sought to make musical capital from their condition—some viewed their polio experience as inspiring a different future career

path. Saxophonist Dave Liebman: "I had polio when I was young and was always around doctors. I wanted to be an orthopaedic surgeon" (quoted in Mandel 2003; see also Liebman 2012, 10). Yet even Liebman has understood his music-making in the context of his disability: "I feel strongly that the artist has a responsibility to look back. To get back to the roots. . . . , [T]here's no question that the need to play is based, say, on a difficult childhood. In my case I had a bad leg from polio" (quoted in Schermer 2008). For Charlie Haden, coming from a country-music family in which he was a well-known local child singer, his polio experience at the age of fifteen affected his facial and throat nerves and muscles, which meant the end of his singing career, but a focus instead on his instrumental career on the double bass (see Davis 2000). Nonetheless, for Haden, the childhood polio is framed by the music shift, as he explained in 2006: "I don't sing now, because I had polio when I was 15, bulbar polio. This [c. 1952] was when the epidemic was happening. And I was lucky that it didn't affect my lungs or my legs. It went to my face and kind of paralyzed my vocal chords, and I wasn't able to sing" (quoted in Goodman 2006).

5. The previous year MacColl and Seeger had written and sung songs about polio survivors for a thirty-minute television feature entitled *Four People,* which in fact used "virtually the same subjects" for interview as the later radio-ballad (Cox 2008, 121).

6. Other cultural expressions—such as by those articulating their own experiences—have viewed the mechanical ventilator more intrusively, less as lifesaver or restorer. American polio survivor Mark O'Brien writes in his poem "The man in the iron lung": "In its repetitive dumb mechanical rhythm, / Rudely, it inserts itself in the map of my body" (quoted in Siebers 2008, 175).

7. Other disability-caused experiences of social isolation have musical impact too of course. A. J. Hood, writing of hearing impaired composers such as Beethoven, Smetana, Gabriel Fauré, and Robert Franz, notes that "the truly remarkable fact is that far from having an adverse effect upon their work, their deafness marked the period of their greatest creativity. . . . It seems almost as if the isolation forced upon them by their deafness drove them to seek consolation and communion in their own work." He concludes wonderfully, in full deconstructive mode: "How much, one wonders, would have been lost to our musical heritage had these composers not been deaf?" (Hood 1977b, 342; emphasis added). There is a difference though: polio isolation was usually a childhood experience—a formative one.

8. Cf. Dave Liebman's experience as a returning polio child in New York City in 1950 or so: "You've got to remember that polio was considered sort of like AIDS in those days. When I did get back [after extended hospitalisation]—we were living on 14th Street—people wouldn't come near the house. It was considered like a plague or something" (Liebman 2012, 7).

9. *Alla zoppa:* a musical term for "uneven rhythms in a melody"; meaning "'limping' or 'halting' in Italian . . . this rhythmic figure is part of the instrumental tradition of representing physical impairments" (Lerner 2006, 88, n. 17). In this context, *alla zoppa* makes us reconsider reggae's characteristic offbeat rhythm guitar and keyboard, and even more so reggae's sometimes out-of-time echo dub practices, as less lilt, more stilt.

Here may be the appropriate moment to suggest that there is a potentially related observation to be made about tonal "imbalance" and disability too: Joseph N. Straus argues that "imbalance and unrest are desirable aesthetically. They propel the piece forward and provide an essential contrast with the normatively balanced and restful beginning and ending" (2011, 49).

10. Dury songs that reference or explore disability, impairment, and/or institutionalization in some way include "Crippled with Nerves" (1975), "Sweet Gene Vincent," "Blockheads," "Clevor Trever" (all 1977), "What a Waste," "Dance of the Screamers," "Inbetweenies," "Mischief" (all 1978), "Hit Me With Your Rhythm Stick" (1979), "Hey, Hey, Take Me Away," "Dance of the Crackpots," "Manic Depression (Jimi)" (the "flaw of the jungle" line is from this song), "I Want to be Straight" (all 1980), "Spasticus Autisticus," "The Body Song" (both 1981), "Geraldine" (1998), "Poo-Poo in the Prawn" (1992), "Drip Fed Fred" (with Madness, 1999).

11. Interestingly, polio survivor and stutterer Marc Shell recalls of his own childhood in the 1950s that "while I was supposed to be recovering from polio, my mother used to call me her 'walkie-talkie.' (A walkie-talkie is a doll that one can make walk and talk.) But I never learned to walk or talk the way my mother wanted" (Shell 2005b, 35).

12. In his autobiography, *Rotten,* the Sex Pistols singer explains: "I was in a hospital for a year from age seven to eight. . . . They would draw fluid out of my spine, . . . it's curved my spine. I've developed a bit of a hunchback. The [Rotten] stare is because I developed bad eyesight, also as a result of the meningitis" (Lydon 1994, 18).

13. It is interesting that the Spastics Society has been no more successful than Dury in overcoming the stigmatized meaning of the word "spastic" in everyday parlance; today the organization has rebranded itself as Scope.

14. How surprised should we be at the single's failure and its negative impact on Dury's career, really, quite apart from its controversial reception? In a discussion of political singles in *Music and Politics,* John Street points out, after identifying a very small number of exceptions, that "a crude generalization might be that the more explicitly political the song, the lower the chart placing" (2012, 47).

15. This is of course a reworking of the famous scene in Stanley Kubrick's 1960 film *Spartacus,* in which the surviving rebel slaves announce en masse to the Roman authorities searching for the rebel leader that "I'm Spartacus!" (see Kubrick 1960).

## *Chapter 2*

1. I write debatably because I am conscious of, if not fully convinced by, Frith's observation that "a voice can never really be heard as a wordless instrument" (1996, 190).

2. Consider the first single released by Buffalo Springfield in 1966, written (though not in this instance sung) by the multiply disabled artist Neil Young, "Nowadays Clancy Can't Even Sing": Clancy was a figure from Young's real life, a boy at school with multiple sclerosis, who "rode his bike to school, sang in the hallway and endured the derision of his fellow students. Clancy was just the kind of misfit Young admired and empathized with" (McDonough 2002, 125). More than that though, the song, one of Young's early

breakthrough pieces in terms of his craft as a songwriter, with its subversive rhythm changes (making it, with those "formal deviations" (Straus 2011, 113), an unusual choice for a single release), addresses the public reception of disability and its cultural expression or compensation—themes Young would return to surprisingly often in his career. See also the discussion of this song in chapter 3.

3. Wyatt in 1996: "when I lost the use of my hi-hat and bass drum legs, I became basically a singer. I was a drummer who did a bit of singing, and then I became a singer who did a bit of percussion. Certainly I would say that I would like to think that the singer is the butterfly, and the drummer was just the little grub in the ground, working to become a caterpillar" (quoted in Unterberger 1996).

4. The fetish of the pure high voice in sung music, and its preservation through a surgically induced emasculation, reached its apotheosis of course with the castrati tradition in Europe from the sixteenth to nineteenth centuries. To maintain the soprano voice of the gifted young male singer, it is estimated that 4,000 operations were carried out annually in the mid-eighteenth century, generally on boys between the ages of seven and nine (Magee 1999, 672). Reginald Magee describes the medical procedure and its physical results: "the child, often drugged with opium or some other narcotic, was placed in a very hot bath for some time, until he was in a state of virtual insensibility. Then the ducts leading to the testicles were severed, so that the latter in the course of time shrivelled and disappeared. Full castration (as in eunuchs proper) does not seem to have been practised in the case of castrato singers. Thus it would seem that the operation involved the complete severance of the spermatic cord only. The resulting consequences of the operation are the following. The body grows somewhat larger than otherwise and the bony structure takes on feminine characteristics. The chest becomes round, the muscles softer, the skin sallow and flabby, the body hairless, the hair on the head thicker and the face beardless. The mammary glands develop in a marked way, which accounted for many of the castrati being able to successfully assume feminine roles on the stage. The most remarkable changes occurred in the larynx . . . [which] was smaller and softer with shorter vocal cords" (Magee 1999, 672). The vocal timbre of the castrati—a voice between boy's and woman's—was notable and venerated, and a dedicated musical practice was made for them: opera seria. The castrato's was not a falsetto head voice, but the chest voice of an impaired body. Magee notes that "Europe was infatuated with the castrati and they were adored wherever they performed. They travelled widely: to England, Austria, Germany, Poland and Russia, singing in the courts of emperors and public theatres, and were idolized as much as today's pop and rock singers" (1999, 673). We see periodically through Shakin' All Over moments when popular music functions as a disabling culture; the castrati figure as a stark—shocking—historic precedent, as workers in a creative industry whose very access to musical careers was predicated on their deliberate initial physical disablement. The last castrato, Allessandro Moreschi, died in 1922, and was the only one ever whose voice was recorded.

5. In a self-ironizing gesture, Chris Martin of Coldplay has sought to undercut the aura of sensitivity around falsetto in some live performances by jokily inhaling helium to alter his voice (Miller 2003).

6. Conjecturing about polio survivor and wheelchair user Connie Boswell, Stras writes: "We might wonder what impact Connie's mobility issues had on her ability to make music; . . . she always performed seated when singing with her sisters (so, according to bel canto singing technique, running the risk of restricting her breathing)" (2009, 316).

7. I write "necessarily" as a marker of qualification, and use this footnote to suggest slyly that maybe I am making that universal claim. Vocal pathologies are of the body too, and their flaws are always medical narratives: "Damaged voices abound in the blues canon; indeed the very sound of the blues singer has been defined by voices in which physical suffering is almost palpable. The early singers were called shouters for good reason; in the words of a Harlem medic, they 'wore themselves ragged trying to rise above the inattentive din of conversation, and soon, literally, yelled themselves hoarse; eventually they lost whatever music there was in their voices and acquired that throaty roughness which is so frequent among blues singers, and which, though admired as characteristically African, is as a matter of fact nothing but a form of chronic laryngitis'" (Stras 2006, 179). Perhaps Barthes's mysterious "grain of the voice" is (just) a medical condition, after all.

8. Note an alternative and significantly less elegant and aesthetically attractive revisioning of Thomson's regularly quoted section by Sharon Snyder and David Mitchell, which contains a more critical perspective on their pragmatism of social strategy, though still rooted in performance (the negative of the masquerade): "Disabled people are recognized as those who must adeptly manipulate suspicious and surly social belief systems about their potential masquerades of incapacity and their parasitism" (2006, 42–43).

9. A few years after his accident Robert Wyatt joined the Communist Party of Great Britain, and became heavily involved in the activist politics of class struggle. His disability may have informed that political choice, though he spoke more of the impact of social issues like racism and imperialism, which he seemed to understand through the experiences of, in particular, black South African musicians with whom he played (see McKay 2005, 222).

10. Such backwards signaling in the context of disability might even also illuminate further for us the pop curiosity of the 1968 album of instrumentals entitled *Eivets Rednow,* by an artist of the same name (aka Stevie Wonder).

11. Mischievously, Dury's take on the stutter when he played "Geraldine" live could involve trying to catch the band out, by maintaining the blocked "G-" and repeating it beyond the rehearsed musical measure. The Blockheads, his band, would have to anticipate where he was going to complete the word and return to the tune accordingly.

12. Apparently there was a personal motivation behind the song. "Songwriter Randy Bachman never wanted the public to hear the song he had composed especially for his brother Gary, the first manager of Bachman-Turner Overdrive. 'He stuttered,' Randy explains. 'He had a speech impediment. We thought, just for fun . . . we'd take this song and I'd stutter and we'd send it to him. He'll have the only copy in the world of this song by BTO'" (Super Seventies website). Thus, a personal or familial experience of disability

informs the cultural expression of the able-bodied. You know, I wonder about mal canto folk-rock innovator Bob Dylan in this kind of context, of the fact that his father, Abe Zimmerman, contracted polio when he was a man and Dylan was a youngster, and the impact of that daily familial experience of disability on the boy.

## Chapter 3

1. TAB = temporarily able-bodied—a critical acronym from disability activism.

2. One of Mayfield's central musical activities was gone forever, though, in an instant: his guitar playing. With a unique tuning kept from his days as a self-taught youngster, and the continuing development of a deceptively soft soul-funk voicing on the instrument, this had long been recognized as significant. Indeed, to some surprise perhaps, he was voted number twenty-five in the British music magazine *Mojo*'s poll of "100 Greatest Guitarists of All Time" in 1996. The lost tuning and technique were noted by Mayfield himself, with some humility: "I'm sorry to say that my style of playing is probably gone forever—the tuning—I can't play it and there's no one to teach it—but there again it was a gift" (Burns 2003, 227–28). I wonder if this is ("probably") as stark a deficit as an instrumental musician could have.

3. A wider and sometimes more critical reading of music celebrity fund-raising campaigns is presented in chapter 5, including reference to Live Aid.

4. Post-aphasia, Collins began also to sing again, which included learning his old songs from scratch, and Maxwell describes the "quite straightforward" way they went about this musical reeducation:

> I typed out the lyrics, big print, lots of spacing. Edwyn would murmur them aloud while listening to the track. . . . [H]e'd move on to simply singing the song over and over until the words began to stick. This took a lot of practice. A lot. . . . The main problem was missing the start of each line. . . . And when he moved on to another song, he would have to remember to keep his hand in with the ones he had already practised, lest all the hard work should simply evaporate. (2009, 291–92)

When I saw Collins play alongside Maxwell discussing her book in Glasgow in 2010 there was a very real sense of the physical and cognitive effort involved in singing, especially the early songs, which sounded now rather difficult in terms of both holding the melody and enunciating the complexity of the lyric. The effort manifested itself in the odd missed cue (his band laughed supportively), once misjudging his pitch for a melody on entry—and this on a new song, "I'm Losing Sleep," written in his new "simple and direct" (quoted in Maxwell 2009, 321) style—as well as some missed notes in the melodic complexity and range of singing. He sneezed uncontrollably toward the end of singing "A Girl Like You." He dropped the harmonica box when removing the instrument on "Low Expectations." But sitting center stage, surrounded by caring musicians who were also friends, with his wife in the wings, and a house full of his own people—

Scots young and old, folk with disabilities—willing him on, there was also a sense that he was giving us what we wanted, what Grace Maxwell called that night and in her book "a happy ending" (2009, 308).

5. Remember Ruby's disabled male veteran from Kenny Rogers in 1969, who is unable to satisfy Ruby sexually, and sings of his self-perception: "Yes it's true I'm not the man I used to be. . . . It's hard to love a man whose legs are bent and paralyzed" (First Edition 1969). Pendergrass was up against the ideology of ability of not only popular music journalism but popular music itself.

6. Of course, to consider the tele-mediated disability of Wyatt alongside that of Teddy Pendergrass for a moment, *Top of the Pops* was no Live Aid—on *Top of the Pops* there was no background agenda of inclusiveness and social critique to inform and illuminate presentational decisions, no awareness of a campaign agenda, and it was a decade earlier, when the identity politics of disability were less articulated and recognized. Wyatt appeared in just another media and music industry working week, which in itself would have been a significant event, even if it would also problematically reveal the limits of everyday attitudes to people with disabilities in much of the entertainment industry then.

7. Behind the cameras and in the dressing rooms things were different, as the pedophilia scandal which rocked the BBC in 2012—centered on *Top of the Pops* presenter and DJ Jimmy Savile—laid bare.

8. And there are other epileptics, such as the blues singer and guitarist Jimmy Reed—who died following a fit in 1976—or (as he sings on "The Sacrifice of Victor") possibly Prince, or the New Zealand indie musician Chris Knox, whose songs about epilepsy may include "Grand Mal" (from the 1989 album Seizure) and "Lapse."

9. The lack of sympathy could apparently be fairly brutal: Stephen Stills "always thought Neil was full of shit, having one of his phony spells." In fact, Young kind of acknowledges that "the seizures became an escape. . . . Some . . . probably weren't real" (see McDonough 2002, 175, 177). Deborah Curtis learned from her experience with husband Ian that "pseudo-seizures can be feigned either consciously or subconsciously and are often used as a way of manipulating people" (1995, 108).

10. In a rare recent interview, Deborah Curtis discussed the film. In her view, it "successfully portrays how Ian and those around him tried to cope with his epilepsy. I particularly like that it shows how the roadies took care of him and worried about him as he tried to carry on. Epilepsy can be managed and monitored and is not always a long term illness, but there was and still is so little out there to help with any associated depression" (quoted in McFadden 2007, n.p.).

11. The self-quotation of a lyric from the song "Insight" (Joy Division 1979a), a line itself quoted on the cover of Joy Division's contribution to the Factory Sampler EP—"I'm not afraid anymore"—is given a startling new insight: it is a lie.

## Chapter 4

1. Both the stigma and the cultural impossibility of deafness in the context of music are expressed by Beethoven, writing in 1801: "I have ceased to attend any social func-

tions just because I find it impossible to say to people: I am deaf. If I had any other profession I might be able to cope with my infirmity; but in my profession it is a terrible handicap" (quoted in Hood 1977b, 342).

2. In an article entitled "Negroes Taught Me To Sing: Famous 'Cry' Crooner Tells What Blues Taught Him," written for *Ebony* in 1953, Ray located a sense of sympathy and critique of injustice and prejudice, as well as a psychological and cultural identification with African America: "Coming up the way I did—the hard way—and having been almost laughed out of existence ever since I was a skinny, unwanted kid, I know how it feels to be rejected. . . . [T]hey have an innate sympathy with the underdog and a delight in seeing a handicapper come from behind" (quoted in Stephens 2005, 305). Also, here Ray is drawing on the common experience of marginalization or discrimination, which would in turn go on to be a central feature of identity politics.

3. The decibel scale is a logarithmic rather than linear form of measurement; a difference of 20 dB between two sounds means that the more intense one has ten times the amplitude (100 times the power) of the softer. Generally, for acoustics concerned with human hearing, dB measurements are "A-filtered," which means that they focus on the midrange frequencies our ears are most physiologically sensitive to. Mostly, as is conventional in much nonspecialist writing about the subject, the dB ratings cited here are technically dB(A).

4. Though see the "rapid response" section of the journal, which includes for this article one from the splendidly named Dr. Funk challenging Patton and McIntosh's findings: "The assertion that concussion can result from an activity as benign as dancing defies common sense" (Funk 2009, n.p.).

5. Let us acknowledge the irony that the youthful generation, the rock and rollers and the baby (sonic) boomers, have aged and deafened. As Pat Benatar puts it on a hearing-impairment booklet: "Our generation has helped shape American culture, especially since we're the first to be raised on rock 'n' roll. From Aerosmith to the Rolling Stones, our music defines us, but all those years of rockin' are beginning to take a toll" (quoted in H.E.A.R. 2004, 2). If our music defines us it is because our music deafens us. Rock 'n' toll.

6. Pete Townshend has given an account of one small excessive aspect of the shortened musical life of Keith Moon, drummer with The Who, who died in 1978: "On the stage once, I saw Keith Moon, who uses earphones to follow a drum track, I saw his earphones catch fire, on God's honour, catch fire on his head there was so much level . . . and he's still going louder, louder, louder!" (quoted in Wilkerson 2009, 249, n2; emphasis added).

## Chapter 5

1. A regular lighthearted column in the form of a questionnaire put to individual stars in the British music weekly *New Musical Express* captures this. It is entitled "Does Rock 'n' Roll Kill Braincells? Testing Musicians' Memories after a Lifetime of Abuse."

2. The overt masculinity is problematized in lyrics by both Curtis and Edwards, in which they explore their own health and disability experiences through a female char-

acter: Joy Division's "She's Lost Control" features a young woman with epilepsy, and as we have seen, Curtis draws in his own experience here; the Manic Street Preachers' "4st 7lbs" is a first-person lyric of a young woman with progressive anorexia, observing her body, and Edwards draws on his own experience here.

3. It is worth pointing out that other types of popular music also have their suicide narratives. One academic study of country music, for example, found a statistical correlation between the prevalence of country-music radio stations and the incidence of white urban suicide (Stack and Gundlach 1992). A subsequent study of the same topic, its authors' curiosity no doubt piqued by the surprising finding that country-music radio kills, found no such correlation at all, and even that country music saves, a little: it has "a negative, though insignificant effect on white urban suicide rates" (Maguire and Snipes 1994, 1239).

4. Consider here another definition of the musical instruction *alla zoppa: zoppa* "in Italian is 'lame,' 'limping,' and so it has been applied to music, meaning 'syncopated'" (Ward 1970, 1128).

5. I offer this indicative range of topics with some confidence, as in 2011 I opened a discussion thread on the International Association for the Study of Popular Music list about music that provided a commentary on the industry, and these were the kinds of common subjects in songs and texts suggested by IASPM members, whom I acknowledge here with thanks.

6. What kind of freakery is this? The confessional lyric of fragmented female experience is presented in the songs of Dory Previn—the best known of which is probably "Twenty-Mile Zone" (1970), about her experience of "screaming" and "letting it all out" while driving her car. With its stop-start structure and speeding-up chorus, even the rhythm of the song contributes to its disturbed meaning. A policeman stops and arrests her for "screaming in your car in a twenty-mile zone"—"Let's have no more of that screaming," he says—male order and rationality in a public place must be maintained. It's interesting here too to note that Carole King, another confessional singer, had been the cowriter of "He Hit Me (It Felt Like a Kiss)"—the Crystals' flopped pop single about relational violence and the internalization of oppression.

7. In my dark reading of the destructive economy of the pop industry, am I getting carried away with the claim here that the industry creates and expects disaster? But there is a Molochian narrative within pop and rock, as we see in the discussion that follows of Kevin Coyne's song "Having a Party" (1978). Whitney Houston acted and sang in a comeback film shortly after leaving rehab in 2011, a few months before her death in February 2012. This was questioned by, for example, Dr. Drew Pinsky, an "addiction specialist," who (according to Christopher Goodwin in the *Sunday Times*) "believes that the pressure on Whitney from her record company, from those close to her and dependent on her, to start making money again, was what drove her back to drugs" (Goodwin 2012, 18). In Pinksy's own words, "That is the reason my celebrity patients relapse. They go back to work far too prematurely. She should have been sent back to rehab. She should have been there for at least six months. The problem is that Whitney and celebrities like her make a lot of money and they have people round them who want them back

at work because they make money for them" (quoted in Goodwin 2012, 18). Note that from 2008 Pinksy hosted a reality television show in the United States entitled *Celebrity Rehab*.

8. I am reminded here of Pete Townshend on rock: "this music I helped to refine seems to demand so much human food" (quoted in Wilkerson 2009, 496). Moloch and roll.

9. A simple fact possibly, but a bewildering and potentially crushing one at the occasion of the second son's diagnosis, as Young recalled: "we made it outside to the car, and we're sitting in the car and I'm going, 'There's something wrong with me. Why did this happen?' Two different mothers. What's going on?" Years later he could say, "Y'know, a lot of families break up when this [a diagnosis of cerebral palsy] happens with one kid, and we've got two" (both quotations in McDonough 2002, 545, 548).

10. Though, perversely, disability, like death (though less so), can sometimes revive a pop career too. Curtis Mayfield's profile and popularity grew again after his adventitious disability: Craig Werner describes how "Mayfield fell into near anonymity before a catastrophic 1990 accident that left him paralyzed for the last decade of his life" (2004, 6; emphasis added). The Scottish singer and songwriter Edwyn Collins, when asked at the 2009 Q music magazine awards why he was being recognized as a "legend" at this moment in his career, replied "cheerfully, 'Because I had a stroke, I suppose'" (Maxwell 2009, 318).

# BIBLIOGRAPHY

Adams, Tim. 2008. "Hearts of Gold." *Observer Music Monthly* (October): 50–55.

Anon. 2006. "Who Guitarist's Deafness Warning." http://news.bbc.co.uk/1/hi/enter tainment/4580070.stm.

Anon. 2011. "Times Topics: People: Conrad Murray." *The New York Times*, November 7. http://topics.nytimes.com/topics/reference/timestopics/people/m/conrad_murray/index.html.

Attinello, Paul. 2006. "Fever/Fragile/Fatigue: Music, AIDS, Present, and . . .". In Lerner and Straus 2006, 13–22.

Auslander, Philip. 2005. "Performance as Therapy: Spalding Gray's Autopathographic Monologues." In Sandahl and Auslander 2005, 163–74.

Balls, Richard. 2000. *Sex & Drugs & Rock 'n' Roll: The Life of Ian Dury*. London: Omni-bus.

Barnes, Colin. 2003. "Effecting Change: Disability, Culture and Art?" Paper presented at *Finding the Spotlight* conference, Liverpool Institute for the Performing Arts, May 2003. www.lipa.ac.uk/effectingchange/effectingchange1/spotlight/abstractpapers/ColinBarnesWEB.doc.

Barnes, Mike. 2009. "Come On, Feel the Noise." *Guardian,* Film and Music section (January 9, 2009), 3.

Barthes, Roland. 1977. "The Grain of the Voice." Translated by Stephen Heath. In Frith and Goodwin 1990, 293–300.

Bayard, Marc. 1999. "Introduction." In O'Hara 1999, 8–13.

Bego, Mark. 2005. *Joni Mitchell*. New York: Taylor Trade.

Berke, Jamie. 2009. "It Had to Happen. iPhone/iPod Touch Becomes a Hearing Aid." July 7. http://deafness.about.com/b/2009/07/07/it-had-to-happen-iphoneipod-touch-becomes-a-hearing-aid.htm.

Bernays, Ueli. 2010. "The Apathy and the Ecstasy." *Sight and Sound*. January 8. www.signandsight.com/features/1981.html.

Berson, Jessica. 2005. "Performing Deaf Identity: Toward a Continuum of Deaf Performance." In Sandahl and Auslander 2005, 42–55.

Better Hearing Institute website. No date. "Celebrities Who Have Supported BHI." www
.betterhearing.org/about/celeb.cfm.

Birch, Will. 2010. *Ian Dury: The Definitive Biography*. London: Sidgwick and Jackson.

Birnbach, Lisa. 2006. "I Just Keep Going" (Neil Young interview). *Parade,* October 2.
www.parade.com/articles/editions/2006/edition_02-19-2006/Neil_Young.

Borsay, Anne. 2005. *Disability and Social Policy in Britain since 1750*. Basingstoke: Pal-
grave Macmillan.

Bradshaw, David, ed. 2008. *Virginia Woolf: Selected Essays*. Oxford: Oxford University
Press.

Bridge School website. 2012. "Annual Bridge School Benefit Concert." http://bridge
school.org/concert/index.php.

Brown, Steven E. 2008. "'Hear us Shout': Music Celebrating Disability Pride and Liberation." Review of Disability Studies: An International Journal 4 (2): 23–28.

Bull, Michael. 2005. "No Dead Air! The iPod and the Culture of Mobile Listening." *Lei-
sure Studies* 24, no. 4 (October): 343–55.

Burns, Peter. 2003. *Curtis Mayfield: People Never Give Up*. London: Sanctuary.

Calvert, Dave. 2010. "Loaded Pistols: The Interplay of Social Intervention and Anti-
Aesthetic Tradition in Learning Disabled Performance." *Research in Drama Education: The Journal of Applied Theatre and Performance* 15 (4): 513–28. http://eprints.
hud.ac.uk/10601/3/Loaded_Pistols.pdf.

Cameron, Colin. 2009. "Tragic but Brave or Just Crips with Chips? Songs and their Lyrics
in the Disability Arts Movement in Britain." *Popular Music* 28, no. 3 (October): 381–96.

Carr, Paul, ed. 2013. *Frank Zappa and the And*. Farnham: Ashgate.

Carroll, Harrison. 1954. "Behind the Hollywood Scene." *Day,* June 16, 15.

Charles, Ray. No date (2004?). Interview. www.raymovie.com/raycharles/the_man_ray_
charles_interview.html.

Charlton, James I. 2000. *Nothing About Us Without Us: Disability Oppression and Em-
powerment*. Berkeley and Los Angeles: University of California Press.

Chatwin, Bruce. 1987. *The Songlines*. London: Vintage, 1998.

Church, David. 2006. "'Welcome to the Atrocity Exhibition': Ian Curtis, Rock Death,
and Disability." *Disability Studies Quarterly* 26, no. 4. www.dsq-sds.org/article/
view/804/979.

Cizmic, Maria. 2006. "Of Bodies and Narratives: Musical Representations of Pain and
Illness in HBO's *W;t*." In Lerner and Straus 2006, 23–40.

Clark, Larry Wayne. 2002. "Mel Tillis: Beyond the Strawberry Patch." http://larrywayne-
clark.com/tillis.html.

Clayson, Alan. 2004. "Kevin Coyne: Singer-Songwriter Respected by his Contempo-
raries but Lacking their Chart Success." *Guardian*, December 6. http://www.guard
ian.co.uk/news/2004/dec/06/guardianobituaries.artsobituaries.

Cooper, B. Lee. 2004. "The Sky is Crying: Tales Told in Tearful Tunes." *Popular Music
and Society* 27, no. 1 (February), 107–15.

Cooper, Mark. 2008. "Against the Tide." Interview with Neil Young. *Observer Music
Monthly*, October, 16–22.

Cooper, Tim. 2005. "The Return of the Likely Lad." *Independent*, November 8.

Cox, Peter. 2008. *Set into Song: Ewan MacColl, Charles Parker, Peggy Seeger and the Radio Ballads*. No place: Labatie Books.

Critchley, Macdonald, and R. A. Henson, eds. 1977. *Music and the Brain: Studies in the Neurology of Music*. London: Heinemann.

Crowe, Cameron. 1979. Interview with Joni Mitchell. *Rolling Stone*, July 26. www.jmdl.com/library/view.cfm?id=300&ss=polio.

Cubitt, Sean. 1984. "*Top of the Pops:* The Politics of the Living Room." In Masterman 1984, 43–45.

Curtis, Deborah. 1995. *Touching from a Distance: Ian Curtis and Joy Division*. London: Faber, 2007.

Daniel, Eileen. 2007. "Noise and Hearing Loss: A Review." *Journal of School Health* 77, no. 5 (May): 225–31.

Davis, Francis. 2000. "Charlie Haden: Bass." *Atlantic Monthly*, August. www.theatlantic.com/issues/2000/08/davis.htm.

Davis, Lennard J. 1995. *Enforcing Normalcy: Disability, Deafness and the Body*. London: Verso.

Davis, Lennard J., ed. 1997. *The Disability Studies Reader*. London: Routledge.

Davis, Lennard J. 2002. *Bending Over Backwards: Disability, Dismodernism and Other Difficult Positions*. New York: New York University Press.

Davis, Miles. 1989. *Miles: The Autobiography*. With Quincy Troupe. London: Picador, 1990.

Doe, Tanis. 2004. "The Difficulty with Deafness Discourse and Disability Culture." *Review of Disability Studies* 1 (1): 34–41. www.rds.hawaii.edu/downloads/issues/pdf/RDSissue012004.pdf.

Drury. Jim. 2003. *Ian Dury and the Blockheads: Song by Song*. London: Sanctuary.

Elflein, Dietmar. 2009. "A Popular Music Project and People with Disabilities Community in Hamburg, Germany: The Case of Station 17." *Popular Music* 28, no. 3 (October): 397–410.

Everitt, Anthony. 1997. *Joining In: An Investigation into Participatory Music*. London: Calouste Gulbenkian Foundation.

Fahy, T. and K. King, eds. 2002. *Peering behind the Curtain: Disability, Illness and the Extraordinary Body in Contemporary Theatre*. London: Routledge.

FDR Library (Franklin D. Roosevelt Presidential Library and Museum) website. http://docs.fdrlibrary.marist.edu/bdayb1.html.

Ferguson, Iain. 2003. "Challenging a 'Spoiled Identity': Mental Health Service Users, Recognition and Redistribution." In Riddell and Watson 2003b, 67–87.

Frith, Simon. 1989. "Why Do Songs Have Words?" *Contemporary Music Review* 5 (1): 77–96.

Frith, Simon. 1996. *Performing Rites: On the Value of Popular Music*. Cambridge, MA: Harvard University Press. Reprint edition, 1998.

Frith, Simon, and Andrew Goodwin, eds. 1990. *On Record: Rock, Pop and the Written Word*. London: Routledge.

Funk, James R. 2009. "The Kids are Alright: Head Banging Poses no Special Risk of Neck or Head Injury." Rapid Responses to Patton and McIntosh a2825. *British Medical Journal,* February 26. www.bmj.com/cgi/eletters/337/dec17_2/a2825#209459.

Garfield, Simon. 2006. "Generation Terrorists." Interview with Pete Townshend and Roger Daltrey of The Who. *Observer Music Monthly* 37 (September): 22–33.

Garofalo, Rebee, ed. 1992a. *Rockin' the Boat: Mass Music and Social Movements.* Boston: South End Press.

Garofalo, Rebee. 1992b. "Understanding Mega-Events: If We Are the World, Then How Do We Change It?" In Garofalo 1992a, 15–35.

Garofalo, Rebee. 2005. "Who is the World? Reflections on Music and Politics Twenty Years after Live Aid." *Journal of Popular Music Studies* 17, no. 3 (December): 324–44.

Gleeson, Brendan. 1999. *Geographies of Disability.* London: Routledge.

Goldmark, Daniel. 2006. "Stuttering in American Popular Song, 1890–1930." In Lerner and Straus 2006, 91–105.

Gomery, Douglas. 1995. "Two Documents: *Your Priceless Gift* and *The 1946 Film Daily Yearbook.*" *Historical Journal of Film, Radio and Television* 15, no. 1 (June): 125–35.

Goodley, Danny. 2003. "Against a Politics of Victimisation: Disability Culture and Self-Advocates with Learning Difficulties." In Riddell and Watson 2003b, 105–30.

Goodman. Amy. 2006. "Jazz Legend Charlie Haden on His Life, His Music and His Politics." *Democracy Now! The War and Peace Report,* September 1. www.democracynow.org/2006/9/1/jazz_legend_charlie_haden_on_his.

Goodwin, Christopher. 2012. "Didn't She Almost Have it All?" *Sunday Times Magazine,* April 15, 12–18.

Gosch, Amy. 1984. "Will the Real Ted Nugent Please Stand Up?" *Stars and Stripes,* March 5. www.stripes.com/news/from-the-s-s-archives-will-the-real-ted-nugent-please-stand-up-1.49746.

Gould, Tony. 1995. *A Summer Plague: Polio and its Survivors.* New Haven, CT: Yale University Press.

Graeae Theatre Company. 2010. *Reasons to be Cheerful.* Written by Paul Sirrett. Directed by Jenny Sealey. Revived 2012.

Gumbel, Andrew. 2011. "Michael Jackson's Doctor Found Guilty of Involuntary Manslaughter." *Guardian,* November 7. http://www.guardian.co.uk/world/2011/nov/07/michael-jackson-conrad-murray-guilty.

Hardy, Phil, and Dave Laing. 1990. *The Faber Companion to 20th-Century Popular Music.* London: Faber.

Harker, Ben. 2007. *Class Act: The Cultural and Political Life of Ewan MacColl.* London: Pluto Press.

Harlow, John, and James Gillespie. 2012. "Hey Joe—Jimi's Alive: Stars Who Died Too Young are Set to Rock a New Generation as Holograms." *Sunday Times,* (June 17, 2012), 3.

Harrison, Robert. 1957. "Hollywood vs. *Confidential:* A Publisher's Statement." *Confidential,* September. www.law.umkc.edu/faculty/projects/ftrials/confidential/hollyvconfid.html.

Hawkins, Stan, and John Richardson. 2007. "Remodeling Britney Spears: Matters of Intoxication and Mediation." *Popular Music and Society* 30, no. 5 (December): 605–29.

Headlam, Dave. 2006. "Learning to Hear Autistically." In Lerner and Straus 2006, 109–20.

H.E.A.R. (Hearing Education and Awareness for Rockers). 1990. PSA featuring Pete Townshend of The Who. www.hearnet.com/features/feature_PSA.shtml.

H.E.A.R. 2004. "It's Hip to H.E.A.R.: Survival Guide: A Lifestyle Guide to Hearing Health." www.hearnet.com/images_site/energizer/hip_to_hear_survival_guide.pdf.

Heartbeats website. No date. www.monstercable.com/productdisplay.asp?pin=5596.

Hebdige, Dick. 1979. *Subculture: The Meaning of Style.* London: Methuen.

Hecht, Alan. 2003. *Polio.* New York: Chelsea House.

Hell On Earth. 2003. "Live Suicide Show and Related News." Band website. http://www.hellonearth.net/archive.html.

Hemphill, Paul. 2005. *Lovesick Blues: The Life of Hank Williams.* London: Penguin.

Herr, Cheryl. 2009. "Roll-Over-Beethoven: Johnnie Ray in Context." *Popular Music* 28, no. 3 (October): 323–40.

Heslam, David, ed. 1992. *The NME Rock 'n' Roll Years.* London: BCA.

Higginbotham, Adam. 2002. "Doctor Feelgood." *Observer,* August 11. http://www.guardian.co.uk/theobserver/2002/aug/11/features.magazine27.

Hollyscoop. 2007. "Britney Shaved Her Head!" *Hollyscoop* website, February 17. www.hollyscoop.com/britney-spears/britney-shaved-her-head.html.

Hood, J. D. 1977a. "Psychological and Physiological Aspects of Hearing." In Critchley and Henson 1977, 32–47.

Hood, J. D. 1977b. "Deafness and Musical Appreciation." In Critchley and Henson 1977, 323–43.

Houston, Frank. 2000. "Brilliant Careers: Joni Mitchell." *Salon.com,* April 4. www.jmdl.com/library/view.cfm?id=485&ss=polio.

Howard, Warren. 2008. "Dan le Sac vs. Scroobius Pip: A New Angle on Hip-Hop." *Independent,* April 25. www.independent.co.uk/arts-entertainment/music/features/dan-le-sac-vs-scroobius-pip-a-new-angle-on-hiphop-815056.html.

*Index on Censorship.* 1998. Vol. 27, no. 6 (November). Special edition called *The Book of Banned Music.*

Ingham, Chris. 2007. Sleeve notes to Slade 1981.

iTunes website. 2010. "Hearing Check" app. http://itunes.apple.com/gb/app/hearing-check/id362792472?mt=8.

Jakubowicz, Andrew, and Helen Meekosha. 2003. "Can Multiculturalism Encompass Disability?" In Riddell and Watson 2003b, 180–99.

Jobes, David A., Alan L. Berman, Patrick W. O'Carroll, Susan Eastgard, and Steve Knickmeyer. 1996. "The Kurt Cobain Suicide Crisis: Perspectives from Research, Public Health, and the News Media." *Suicide and Life-Threatening Behavior* 26 (Fall): 260–71.

Johnnie Ray fan-club website. www.johnnieray.com.

Johnson, Phil. 1997. "The Only Way is Up When You've Hit Rock Bottom." *Independent,*

September 30. http://www.independent.co.uk/life-style/interview-robert-wyatt-the-only-way-is-up-when-youve-hit-rock-bottom-1241992.html.

Johnson, Bruce, and Martin Cloonan. 2009. *Dark Side of the Tune: Popular Music and Violence*. Farnham: Ashgate.

Juman, Solaiman, Collin S. Karmody, and Donald Simeon. 2004. "Hearing Loss in Steelband Musicians." *Otolaryngology: Head and Neck Surgery* 131, no. 4 (October): 461–65.

Kähäri, Kim, Gunilla Zachau, Mats Eklöf, and Claes Möller. 2004. "The Influence of Music and Stress on Musicians' Hearing." *Journal of Sound and Vibration* 277: 627–31.

Kahn-Harris, Keith. 2007. *Extreme Metal: Music and Culture on the Edge*. London: Berg.

Kincaid, Jason. 2009. "Hear That? It's the Sound of Your New Hearing Aid, the iPhone." July 7. http://techcrunch.com/2009/07/07/hear-that-its-the-sound-of-your-new-hearing-aid-the-iphone/#comments.

King, Michael. 1994. *Wrong Movements: A Robert Wyatt History*. London: SAF Publishing.

Kirchner, Bill. 2011. Transcribed interview with Dave Liebman, "as part of NEA Masters of Jazz Project." www.daveliebman.com/interview.php?WEBYEP_DI=36.

Koestenbaum, Wayne. 1993. *The Queen's Throat: Opera, Homosexuality and the Mystery of Desire*. No place: Da Capo Press, 2001.

Kuppers, Petra. 2003. *Disability and Contemporary Performance: Bodies on Edge*. London: Routledge.

Kuppers, Petra. 2005. "Bodies, Hysteria, Pain: Staging the Invisible." In Sandahl and Auslander 2005, 147–62.

Lamacq, Steve. 2000. "The Last Time I Saw Richey." *Guardian*, September 29. http://www.guardian.co.uk/friday_review/story/0,,374432,00.html.

Lane, Harlan. 1995. "Constructions of Deafness." In Davis 1997, 153–71.

Leigh, Rob. 2011. "Sarah Harding in Rehab: Amy Winehouse, Robbie Williams, Shaun Ryder and More UK Pop Stars That Have Checked in for Treatment." Daily Mirror, October 12. www.mirror.co.uk/3am/celebrity-news/sarah-harding-in-rehab-amy-winehouse-274634.

Leitch, Donovan. 2005. *The Autobiography of Donovan: The Hurdy-Gurdy Man*. New York: St Martin's Press.

Lerner, Neil. 2006. "The Horrors of One-Handed Pianism: Music and Disability in *The Beast with Five Fingers*." In Lerner and Strauss 2006, 75–89.

Lerner, Neil, and Joseph N. Straus, eds. 2006. *Sounding Off: Theorizing Disability in Music*. London: Routledge.

Lerner, Neil. 2006a. "Introduction: Theorizing Disability in Music." In Lerner and Straus 2006, 1–10.

Levy, Andrew. 2008. "Girl, 13, Hangs Herself after Becoming Obsessed with Emo 'Suicide Cult' Rock Band." Daily Mail, May 9. www.dailymail.co.uk/news/article-564611/Girl-13-hangs-obsessed-Emo-suicide-cult-rock-band.html.

Liebman, Dave. 2012. *What It Is: The Life of a Jazz Artist*. With Lewis Porter. Plymouth: Scarecrow Press.

Linder, Douglas O. 2010. "The *Confidential* Magazine Trial of 1957: An Account." www .law.umkc.edu/faculty/projects/ftrials/confidential/confidentialaccount.html.

Lipsitz, George. 1994. *Rainbow at Midnight: Labor and Culture in the 1940s*. Urbana: University of Illinois Press.

Lubet, Alex. 2008. "To Dance Beneath the Diamond Sky with One Hand: Writings in Disability and Music." *Review of Disability Studies: An International Journal* 4 (1): 3–5.

Lubet, Alex. 2011. *Music, Disability, and Society*. Philadelphia: Temple University Press.

Lydon, John. 1994. *Rotten: No Irish, No Blacks, No Dogs*. With Keith and Kent Zimmerman. London: Hodder and Stoughton.

Magee, Reginald. 1999. "Deriving Opera from Operation." *Australian and New Zealand Journal of Surgery* 69, no. 9 (September): 672–74.

Maguire, Edward R., and Jeffrey B. Snipes. 1994. "Reassessing the Link between Country Music and Suicide." *Social Force* 72, no. 4 (June): 1239–43.

Malings, Ron. 2009. "Steve Race." *Independent*, June 26. http://www.independent.co.uk/ news/obituaries/steve-race-1719918.html.

Maloney, S. Timothy. 2006. "Glenn Gould, Autistic Savant." In Lerner and Straus 2006, 121–35.

Mandel, Howard. 2003. "*Downbeat* interview with Dave Liebman." www.daveliebman .com/Other_Sites/downbeat.htm.

Manderson, Lenore, and Susan Peake. 2005. "Men in Motion: Disability and the Performance of Masculinity." In Sandahl and Auslander 2005, 230–42.

Maney, Patrick J. 2000. "They Sang for Roosevelt: Songs of the People in the Age of FDR." *Journal of American and Comparative Cultures* 23, no. 1 (Spring): 85–89.

Masterman, Len, ed. 1984. *Television Mythologies: Stars, Shows and Signs*. London: Routledge.

Matteo, Steve. No date. "Women of Heart and Mind: A Rare Interview with Joni Mitchell." *Inside Connection*. http://www.insidecx.com/interviews/i49.asp.

Maxwell, Grace. 2009. *Falling & Laughing: The Restoration of Edwyn Collins*. London: Ebury.

Mayfield, Curtis. No date. Curtis Mayfield website.

McDonough, Jimmy. 2002. *Shakey: Neil Young's Biography*. London: Vintage.

McFadden, Lee. 2007. Interview with Deborah Curtis. First published in *Morning Star*. Joy Division Central website. www.joydiv.org/dcint3.htm.

McKay, George. No date a. *OR Boy: A Norfolk Punk Spills the Beans*. Unpublished manuscript.

McKay, George. No date b. Personal website. http://georgemckay.org.

McKay, George, ed. 1998. *DiY Culture: Party & Protest in Nineties Britain*. London: Verso.

McKay, George. 2000. *Glastonbury: A Very English Fair*. London: Victor Gollancz.

McKay, George. 2005. *Circular Breathing: The Cultural Politics of Jazz in Britain*. Durham NC: Duke University Press.

McKay, George. 2009a. "'Crippled with Nerves': Popular Music and Polio, with Particular Reference to Ian Dury." *Popular Music* 28, no. 3 (October): 341–65.

McKay, George, ed. 2009b. Special issue of *Popular Music* 28, no. 3 (October), on disability and popular music.

McKay, George. 2010a. Review of Terry Rowden, *The Souls of Blind Folk: African American Musicians and the Cultures of Blindness*. *Times Higher Education* July 8, 54–55.

McKay, George. 2010b. Personal interview with David Rohoman, London, September 14. Transcription available at http://georgemckay.org/jazz/interviews/.

McKay, George. 2011. Review of Alex Lubet, *Music, Disability, and Society*. *new formations* 73: 136–37.

McKay, George, and Ben Higham. 2011. *Community Music: History and Current Practice, its Constructions of 'Community', Digital Turns and Future Soundings*. Swindon: Arts and Humanities Research Council. http://www.ahrc.ac.uk/FundingOpportunities/Documents/CC%20scoping%20studies/McKay.pdf.

McLeod, Ken. 2001. "Bohemian Rhapsodies: Operatic Influences on Rock Music." *Popular Music* 20, no. 2 (May): 189–203. http://home.comcast.net/~collaros623/bohemianRhapsodies.pdf.

McRuer, Robert. 2006. *Crip Theory: Cultural Signs of Queerness and Disability*. New York: New York University Press.

Mel Tillis website. No date. www.meltillis.com.

Middles, Mick, and Lindsay Reade. 2009. *Torn Apart: The Life of Ian Curtis*. 2nd edition. London: Omnibus.

Millard, Andre. 2005. *America on Record: A History of Recorded Sound*. 2nd edition. Cambridge: Cambridge University Press.

Miller, Edward D. 2003. "The Nonsensical Truth of the Falsetto Voice: Listening to Sigur Rós." *Popular Musicology Online*. www.popular-musicology-online.com/issues/02/miller.html.

Monacelli, Antonia. 2010. "Music Makes You Kill Yourself." http://antonia-monacelli.hubpages.com/hub/Music-Makes-You-Kill-Yourself.

Monster website. No date. www.monstercable.com/headphones/.

Moore, Timothy E. 1996. "Scientific Consensus and Expert Testimony: Lessons from the Judas Priest Trial." *Skeptical Enquirer* 20, no. 6 (November/December). http://www.csicop.org/si/show/scientific_consensus_and_expert_testimony.

Moser, Pete, and George McKay, eds. 2005. *Community Music: A Handbook*. Lyme Regis: Russell House.

Muirhead, Bert. 1983. *Stiff: The Story of a Record Label*. Poole: Blandford.

Nash, Melissa. C. 2005. "Beyond Therapy: 'Performance' Work with People who Have Profound and Multiple Disabilities." In Sandahl and Auslander 2005, 190–201.

Nash, Meredith. 2005. "Oh Baby, Baby: Unveiling Britney Spears' Pregnant Body." *Michigan Feminist Studies* 19 (Fall 2005–Spring 2006). http://quod.lib.umich.edu/cgi/t/

text/textidx?cc=mfsfront;c=mfs;c=mfsfront;idno=ark5583.0019.002;rgn=main ;view=text;xc=1;g=mfsg.

NSE (National Society for Epilepsy) website. 2010. www.epilepsysociety.org.uk/About-Epilepsy/Whatisepilepsy.

O'Brien, Karen. 2001. *Shadows and Light. Joni Mitchell: The Definitive Biography.* London: Virgin.

O'Brien, Lucy. 2002. *She Bop II: The Definitive History of Women in Rock, Pop and Soul.* London: Continuum.

*Observer Music Monthly.* October 2008.

O'Hara, Craig. 1999. *The Philosophy of Punk: More than Noise.* Revised edition. Edinburgh: AK Press.

Oppenheimer, Joseph. 1953. "Singer Not Hurt by Poor Hearing." *Kentucky New Era.* October 27, 12.

Oster, Andrew. 2006. "Melisma as Malady: Cavalli's *Il Giasone* (1649) and Opera's Earliest Stuttering Role." In Lerner and Straus 2006, 157–71.

Palmer, Robert. 2004. "CeDell Davis." www.fatpossum.com/artists/cedell.html.

Paton, Rod. 2000. *Living Music: Improvisation Guidelines for Teachers and Community Musicians.* No place: West Sussex County Council.

Patton, Declan and Andrew McIntosh. 2008. "Head and Neck Injury Risks in Heavy Metal: Head Bangers Stuck between Rock and a Hard Bass." *British Medical Journal* 337, a2825, December 17. www.bmj.com/cgi/content/full/337/dec17_2/a2825.

Pence, Ray. 2008. "People with Disabilities Get Ready: Curtis Mayfield in the 1990s." *e Review of Disability Studies: An International Journal* 4 (2): 10–24. www.rds.hawaii.edu/downloads/issues/doc/RDSv04iss02.doc.

Pendergrass, Teddy. 1998. *Truly Blessed.* With Patricia Romanowski. New York: Putnam.

Pendergrass, Teddy. 2002. "Interview" on *Profile,* U.S. television show. www.youtube.com/watch?v=f46igblS8Ws.

Pendergrass, Teddy. 2007. "Interview" on *Art Fennell Reports.* Broadcast June 7, 2010. www.youtube.com/watch?v=jSE6QQUHUME.

Perring, Giles. 2005. "The Facilitation of Learning-Disabled Arts: A Cultural Perspective." In Sandahl and Auslander 2005, 175–89.

Phelan, Peggy. 2005. "Reconsidering Identity Politics, Essentialism, & Dismodernism: An Afterword." In Sandahl and Auslander 2005, 319–26.

Polydor. 1981. Press release for Ian Dury single "Spasticus Autisticus." POSP/X 285. August 21, 1981.

Quayson, Ato. 2007. *Aesthetic Nervousness: Disability and the Crisis of Representation.* New York: Columbia University Press.

Riddell, Sheila, and Nick Watson. 2003a. "Disability, Culture and Identity: Introduction." In Riddell and Watson 2003b, 1–18.

Riddell, Sheila, and Nick Watson, eds. 2003b. *Disability, Culture and Identity.* Harlow: Pearson.

Ringen, Jonathan. 2005. "Music Making Fans Deaf?" *Rolling Stone,* November 18. www.rollingstone.com/news/story/_/id/8841090.

*Riverfront Times.* 1996. "Israel Vibration: Modern Roots with a Message." www.skank-productions.com/articleiv.htm.

RNID (Royal National Institute for Deaf People) website. No date. "Hearing Matters. That's Why You Should Take Our Hearing Check Today." www.rnid.org.uk/how wehelp/hearing_check/.

Rogers, Naomi. 2007. "Race and the Politics of Polio: Warm Springs, Tuskegee, and the March of Dimes." *American Journal of Public Health* 97, no. 5 (May): 784–95.

Roosevelt, Franklin D. Birthday balls radio addresses. http://docs.fdrlibrary.marist.edu/bdsptxt.html.

Ross, Michael E. 1996. "An Indelible Impression." *Salon.com*, October 14. www.salon.com/entertainment/music/feature/1996/10/14/music961014.

Rowden, Terry. 2009. *The Songs of Blind Folk: African American Musicians and the Cultures of Blindness.* Ann Arbor: University of Michigan Press.

Rutty, Christopher J. 1988. "'Helpless'; The 1951 Polio Outbreak; the Neil Young Case." Original essay supplied by the author; also published in A. Jenkins, ed., *Neil Young and Broken Arrow: On a Journey Through the Past.* Mid Glamorgan, Wales: Neil Young Appreciation Society, 1994, 95–112. See also Rutty's website on polio history: www.healthheritageresearch.com.

Sacks, Oliver. 2007. *Musicophilia: Tales of Music and the Brain.* London: Picador.

Sanborn, David. No date. Official website: www.davidsanborn.com.

Sandahl, Carrie, and Philip Auslander, eds. 2005. *Bodies in Commotion: Disability & Performance.* Ann Arbor: University of Michigan Press.

Sanjek, David. 2013. "Zappa and the Freaks: Recording Wild Man Fischer." In Carr 2013, 149–65.

Sartin, Jeffrey S. 2010. "Contagious Rhythm: Infectious Diseases of 20th century Musicians." *Clinical Medicine & Research* 8, no. 2 (July): 106–13. www.ncbi.nlm.nih.gov/pmc/articles/PMC2910108/pdf/0070106.

Savage, Jon. 1991. *England's Dreaming: Sex Pistols and Punk Rock.* London: Faber.

Savage, Jon. 1995. "Foreword." In Curtis 1995, xi–xiii.

Schermer, Victor L. 2008. "Dave Liebman/Jim Ridl: The Creative Process in Jazz." www.allaboutjazz.com/php/article.php?id=28416.

Scientific Committee on Emerging and Newly Identified Health Risks. 2008. *Scientific Opinion on the Potential Health Risks of Exposure to Noise from Personal Music Players and Mobile Phones Including a Music Playing Function,* September 23. http://ec.europa.eu/health/ph_risk/committees/04_scenihr/docs/scenihr_o_018.pdf.

Scott-Hill, Mairian. 2003. "Deafness/Disability: Problematising Notions of Identity, Culture and Structure." In Riddell and Watson 2003b, 88–104.

Shakespeare, Tom. 2006. *Disability Rights and Wrongs.* London: Routledge.

Shearing, George. 2004. *Lullaby of Birdland: The Autobiography of George Shearing.* Written with Alyn Shipton. London: Continuum, 2005.

Shell, Marc. 2005a. *Polio and its Aftermath: The Paralysis of Culture.* Cambridge, MA: Harvard University Press.

Shell, Marc. 2005b. *Stutter*. Cambridge, MA: Harvard University Press.

Sher, Antony. 1985 [2006]. *Year of the King: An Actor's Diary and Sketchbook*. 4th edition. Pompton Plains, NJ: Limelight.

Shipton, Alyn. 2001. *A New History of Jazz*. London: Continuum.

Sieber, Tobin. 2008. *Disability Theory*. Ann Arbor: University of Michigan Press.

Slash. 2010. "This Much I Know." *Observer Magazine*, November 21, 8–9.

Smith, Owen. 2005. "Shifting Apollo's Frame: Challenging the Body Aesthetic in Theatre Dance." In Sandahl and Auslander 2005, 73–85.

Snyder, Sharon L,. and David T. Mitchell. 2006. *Cultural Locations of Disability*. Chicago: University of Chicago Press.

Spelman, Nicola. 2009. *"All the Madmen: Popular Music, Anti-Psychiatry, and the Myths of Madness."* PhD diss., University of Salford.

Stack, Steven and Jim Gundlach. 1992. "The Effect of Country Music on Suicide." *Social Force* 71, no. 1 (September): 211–18.

Stein, Isaak. 2008. "Transformer Man: An Exploration of Disability in Neil Young's Life and Music." *Review of Disability Studies: An International Journal* 4 (2): 2–10. www.rds.hawaii.edu/downloads/issues/doc/RDSv04iss02.doc.

Stephens, Vincent Lamar. 2005. *"Queering the Textures of Rock and Roll History."* PhD diss., University of Maryland. www.lib.umd.edu/drum/handle/1903/2444.

Stiker, Henri-Jacques. 1997. *A History of Disability*. Revised edition; first published in 1982. Translated by William Sayers. Ann Arbor: University of Michigan Press.

Stras, Laurie. 2006. "The Organ of the Soul: Voice, Damage, and Affect." In Lerner and Strauss 2006, 173–84.

Stras, Laurie. 2009. "Sing a Song of Difference: Connie Boswell and a Discourse of Disability in Jazz." *Popular Music* 28, no. 3 (October): 297–322.

Straus, Joseph N. 2011. *Extraordinary Measures: Disability in Music*. Oxford: Oxford University Press.

Street, John. 2012. *Music and Politics*. Cambridge: Polity.

Super Seventies website. No date. "You Ain't Seen Nothing Yet." www.superseventies.com/sw_youaintseennothinyet.html.

Taleporos, George, and Marita P. McCabe. 2002. "Body Image and Physical Disability: Personal Perspectives." *Social Science & Medicine* 54: 971–80.

Thomson, Rosemarie Garland, ed. 1996. *Freakery: Cultural Spectacles of the Extraordinary Body*. New York: New York University Press.

Thomson, Rosemarie Garland. 1997. *Extraordinary Bodies: Figuring Physical Disability in American Culture and Literature*. New York: Columbia University Press.

Thomson, Rosemarie Garland. 2000. "Staring Back: Self-Representations of Disabled Performance Artists." *American Quarterly* 52 (2): 334–38.

Thomson, Rosemarie Garland. 2005. "Dares to Stares: Disabled Women Performance Artists and the Dynamics of Staring." In Sandahl and Auslander 2005, 30–41.

Thomson, Rosemarie Garland. 2006. "Foreword." In Lerner and Straus 2006, xiii–xv.

Today News website. 2011. "'I am asleep', Jackson Says in Slurring Audio." http://today

.msnbc.msn.com/id/44785478/ns/today-entertainment/t/i-am-asleep-jackson
-says-slurring-audio/#.ToTgkJhRxHg.

Ullestad, Neal. 1992. "Diverse Rock Rebellions Subvert Mass Media Hegemony." In Garofalo 1992a, 37–53.

Unterberger, Richie. 1996. "Robert Wyatt interview." *Perfect Sound Forever.* http://www
.furious.com/perfect/wyatt.html.

Veal, Michael E. 2000. *Fela: The Life and Times of an African Musical Icon.* Philadelphia: Temple University Press.

Vogel, Ineke, Johannes Brug, Catharina P. B. van der Ploeg, and Hein Raat. 2007. "Young People's Exposure to Loud Music: A Summary of the Literature." *American Journal of Preventive Medicine* 33 (2): 124–33.

Wald, Elijah. 2004. *Escaping the Delta: Robert Johnson and the Invention of the Blues.* New York: HarperCollins.

Walser, Robert. 1993. *Running with the Devil: Power, Gender, and Madness in Heavy Metal Music.* Middletown CT: Wesleyan University Press.

Waltz, Mitzi, and Martin James. 2009. "The (Re)marketing of Disability in Pop: Ian Curtis and Joy Division." *Popular Music* 28, no. 3 (October): 367–80.

Ward, John Owen. 1970. *The Oxford Companion to Music.* Revised edition of Percy A. Scholes, ed. (1938). Oxford: Oxford University Press.

Watson, Nick. 2003. "Daily Denials: The Routinisation of Oppression and Resistance." In Riddell and Watson 2003b, 34–52.

Werner, Craig. 2004. *Higher Ground: Stevie Wonder, Aretha Franklin, Curtis Mayfield, and the Rise and Fall of American Soul.* New York: Crown.

Whiteside, Jonny. 1994. *Cry: The Johnnie Ray Story.* New York: Barricade.

Wilkerson, Mark. 2009. *Who Are You: The Life of Pete Townshend.* London: Omnibus.

Wimmer, Bill. No date. "Pianist Horace Parlan Created His Own Technique." Berman Music Foundation. www.bermanmusicfoundation.org/hprlnus.htm.

Wise, Tim. 2007. "Yodel Species: A Typology of Falsetto Effects in Popular Music Vocal Styles." *Radical Musicology* 2, 57 pars. www.radical-musicology.org.uk/2007/Wise
.htm.

Wolkewitz, Martin, Arthur Allignol, Nicholas Graves, and Adrian G. Barnett. 2011. "Is 27 Really a Dangerous Age for Famous Musicians? Retrospective Cohort Study." *British Medical Journal* 343:d7799. http://www.bmj.com/content/343/bmj.d7799.

Woolf, Virginia. 1931. "Professions for Women." In Bradshaw 2008, 140–45.

Wyatt, Robert. 1998. "*Rock Bottom* (The Odd History of a Piece of Music)." Sleeve notes to rereleased album *Rock Bottom* (Wyatt 1974).

# DISCOGRAPHY/FILMOGRAPHY

Bachman-Turner Overdrive. 1974. "You Ain't Seen Nothing Yet." *Not Fragile.* Mercury Records.

Buffalo Springfield. 1967. "Expecting to Fly." *Buffalo Springfield Again.* Atco Records.

Cockney Rebel. 1974. "Psychomodo." *The Psychomodo.* EMI Records: EMC 3033.

Cockney Rebel. 2005. "The last feast." *The Quality of Mercy.* GOTT Discs. GOTT CD040.

Coyne, Kevin. 1972. *Case History.* Rereleased in Kevin Coyne. n.d. *Dandelion Years* box set. Butt Records: BUTBOX 1.

Coyne, Kevin. 1976. "Fat Girl." *In Living Black and White.* Virgin Records. VD2505.

Coyne, Kevin. 1978. "Having a Party." *Millionaires and Teddy Bears.* Virgin Records. V2110.

Dury, Ian. 1977. "Sweet Gene Vincent." *New Boots and Panties.* Stiff Records.

Dury, Ian. 1979. "Dance of the Screamers." *Do It Yourself.* Stiff Records.

Dury, Ian. 1980. "Hey, Hey, Take Me Away." *Laughter.* Stiff Records.

Dury, Ian. 1981. "Spasticus Autisticus." Polydor Records. POSP/X 285.

Epileptics. 1981. *Last Bus to Debden* EP. Spider Leg Records.

Faithfull, Marianne. 1979. *Broken English.* Island Records.

Faithfull, Marianne. 1995. "Bored by Dreams." *A Secret Life.* Island Records.

First Edition. 1969. "Ruby, Don't Take Your Love to Town." Available on Kenny Roger and The First Edition. *Anthology.* Master Classics (2004).

Holiday, Billie. 1957. "Fine and Mellow." *The Sound of Jazz,* CBS television show, December 8.

Israel Vibration. 2002. "Level Every Angle." *Fighting Soldiers.* Nocturne NTCD 131.

Joy Division. 1978. "At a Later Date." Various artists. *Short Circuit: Live at the Electric Circus.* Virgin Records VCL 5003.

Joy Division. 1979a. "Insight." *Unknown Pleasures.* Factory Records. FACT 10.

Joy Division. 1979b. "She's Lost Control." *Unknown Pleasures.* Factory Records. FACT 10.

Joy Division. 1980a. "Atrocity Exhibition." *Closer.* Factory Records. FACT 25.

Joy Division. 1980b. "Atmosphere" / "She's Lost Control" (12" extended version). Factory Records.

Kolbert, Kata. 1987. "Live Your Life" / "The Deed is Done." Nevermore Records. NE1.

Kubrick, Stanley, director. 1960. *Spartacus*.

MacColl, Ewan, Charles Parker, and Peggy Seeger. 1999. *The Body Blow*. First broadcast, BBC Radio, Home Service, March 27, 1962. Topic Records. TSCD 805.

Mayfield, Curtis. 1996. "Here but I'm Gone." *New World Order*. Warner Bros. Records. 9362–46348–2.

Miller, Glenn. 1942. "The President's Birthday Ball." Available on *The Hits*. Master Series, Inc. (2011).

Morrison, Van. 1997. "Sometimes We Cry." *The Healing Game*. Exile Records.

Mötorhead. 1986. "Deaf Forever." Available on *Deaf Forever: The Best of Mötorhead*. Castle Records. SELCD502 (1999).

Nugent, Ted. 1976. "Turn it Up." *Free For All*. Epic Records.

Osbourne, Ozzy. 1980. "Suicide Solution." *Blizzard of Ozz*.

Perkins, Carl. 1956. *Introducing . . . Carl Perkins*. Dootone Records. Reissued by Boplicity Records in 1996. CDBOP 008.

Presley, Elvis. 1956. "All Shook Up." Available on *Elvis: 30 #1 Hits*. RCA Records (2002).

Ray, Johnnie. 1953. "It's the Talk of the Town." Available on *Johnnie's Coming Home*. Cool Cats Records (2007).

Ray, Johnnie. 1956. "Just Walking in the Rain." Available on *The Best of Johnnie Ray*. Sony Records (1996).

Scorsese, Martin, director. 1978. *The Last Waltz*. Film rereleased, MGM, 2002.

Sex Pistols. 1977. "Bodies." *Never Mind the Bollocks . . . Here's the Sex Pistols*. Virgin V2086.

Slade. 1981. *Till Deaf Do Us Part*. Rereleased on Salvo (2007). SALVOCD008.

Spears, Britney. 2007. "Piece of Me." *Blackout*. Jive Records.

Staff Benda Bilili. 2009. *Très Très Fort*. Crammed Discs. CRAW51.

Talking Heads. 1979. "Electric Guitar." *Fear of Music*. Sire Records. SRK 6076.

The Who. 1965. "My Generation." Available on *My Generation (Deluxe Edition)*. Polydor Records (2002).

The Who. 1975. *Tommy*. Directed by Ken Russell, music by Pete Townshend. Hemdale Film.

Whitehouse, Mat, director. 2010. *Sex & Drugs & Rock & Roll*.

Williams, Hank. 1951. "Howlin' at the Moon." Available on *The All-Time Greatest Country Artists—Volume 23: Hank Williams*. Rachelle Productions (2011).

Winehouse, Amy. 2006a. "Me and Mrs Jones." *Back to Black*. Island Records.

Winehouse, Amy. 2006b. "Rehab." *Back to Black*. Island Records.

Wyatt, Robert. 1974. *Rock Bottom*. Hannibal Records, 1998. HNCD 1426.

Young, Neil. 1970. "Helpless." On Crosby, Stills, Nash & Young. 1970. *Déjà Vu*. Atlantic Records.

Yunupingu, Geoffrey Gurrumul. 2008. *Gurrumul*. Skinnyfish Music.

# INDEX

*Entries in bold indicate an image.*

**Song titles**